Basic CAD for Interior Designers

Basic CAD for Interior Designers

AutoCAD®, Architectural Desktop, and VIZ® Render 2007

Jin Feng

Lawrence Technological University

Jiang Lu

Eastern Michigan University

PEARSON

Prentice
Hall

Upper Saddle River, New Jersey
Columbus, Ohio

Library of Congress Cataloging Control Number: 2007924059

Editor in Chief: Vernon R. Anthony
Acquisitions Editor: Jill Jones-Renger
Editorial Assistant: Doug Greive
Production Editor: Louise N. Sette
Production Supervision: Karen Fortgang, bookworks publishing services
Design Coordinator: Diane Ernsberger
Art Coordinator: Janet Portisch
Cover Designer: Jeff Vanik
Production Manager: Deidra M. Schwartz
Director of Marketing: David Gesell
Marketing Manager: Jimmy Stephens
Marketing Coordinator: Alicia Dysert

Certain images and materials contained in this publication were reproduced with the permission of Autodesk, Inc. © 2006. All rights reserved.

Autodesk and AutoCAD are registered trademarks of Autodesk, Inc., in the U.S.A. and certain other countries.

This book was set by Aptara, Inc. It was printed and bound by Bind-Rite Graphics. The cover was printed by Coral Graphic Services, Inc.

Disclaimer:

The publication is designed to provide tutorial information about AutoCAD® and/or other Autodesk computer programs. Every effort has been made to make this publication complete and as accurate as possible. The reader is expressly cautioned to use any and all precautions necessary, and to take appropriate steps to avoid hazards, when engaging in the activities described herein.

Neither the author nor the publisher makes any representations or warranties of any kind, with respect to the materials set forth in this publication, express or implied, including without limitation any warranties of fitness for a particular purpose or merchantability. Nor shall the author or the publisher be liable for any special, consequential or exemplary damages resulting, in whole or in part, directly or indirectly, from the reader's use of, or reliance upon, this material or subsequent revisions of this material.

Pearson Education Ltd.
Pearson Education Singapore Pte. Ltd.
Pearson Education Canada, Ltd.
Pearson Education—Japan

Pearson Education Australia Pty. Limited
Pearson Education North Asia Ltd.
Pearson Educación de Mexico, S.A. de C.V.
Pearson Education Malaysia Pte. Ltd.

10 9 8 7 6 5 4 3 2 1
ISBN-13: 978-0-13-225183-9
ISBN-10: 0-13-225183-3

Preface

AutoCAD and Learning AutoCAD

Since its introduction into the world of design by Autodesk in 1982, AutoCAD has become the most widely used PC design software for many disciplines, including interior design and architecture. In today's building industry, AutoCAD is a standard tool of design, drafting, and management. Without competent AutoCAD skills, a college graduate may find it difficult to find an entry-level job; a veteran designer may feel at a disadvantage. The importance of adequate AutoCAD training can never be exaggerated. On the other hand, AutoCAD is a comprehensive and complex computer- aided design system used in many different fields, among which interior design is only a small area of application. This makes learning AutoCAD a difficult task for interior designers and interior design students because, in spite of the many books on AutoCAD, very few are written specifically for interior designers. Most books on AutoCAD are overloaded with information that is irrelevant to interior design. Those who are inexperienced in computing can easily be overwhelmed by the complex functions of AutoCAD and the cumbersome volume of most "complete" or "one-stop" books on AutoCAD. Tutorials on how to create machine parts can very easily bore interior designers. To meet the special requirements of interior design students and professional interior designers, this book simplifies the learning of AutoCAD to relate it as closely as possible to interior design applications. In recent years, Autodesk Architectural Desktop (ADT) has become more and more common in both schools and design firms. Learning the new parametric design approach implemented in Architectural Desktop and taking advantage of the integration of the 2D plan and 3D modeling become imperative. The advanced functions in the Autodesk VIZ Render program associated with Architectural Desktop will also significantly improve the design visualization. Therefore, this book provides a brief introduction to Architectural Desktop and VIZ Render in the last three chapters.

About This Book

Written for interior design students, this text is also intended as their first book on AutoCAD. It is an easy-to-understand tutorial with step-by-step instructions. It may also be used as a tutorial for interior design professionals who need to catch up with the technological advancement of the field. The book is very pragmatic and focused. It combines explanations of commands with practical and systematic drafting procedures to teach students an adequate set of skills that they can use immediately in school and in their profession.

This book has the following unique features:

1. A humanistic philosophy that respects the interior designer as an AutoCAD user.

2. A focus on what an interior designer can do with AutoCAD rather than on what AutoCAD can do.

3. An emphasis on the procedures of drafting tasks using appropriate AutoCAD commands rather than functions of individual AutoCAD commands.

4. A careful selection of commands to simplify the learning process.

5. A brief introduction to Architectural Desktop with outcomes comparable to those of AutoCAD tutorials so that the student can learn the difference between the two systems.

6. A brief introduction to VIZ Render that allows the student to create photo-accurate rendering.

Exercises with step-by-step instructions and comments are the primary format of instruction. These exercises can also be used as a practical how-to guide for future reference.

This book treats AutoCAD as a drafting and presentation tool. Intended for readers with minimal computing experience, only basic knowledge and experience of Windows are expected. After completing the tutorials, the reader will have adequate skills to start as a CAD drafter in the design profession. Although AutoCAD can surely be used as a design tool, the creative design process is beyond the intended scope of this book. Meanwhile, the reader should remember that this book is an introductory text, so it does not cover all the AutoCAD skills and procedures that are used in the field of interior design.

This book is developed from its predecessors *Basic AutoCAD for Interior Designers Using Release 14* and *Basic AutoCAD for Interior Designers Using AutoCAD 2002*. It is more than a simple update to accommodate a new version of AutoCAD. There are substantial changes in content and scope. The type of designed space is now commercial rather than residential. A chapter on creating a reflected ceiling plan is added. An introduction to Autodesk Architectural Desktop and VIZ Render is also added to embrace the parametric design paradigm and physically based rendering techniques. These changes will greatly enhance the student's learning experience and outcome.

How to Use This Book

This book is organized around the task of presenting a simple designed space in both 2D drawings and 3D modeling. The task is divided into chapters. Although the space is extremely simple, the presentational tasks require almost all the basic AutoCAD skills frequently used in the design profession. The chapters are sequential, and the reader can simply follow the chapters in order. Learning AutoCAD is similar to learning to play the piano; you need to know the AutoCAD functions and commands by heart just as a pianist must know the keyboard and memorize the music. If you practice these exercises repeatedly, you can become fluent in AutoCAD in a short period of time. While practicing the exercises, the reader needs to reflect on what he or she is doing and on what the potential usage for a certain command or procedure might be. After finishing the tutorials, it is important to put what you have learned into use for your own design to truly internalize the procedures.

The Format of the Tutorials

In these tutorials, instruction of operation is presented using the following conventions:

1. AutoCAD command prompt output (what AutoCAD says) and input (what you reply) are printed in a special typeface (Arial Narrow), the output is printed in plain

type, and your actions or inputs are printed in **bold**; descriptions and explanations of both your actions and AutoCAD's are *italicized*.

2. Operations using Menu or dialog boxes are listed with numbers. These numbers usually correspond to the bold numbers in the figures.

3. AutoCAD commands are in uppercase letters.

4. Explanatory notes are all preceded with a round bullet point.

See the following figure for an example:

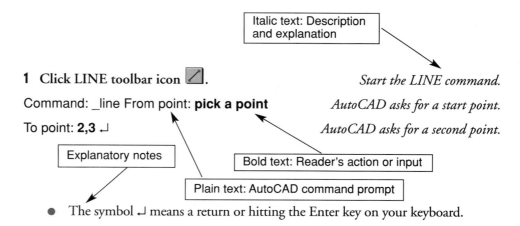

Italic text: Description and explanation

1 Click LINE toolbar icon ▨.   *Start the LINE command.*

Command: _line From point: **pick a point**   *AutoCAD asks for a start point.*

To point: **2,3** ↵   *AutoCAD asks for a second point.*

Explanatory notes

Bold text: Reader's action or input

Plain text: AutoCAD command prompt

● The symbol ↵ means a return or hitting the Enter key on your keyboard.

Note on the Software and Hardware

This tutorial is based on AutoCAD 2007, Architectural Desktop 2007, and VIZ Render 2007. To make this book useful for most readers, the tutorials are written based on the minimal hardware configuration required by AutoCAD: a Windows XP–based personal computer with a three-button mouse. If the reader has Architectural Desktop 2007, AutoCAD 2007 is included in the software. There is no need for a separate installation of AutoCAD. VIZ Render 2007, as a component of the Architectural Desktop package, is no longer installed with Architectural Desktop by default. It requires an additional installation after ADT is installed. If the reader has AutoCAD only, he or she can still use the first part of the book to learn AutoCAD. Some of the new 3D functions of AutoCAD 2007 are supported only by a professional workstation–grade graphic processor that is usually not included in personal desktop and notebook computers. Therefore, those functions may not be available to the reader. In addition, the time required to perform some of the demanding 3D tasks may be substantially increased when compared with previous versions of AutoCAD.

Basic Terms

Certain terms are used throughout this book to describe the actions you need to take in operating the AutoCAD system. These terms are clarified as follows:

CHECK—Click a check box in dialog boxes to make a check mark or cross appear in that box. It means that the option associated with the check box is taken.

CHOOSE (an item from a list or menu)—Left-click on an item from a list.

CLEAR (a check box)—Click a check box to make the check mark or cross disappear. It means that the option associated with the check box is not taken.

CLICK—Click the left button of a mouse or the equivalent button of another pointing device.

DOUBLE-CLICK—Click the left mouse button or the equivalent button of another pointing device twice quickly to open a drawing or to highlight an existing text string.

DRAG—Move the mouse while holding down the left button. This action is usually taken to move windows by the title bar or in a drag-and-drop operation.

ENTER—Type an input (a command, a number, or any kind of data) from the keyboard and finish with a hit on the [Enter] key (symbolized by ⏎) at a command prompt or in a text window in a dialog box.

PICK (a point)—Use the mouse to click at a point in the drawing area to identify the point. The *x,y* coordinates of the point will be entered into the system.

POINT TO (a menu item)—Move the cursor with the mouse over a menu item without clicking. The item is usually highlighted.

PULL—Move the mouse without holding down any button. This action is used to create selection-windows.

RIGHT-CLICK—Click the right mouse button or the equivalent button of another pointing device. It is equivalent to hitting the [Enter] key, and it sometimes may bring out a menu.

SELECT—Use the pointing device to pick a drawing entity, or entities, as required by certain AutoCAD commands. Usually, the selection process has to be signaled to end with a hit on the [Enter] key.

SHIFT-SELECT (an object)—Hold down the [Shift] key while clicking on the object you want to select.

Online Instructor Resources

To access supplementary materials online, instructors need to request an instructor access code. Go to **www.prenhall.com**, click the **Instructor Resource Center** link, and then click **Register Today** for an instructor access code. Within forty-eight hours after registering, you will receive a confirming e-mail including an instructor access code. Once you have received your code, go to the site and log on for full instructions on downloading the materials you wish to use.

Acknowledgments

We would like to acknowledge the reviewers of this text: Nancy Nehring, East Tennessee State University, and Helen Evans Warren, Mount Royal College, Calgary, AB, Canada.

Contents

Chapter 3   Modify and Add to the Floor Plan   33

Chapter 4   Get Organized with Layers   53

Chapter 5   Draw the Furniture Plan

Chapter 6   Draw the Reflected Ceiling Plan

Chapter 9 Draw a Detail 129

Chapter 10 Legend and Schedule 145

Chapter 11 Plotting 155

Chapter 12   Assemble the Finished Drawing   171

Chapter 13   Build a 3D Model   199

Chapter 14   Rendering   233

Chapter 15   Construct the Space Model with ADT   259

Chapter 16   Create the Reflected Ceiling Plan   283

Chapter **17**   Rendering with VIZ Render   **297**

Appendixes

Basic CAD for Interior Designers

Basic Knowledge to Start

Standard toolbar

Layer toolbar

Title bar

Properties toolbar

Menu bar

Styles toolbar

Workplace toolbar

Draw toolbar

Sheet Set manager

Modify toolbar

Cursor

Draw Order toolbar

Tool Palette

UCS icon

Layout tabs

Prompt area

Status line

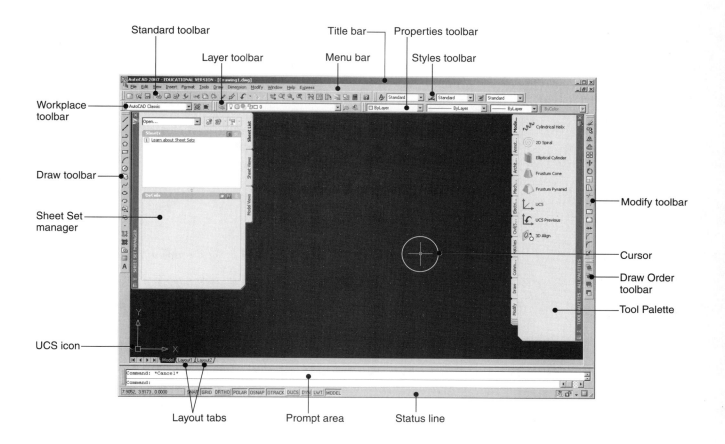

- **Start the Program**
- **Get to Know the AutoCAD Program Window**
- **Experiment with an AutoCAD Command**
- **Look Around in an AutoCAD Drawing**
- **Commands for Correcting Your Mistakes: Cancel, Undo, Redo, Erase, and Oops**
- **Handling Files**

This chapter provides an illustrated description of the AutoCAD drawing environment. You will be guided through an adventure into the AutoCAD drawing environment, where you will communicate and work with AutoCAD.

Start the Program

Before you start to explore AutoCAD with the following tutorial, you should have some basic computing skill to maneuver in the Windows environment. If you are not sure about your skills, you may find tutorials, such as the *Windows for Dummies* books, to learn the most basic skills.

The exact location of the AutoCAD program in your computer system depends on how it was installed. In a typical installation, a shortcut icon 🅐 is placed on the Windows desktop. You can simply double-click the shortcut icon to start AutoCAD. If you do not see the shortcut icon on the desktop, the AutoCAD program can usually be found as described below.

1 **Click the Start button at the**
lower left corner of the screen.

2 **Point to All Programs.** *A list of the program folders appears.*

3 **Point to Autodesk.** *A submenu appears.*

4 **Point to AutoCAD 2007.**

5 **Click AutoCAD 2007.** *Your computer should start to boot AutoCAD.*

For Autodesk Architectural Desktop users: *If you have only Autodesk Architectural Desktop 2007 installed on your computer, you may follow the instructions in Appendix A to change the Architectural Desktop user interface to the AutoCAD user interface.*

Get to Know the AutoCAD Program Window

AutoCAD 2007 has two distinctly designed user interfaces known as workspaces. They are 3D Modeling and AutoCAD Classic. When you start AutoCAD for the first time, you are asked to make a choice between the two (Figure 1.1). For this tutorial, we will use AutoCAD Classic.

1 **Click AutoCAD Classic to highlight it.**

2 **Click OK.**

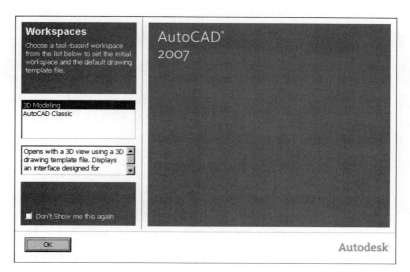

Figure 1.1
Choose an AutoCAD
workspace.

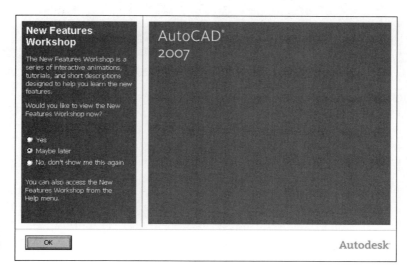

Figure 1.2
Skip the New Features
Workshop.

You may be prompted to decide if you want to view the new features of AutoCAD 2007 (Figure 1.2). Because you have little knowledge about AutoCAD at this moment, you may want to see it at a later time.

3 **Click to check Maybe later.**

4 **Click OK.**

A typical AutoCAD Classic program window without customization contains many parts, as shown in Figure 1.3. You will understand these parts more fully after doing the tutorials. If you encounter the terms referring to these parts, you may come back to this section for exact definitions.

- If your AutoCAD program window looks different, it must have been customized by someone else. You may try to reset the AutoCAD profile to return to the original interface.

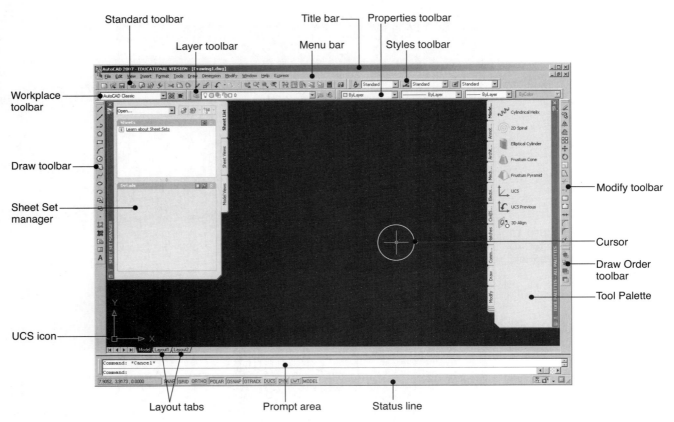

Figure 1.3
AutoCAD drawing window.

Title bar   shows the current drawing name. (In the above example, the drawing name is "Drawing1.dwg." Window control buttons for closing ☒, minimizing ▣, maximizing ▣ , or restoring ▣ the AutoCAD window are located at the right side. You may also move the AutoCAD window by dragging the title bar.

Menu bar   has a row of menu names. It is similar to all other Windows programs. Clicking on any of them brings out a pop-up menu. A pop-up menu is a list of commands that pops up for you to choose from. A second set of window control buttons that control the current drawing are located at the right side.

Standard toolbar   contains a row of toolbar icons, including some of the standard Windows tools such as print, cut, copy, and paste.

Properties toolbar   shows the properties of the current layer or selected objects, and you can manipulate the properties though the lists and tools.

Workplaces toolbar   allows you to switch between AutoCAD Classic user interface and 3D modeling user interface.

Layer toolbar   shows the current layer status and allows you to change object layers or access layer manager.

Styles toolbar   shows the current text, dimension, and table styles, and you can change the current styles through the pull-down style lists.

Draw toolbar   has a collection of icons to activate some frequently used drawing commands.

Modify toolbar   has a collection of icons to activate some frequently used editing commands.

Draw Order toolbar   has tools to control the visibility of overlapping drawing elements.

Sheet set manager   manages the drawings of a project.

Tool Palettes   contain convenient tools.

UCS icon   shows the positive directions of the x, y, and z axes of the coordinate system.

Cursor   is a pointer on the screen controlled by the digitizer, such as a mouse. The cursor may change into a small box when AutoCAD prompts you to pick objects.

Prompt area   is the place where you "talk" with AutoCAD; key in your command there, and AutoCAD talks back with questions and requests.

Layout tabs   allow you to switch to different layout pages of the drawing.

Status line   provides some important information about your drawing environment, including the coordinates of the cursor in the drawing area and modes of drawing aids.

The functions of the tools will be discussed in the following chapters. At this moment, the most important task is to get familiar with the names of the components of the AutoCAD user interface.

Experiment with an AutoCAD Command

AutoCAD works by following your command. Let us try to use the LINE command to draw a line. With this experiment, you will learn how people interact with the program.

Step 1: Clean up the drawing area

Before we begin, we need to clean up the drawing area that is now occupied by the palettes. Since we will not use the Sheet set manager until we have a set of drawings, we can simply close it.

1 Click the close button ⊠ at the upper left corner of the Sheet Set Manager palette.

- The Tool Palettes are useful for us to launch AutoCAD commands. Although we will not use the tool palettes in the following experiment, we may need it in the future. Instead of closing it, we can push it to the side to make space for the drawing elements.

2 Click the Properties icon ▤ at the lower right corner of the palette and choose Anchor Right >.

The palette is embedded into the window frame on the right.

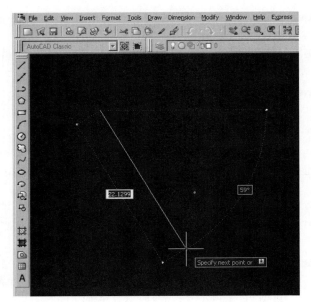

Figure 1.4
Draw a line.

● When you move the cursor over the window frame, the palettes will pop out
automatically.

Step 2: Draw a line

There are many different ways to launch an AutoCAD command. For this experiment,
we will try to use the toolbar that is already placed on the left side of the drawing window. The LINE tool is the first one on top.

1 Click the LINE toolbar
icon ◿ and move the
cursor into the drawing
area.

*Near the crosshair are three boxes. The first
one is AutoCAD's prompt that asks you to
specify the first point. The second and third
are the x and y coordinates of the current
cursor position (Figure 1.4). These boxes are
called Dynamic Input, and they can be toggled on and off through the [DYN] button
on the status bar.*

2 Click to specify a point
(somewhere in the upper
left corner of the drawing area).

*A rubber band line is now stretching from
the specified point, and AutoCAD is
prompting you to specify the next point and
showing you the angle and length of the line.*

3 Click to specify a second point.

*AutoCAD continues to prompt you for the
next point.*

4 Right-click and choose Enter.

The command is terminated.

Look Around in an AutoCAD Drawing

To work on an AutoCAD drawing on a monitor of limited size, you need to zoom in and out to see both tiny details and the entire sheet. The most popular method to zoom in and out is to use the mouse wheel. To zoom in, roll the wheel forward (toward the screen); to zoom out, roll the wheel backward (toward yourself). The zooming is always centered at the cursor. Therefore, before you turn the wheel, move the cursor to the point of interest. Otherwise, what you really want to see will go out of the screen. When that happens, you need to use the PAN function to adjust the view. To do that, hold down the mouse wheel (the cursor will turn into a little hand icon) and drag.

You may also use the ZOOM command to manipulate the view. The ZOOM command is a complex command with many suboptions. You need to learn only three of the suboptions to navigate freely in a large drawing. These subcommands are ZOOM-WINDOW, ZOOM-PREVIOUS, and ZOOM-ALL.

EXPERIMENT 1: ZOOM with the mouse wheel

1 Move cursor over one end of the line.

2 Roll the mouse wheel forward to zoom in.

3 Roll the mouse wheel backward to zoom out.

EXPERIMENT 2: PAN with the mouse wheel

1 Hold down the mouse wheel. The cursor turns into a hand icon.

2 Drag to move the relative position of the line to the drawing window.

- This does not change the position of the line in the drawing.

EXPERIMENT 3: ZOOM-Window

This suboption of the ZOOM command allows you to define the area you want to zoom into. Because it is the most frequently used option, it has been set as a default that is automatically chosen for you by AutoCAD unless you make a different choice. You can start to pick the window definition points right after the ZOOM command is entered. The task of this experiment is to Zoom in to see the end of the line.

1 Click the ZOOM-Window toolbar icon on the Standard toolbar.

2 Move the cursor near the line.

The cursor prompt appears to request you to specify the first point of a zoom window (Figure 1.5a).

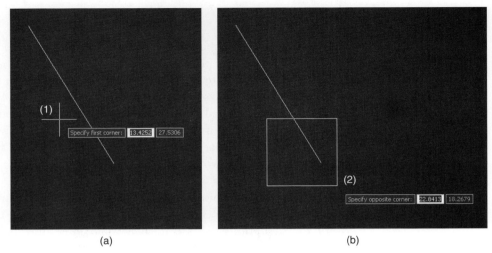

(a)   (b)

Figure 1.5
Use the ZOOM-Window command to zoom in.

3 Pick point (1).

Pick a point close to one end of the line. AutoCAD shows a rubber band window stretching with the movement of your mouse, and asking you to pick the opposite corner of the window (Figure 1.5b).

4 Pick point (2).

AutoCAD zooms into the window you just defined.

EXPERIMENT 4: ZOOM-Previous

This ZOOM function allows you to step back to a previous view. You may keep repeating this subcommand to go back many steps. The task of this experiment is to see what we were looking at previously.

1 Click the ZOOM-Previous toolbar icon 🔍 on the Standard toolbar.

AutoCAD zooms to the previous view.

EXPERIMENT 5: ZOOM-All

ZOOM-ALL command means "zoom out to see the whole drawing." It allows you to see the whole drawing you are working on to its outermost limits. In a drawing session, after you zoom in and out many times, you may get lost. The easiest way to get out of the uncertainty is to see the whole picture. Then you can jump in again.

This time, we will try to communicate with AutoCAD through the keyboard by typing in our input. When you enter the input, read the command line output and respond accordingly.

Command: ↵

Hitting the [Enter] key makes AutoCAD repeat the last command.

ZOOM

Specify corner of window, enter
a scale factor (nX or nXP), or

[All/Center/Dynamic/Extents/
Previous/Scale/Window]
<realtime>: **A** ↵   *Choose the subcommand All by entering A.*
Command: *AutoCAD zooms to the outermost limits.*

Commands for Correcting Your Mistakes: Cancel, Undo, Redo, Erase, and Oops

Before you begin, you need to know a few commands that will help you correct common mistakes in AutoCAD sessions. As a novice, you cannot avoid making mistakes. In most scenarios, you can step back from your mistakes. In the following miniexercise, you will practice how to correct your mistakes. AutoCAD is very forgiving.

Let's assume that you want to draw a series of lines.

EXPERIMENT 6: Escape from a wrong command

Let us assume that you clicked the construction line tool instead of the LINE tool by mistake, and the construction line command started.

1 **Click the construction line**   *The construction line command started.*
   tool ◩ icon that is right below   *You are prompted to specify a point.*
   the LINE tool on the drawing
   toolbar.

2 **Hit the Esc key.**   *The command is cancelled.*

EXPERIMENT 7: UNDO a mistaken step within a LINE command

Let us use the LINE command to draw a series of lines, and assume that after drawing the second segment, you discover that the second line segment was not drawn correctly. You want to go back one step and redraw that line segment without exiting the command.

1 Click the LINE toolbar icon ◩ to start the LINE command.

2 Pick a starting point as requested.

3 Pick a second point.

4 Pick a third point.

5 Right-click and choose Undo from the pop-up menu.

6 Pick another point.

7 Right-click and choose Enter to terminate the command.

EXPERIMENT 8: UNDO a command

Let us assume that you discover both line segments are incorrect. You want to UNDO the LINE command.

Right-click in the drawing window
and choose Undo Line.
The lines disappear.

EXPERIMENT 9: REDO the undone command

Let us assume that the two line segments are not totally incorrect. Therefore, you want to bring them back.

Right-click in the drawing window
and choose Redo Line.
The lines reappear.

EXPERIMENT 10: ERASE a line segment

Let us assume that the first line segment is wrong and that you want to erase it and draw another line segment.

1 Click the ERASE toolbar icon 🖉 **on the Modify toolbar (located on the right side of the drawing window).**
The cursor turns into a small box and the cursor prompt asks you to select objects.

2 Move the cursor over the line segment you want to erase.
The line segment is highlighted (Figure 1.6).

3 Click to select the line segment.
The line segment turns into a dotted line.

4 Right-click to finish the command.

5 Use the LINE command to draw a new line segment.
See Figure 1.7.

EXPERIMENT 11: Use the OOPS command to bring back the last erased object

Let us assume that you suddenly realize you should not have erased the first line segment, and you want to bring it back while keeping the new line segment you just created. At

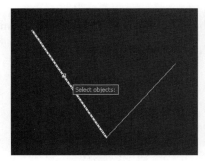

Figure 1.6
ERASE a line.

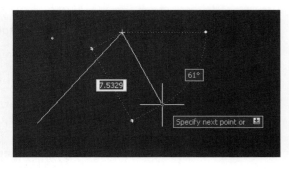

Figure 1.7
Draw a new line segment.

this moment, you cannot use UNDO to bring back the first line segment because that will UNDO the new line segment before you can UNDO the ERASE command. You need to use the OOPS command to bring back the last erased object. Because OOPS is an old command that is not on the right-click pop-up menu, we need to use the old-fashioned key-in method to type in the command using the keyboard.

1 Type OOPS.

2 Hit the Enter key.   *The line segment reappears.*

Handling Files

While you are working on your drawing on the monitor, the result of a working session will be stored in electronic files. Handling files is fundamental to your work with AutoCAD. When you first start your drawing, you need to create an AutoCAD drawing with a name. In a drawing session, you need to save the changes you made to the drawing file. When you finish a drawing session, you need to make sure you save your work before exiting the program. When you continue your work on an unfinished drawing you saved in a previous session, you need to open an existing drawing file.

EXPERIMENT 12: Save and name a new file

After you start a new drawing from scratch, you need to save it and give it a name. The command for this purpose is SAVE.

1 Click the SAVE toolbar icon 🖫 on the   *The Save Drawing As dialog box*
  Standard toolbar.   *pops up (Figure 1.8).*

2 Clear the text field File name.

3 Type the drawing name: myfirst.

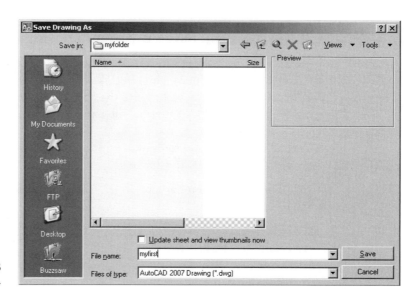

Figure 1.8
Save drawing.

4 Look at the text box Save in: to see where the file will be saved (write it down if you are not sure you can remember it). If the directory is not where you want to store your files, you may find the directory through the "Save in" drop-down list or the shortcut icons in the window on the left side of the dialog box to go to directories such as My Documents.

- A common problem for beginners is that they overlook this information and they cannot find their drawing files after saving them. If you have problems navigating in the Windows directory system, see your reference on basic Windows operation.

5 Click the button Save.

- The dialog box disappears and the new drawing name appears in the title bar. A file is created with the name **myfirst.dwg**. The file name extension **.dwg** (meaning "drawing") is automatically added by AutoCAD.

EXPERIMENT 13: Save changes to a named drawing file

The command QSAVE (meaning "quick save") allows you to save the most recent changes to the named drawing file. It does not call up the Save Drawing As dialog box unless you have not named your file. Note that the QSAVE command is launched by clicking the same toolbar icon 🔲 that evoked the SAVE command. AutoCAD knows you have already named the drawing file and will automatically use the QSAVE command instead of the SAVE command when you click the toolbar icon.

1 Click the toolbar icon 🔲 on the   *AutoCAD updates the file.*
Standard toolbar.

- When a file is updated, an old version of the file (that you saved last time) will be created with the same file name and the extension **.bak** (meaning "backup"). In this experiment, a file named **myfirst.bak** is created in the same folder as the .dwg file.

EXPERIMENT 14: Save the current drawing as a new file

Sometimes you may want to save a copy of the current drawing (displayed on the monitor screen) and give it a new name. In this situation, use the SAVEAS command. The SAVEAS command allows you to give the current drawing a new name and keep the original file as it was with its original file name.

1 Use the LINE command to draw a
line to make a change to the drawing.

2 Click File on the menu bar and   *The Save Drawing As dialog box pops up*
choose Save As . . .   *(Figure 1.9).*

3 Enter a new drawing name
"mysecond" in the text field
"File name."

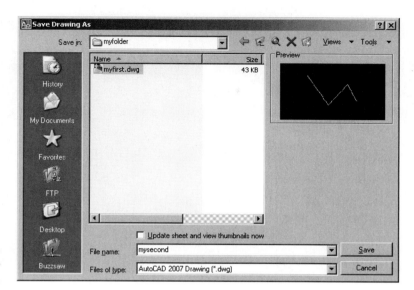

Figure 1.9
Save a file as a new
drawing.

4 Make sure you know the folder
name in the field "Save in."

5 Hit the [Enter] key on the
keyboard.

*This action remotely "hits" the highlighted
"Save" button (with the dark shadow). The
dialog box disappears, a drawing file named
"mysecond" is created and opened as the current drawing, and the file "myfirst" is closed
and preserved as it was saved last time
(without the last line added to the drawing).*

● The command SAVEAS is very similar to SAVE when you use them to save the
current drawing under a name different from the original; they both use the
same Save Drawing As dialog box. The difference between the two commands is
that the SAVE command saves the contents (with changes) of the current drawing in a new file with the new name and puts it away, while the SAVEAS command saves the contents (with changes) of the current drawing in a new file
with the new name, puts it in the current drawing window, and puts away the
original drawing file (without changes).

EXPERIMENT 15: Open a drawing file

The command OPEN allows you to open existing files. When you click on the Standard toolbar icon 🖝, AutoCAD will respond with a dialog box. You may select any
drawing on the list and open it with the **Open** button. Or you can go to different directories to locate your file and open it. When a new drawing is open, the previously
opened drawing will recede to the background but remain open. To support multiple
drawing sessions, AutoCAD has to divide the computing power to juggle the tasks and
thus reduces the computer's performance. Therefore, you should close the previously
opened drawings before opening a new drawing if the previously opened drawing is
no longer needed.

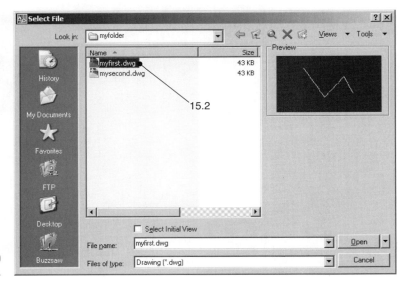

Figure 1.10
Open a file.

1 Click the OPEN toolbar icon ![icon].	*The "Select file" dialog pops up (Figure 1.10).*
2 Click file myfirst **on the list.**	*The file name appears in the "File name" field. You may see the image in the "Preview window."*
3 Hit Enter.	*The highlighted [Open] button is remotely hit. The selected drawing file opens.*

EXPERIMENT 16: SAVE a file to a flash drive

At the end of a working session, you may want to save your drawing file to your USB flash drive. The command SAVE can be used for this task. The procedure is similar to the one shown in Experiment 8.

1 Insert a flash drive into the USB port.	
2 Click File on the menu bar and choose Save As	*The Save Drawing As dialog box pops up.*
3 Click the drop-down arrow next to the list box Save in: to find flash drive.	*It is usually shown as "Removable Disk."*
4 Click flash drive on the list.	*It appears in the list box.*
5 Click the button Save.	*AutoCAD will start to save the file to the floppy disk.*

EXPERIMENT 17: SAVE a drawing file in AutoCAD 2004 format

Because previous versions of AutoCAD, such as 2004, are still in use, and they cannot open .dwg files saved in Release 2007, you may need to save your file in the format of AutoCAD 2004, for example. This can be accomplished in the Save Drawing As dialog box, where you simply click the drop-down list **Save as type:** and select the appropriate file type.

1 **Click File on the menu bar and choose** Save As . . . .

The Save Drawing As dialog box pops up.

2 **Click the drop-down arrow next to the list box** Save in: **to find your disk drive.**

3 **Click the** Save as type: **drop-down list.**

The list drops down.

4 **Click on** AutoCAD 2004/LT2004 Drawing [*.dwg].

5 **In the text box** File name: **change the file name from** myfirst **to** myfirst2004.

6 **Click the button** Save.

AutoCAD will start to save the file to your disk.

EXPERIMENT 18: QUIT

The command QUIT terminates the AutoCAD program when you finish a drawing session. The QUIT command can be launched by using the key combination Ctrl + Q. If you have not saved all the changes, a warning will pop up. You may then choose whether to save.

1 **Use the LINE command to draw a line** to make a change to the drawing.

2 **Hold down the Ctrl key and hit Q on the keyboard.**

A warning pops up (Figure 1.11).

3 **Click** Yes.

● You may also end a drawing session by clicking the close button ⊠.

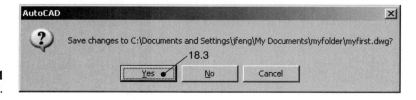

Figure 1.11
AutoCAD warning on quit.

EXPERIMENT 19: Copy file to a recordable CD

If you use a recordable CD to store your files, you need to save the finished drawing to the hard disk of the computer and then copy the file to the CD.

1 **Insert a blank CD into the CD drive.**

Windows XP will show a dialog box to let you choose what to do with the CD.

2 **Choose** Open writable CD folder.

3 **Click** OK.

The explorer will show the files on the CD.

4 **Find the drawing file and drag it on to the CD folder.**

The explorer window shows a message saying, "Files ready to be written to CD."

5 **Click** Write these files to CD.

The CD Writing Wizard dialog box pops up.

6 **Click** Next **and wait.**

The wizard will show progress, and the CD drive will open when the copy is made.

7 **Click** Finish.

Start a Floor Plan

- Set up a Drawing
- Draw Wall Lines

In this chapter, a very simple method of drawing wall lines will be introduced as a starting point to your adventure into the world of AutoCAD drafting. In the following tutorial, you will draw a simple floor plan, as shown in Figure 2.1. In the drawing process, you will learn a few frequently used commands. While you are practicing, reflect on what you are doing, and memorize the commands and the corresponding responses from AutoCAD. If you are bogged down by mistakes, apply the rescue skills you practiced in Chapter 1.

Set up a Drawing

Before you start to draw in AutoCAD, you should set up the drawing first to meet your needs in the drafting process. It is a good idea to start a drawing from a ready-made template. A template contains many fundamental settings that determine how the drawing behaves. Starting with incorrect settings will give you all sorts of problems and it will be tedious to correct them. A careful start ensures future smooth operation.

When the AutoCAD program starts, a default drawing opens with the name "Drawing1.dwg." The settings of this default drawing may vary according to the preference settings of the AutoCAD program. Therefore, it may not meet your require-

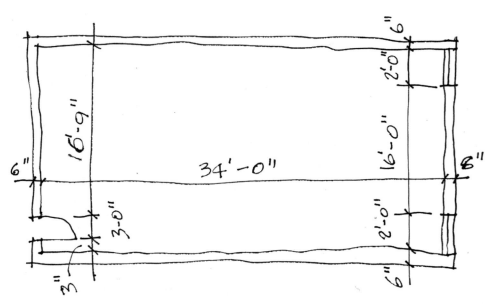

Figure 2.1
A simple floor plan.

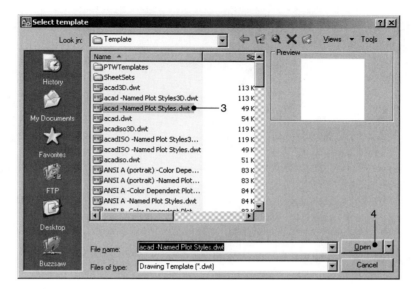

Figure 2.2
Select template.

ments. You should *not* use it unless you are sure how it was set up. Instead, you should use the NEW command to start a drawing from the beginning using a template.

1 **Start AutoCAD.**

2 **Click the NEW toolbar icon** ▢ **on**   *The Select template dialog box pops up*
   the Standard toolbar.   *(Figure 2.2).*

3 **Select** acad-Named Plot Styles.dwt.

4 **Click Open.**   *A new drawing opens.*

   ● The template we just selected is a rather generic template. We need to set the
     following settings.

Step 1: Set drawing measurement UNITS

AutoCAD can report measurement output and accept dimension input in a few different formats. Because we use the architectural style (feet and inches) in interior design drawings, we need to tell AutoCAD our preference.

1 **Enter Command: UNITS.**   *The Drawing Units dialog box pops up*
                                                 (Figure 2.3).

2 **Click the** Length-Type **drop-down**
   list and choose architectural.

3 **Click OK.**

   ● From this point, AutoCAD begins to take in measurement input and to report
     measurement output in the architectural format (for example: 2′-3″). Numerical
     inputs without foot or inch designators will be taken as inches. Therefore, you

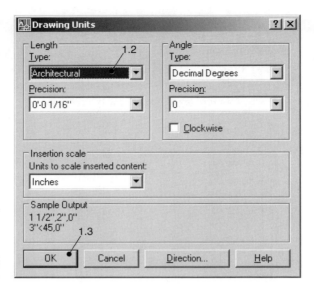

Figure 2.3
Set drawing units.

will never need to enter the inch mark when entering a dimension unless you do not mind wasting one keystroke.

Step 2: Set drawing LIMITS

Unlike drafting on paper that is always limited in size, you have an almost unlimited space in AutoCAD. If you like, you can map the whole earth in an AutoCAD drawing in full scale. (Printing it out, however, is another matter!) Because the space is unlimited in AutoCAD, we *always draw in actual size* in AutoCAD. If a door opening in reality is three feet wide, you draw it in AutoCAD three feet wide, too. Only when you start to think about how to print out the drawing do you think about it in terms of scale. (This will be discussed in Chapter 11.) Although space is unlimited in Auto-CAD, the space you will be working on is likely to be limited in size. A set of drawing limits will help AutoCAD to focus on the area of work. Some AutoCAD commands, such as ZOOM, also use the drawing limits as a guide. In setting up a drawing, there-fore, you need to define the limits of your drawing area. For this tutorial, a 40' × 30' drawing area will be more than adequate to contain the 34' × 20' floor plan. These limits are arbitrarily set based on a commonsense estimate. You may change it any time you need more or less space. To define the working area, use the command LIMITS, which defines a rectangular area with its lower left and upper right corners.

Command: **LIMITS** ↵   *Enter the command LIMITS.*
Reset Model space limits:

Specify lower left corner or
[ON/OFF] <0'-0",0'-0">: ↵   *Accept the default value 0,0.*

Specify upper right corner
<1'-0",0'-9">: **40',30'** ↵   *Enter the upper right corner coordinates.*

Command: *AutoCAD is ready for new command.*

- Usually, you accept the point 0,0 as the lower left corner.

Step 3: Turn on ORTHO

In manual drafting, we need tools such as a T-square and triangles to draw horizontal and vertical lines. In AutoCAD drafting, we can turn on the ORTHO (orthogonal) mode to restrain the cursor to horizontal or vertical movement. The ORTHO mode status is indicated on the status line at the bottom of the AutoCAD drawing window. If the ORTHO button on the status line is not depressed, it indicates that ORTHO mode is off. You can click the button to turn it on. If you click it again, it will be turned off.

Click the ORTHO **button.**   *The button turns depressed.*

- The ORTHO mode can also be toggled by pressing the function key [F8].

Step 4: Set up GRID

In manual drafting on paper, we have a good sense of space and dimension because we know how big the paper is. In CAD drafting, we may easily lose this sense of space and dimension after we zoom in and zoom out a few times. The **GRID** setting allows AutoCAD to display a grid in the drawing area to give us a sense of space and dimension.

Command: **GRID** ↵   *Enter the command GRID.*
Specify grid spacing(X) or [ON/OFF/
Snap/Major/aDaptive/Limits/Follow/Aspect]
<0'-0 1/2">: **24** ↵   *Set the grid spacing.*

- Entering 24 at the prompt not only sets the grid spacing but also turns on the grid. Because the current drawing window only displays an area of 12 inches wide by 9 inches high (by default), the grid is not visible until you ZOOM out to look at a greater area of the drawing.

Command: **Z** ↵

ZOOM

Specify corner of window, enter a scale
factor (nX or nXP), or

[All/Center/Dynamic/Extents/Previous/
Scale/Window] <real time>: **A** ↵

Regenerating model.   *The grid shows.*

- The grid display can be toggled off and on by hitting the function key [F7], or clicking the [GRID] button embedded in the status line at the bottom of the AutoCAD window.

Step 5: Set up SNAP

In CAD drafting, the drawing elements are generated in a coordinate system. Randomly picking a point may result in coordinates of fractioned values, such as 13/16". This will make reading the coordinates very difficult. The **SNAP** setting restricts cursor movement to specified intervals and therefore controls the accuracy of the points you pick. You can use the command SNAP to set the snap settings.

Command: **SNAP** ↵   *Enter the command SNAP.*
Specify snap spacing or [ON/
OFF/Aspect/Rotate/Style/Type]
<0'-0 1/2">: **1** ↵

- Similar to setting the grid, entering 1 at the prompt sets the snap spacing and turns on the snap function. You can see the effect of this command at the status line where the coordinates of the cursor position are reported. Now, you no longer have the fractioned measurements. The snap mode can be toggled off and on by hitting the function key [F9] or clicking the button [SNAP] embedded in the status line at the bottom of the AutoCAD window.

It is important to know the difference between the grid shown in the drawing area and the snap grid. The grid controlled by the GRID setting is a visual aid, and it does not restrict cursor movements. The visual grid may have a different spacing from that of the snap grid. The two can be turned on or off independently.

Draw Wall Lines

Step 1: Create base wall lines with LINE

LINE is the most fundamental command in AutoCAD. We experimented with it in the previous chapter and you will use it a lot in the future.

Clicking the LINE toolbar icon ◪ **on the Draw toolbar.**

Command: _line Specify first point: *Note: Point location does not need*
pick a point at the lower left   *to be exact.*
corner of the drawing field.

Specify next point or [Undo]:   *See Figure 2.4.*
move mouse to the right to make
a rubber band stretching
horizontally and key in 34'.

Specify next point or [Undo]:
move mouse up to make the
rubber band stretching
right up and key in 20'.

Figure 2.4
Move mouse to the right
and key in the distance.

Figure 2.5
The completed interior wall lines.

Specify next point or [Undo]:
**move mouse to the left to make
a rubber band stretching
horizontally and key in 34′.**

Specify next point or [Close/Undo]: **C⏎**   *To close the rectangle and terminate
the command. See Figure 2.5.*

Command: *AutoCAD is ready for the next
command.*

Step 2: Create more wall lines with OFFSET

The OFFSET command allows you to create another line or other linear elements that are offset from the original. The offset line will be parallel to the original line. When you launch the OFFSET command by clicking the OFFSET toolbar icon ⬛, you are prompted for the distance between the original line and the offset line. You should type in the value of the distance. (This key-in operation saves you effort in maneuvering the mouse and guarantees accuracy.) Then you will be prompted to pick the original line. After picking the line, you will be prompted to indicate on which side of the original line you want the offset line to be placed. You can pick any point that is to the side of the original line. To terminate the command, you need to hit [Enter] or to right-click.

When drawing the two base lines in the previous step, you may have noticed that a small yellow-colored square appeared at the end of the lines. That is the Object Snap function that is intended to assist you to snap to certain critical points on an object. Before you start to use the OFFSET command, make sure the object snap mode (OSNAP) is off to avoid unwanted snapping. Click [OSNAP] on the status line, or hit [F3] to toggle the OSNAP off. The functions of the object-snap mode will be discussed later.

Click the OFFSET toolbar icon 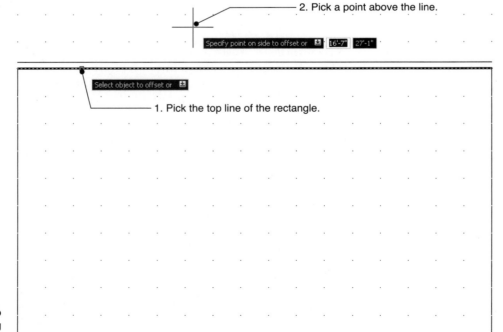 on the Modify toolbar.

Command: Offset	
Specify offset distance or [Through] <0'-1">: **6** ↵	*Input distance.*
Select object to offset or <exit>: **pick the top line of the rectangle**	*Pick original line.*
Specify point on side to offset: **pick a point above it**	*Indicate side of offset and the offset line is created. See Figure 2.6.*
Repeat two more times to create offset lines on the left and lower sides of the room.	
Select object to offset or <exit>: ↵	*Terminate the command.*
Command: ↵	*Restart the last command to enter a different distance.*
OFFSET	
Specify offset distance or [Through] <6">: **8** ↵	*Input distance.*
Select object to offset or <exit>: **pick the vertical line on the right**	*Pick original line.*

2. Pick a point above the line.

Specify point on side to offset or 16'-7" 27'-1"

Select object to offset or

1. Pick the top line of the rectangle.

Figure 2.6
Create wall lines by
OFFSET.

Figure 2.7
Create wall lines by
OFFSET: the result.

Specify point on side to offset: **pick a point to the right of the line**	*Indicate side of offset and offset line is created.*
Select object to offset or <exit>: ⏎	*Terminate the command (Figure 2.7).*
Command:	

Step 3: Fix corner joints of wall lines with FILLET

The command FILLET is intended to link two lines with an arc. When the radius of the arc is set to 0, the command can be used to join two lines at the actual or implied intersection. The default value for the radius of the arc is 0. The easiest way to launch the FILLET command is to click the toolbar icon ▣ on the Modify toolbar. Auto-CAD will prompt you to pick two lines. When the lines are picked, they will be perfectly connected. If the two lines intersect, a section of each line will be cut off. It is important to remember that the section that you pick will remain while the other section beyond the intersection will be removed.

Click the FILLET toolbar icon ▣ .

Command: FILLET	
Current settings: Mode=TRIM, Radius=0′-0″	
Select first object or [Polyline/ Radius/Trim/mUltiple]: **pick a line**	*(Figure 2.8).*
Select second object: **pick the line to be connected**	*The lines are connected.*
Command: ⏎	*Restart FILLET command.*

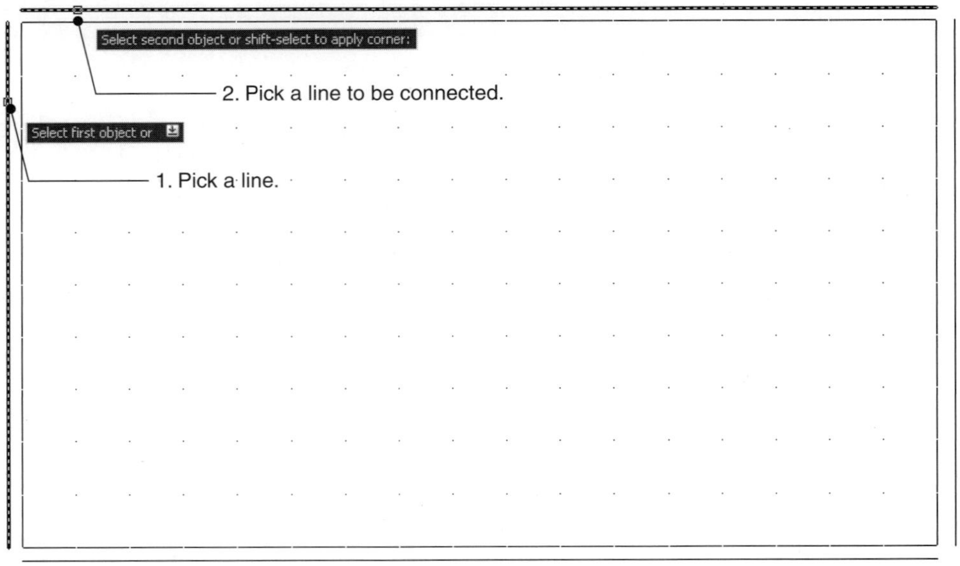

Figure 2.8
Use FILLET to connect the corners.

Select second object or shift-select to apply corner:

2. Pick a line to be connected.

Select first object or

1. Pick a line.

FILLET

Polyline/Radius/<Select first object>: **continue to connect the other corners.**

...

Figure 2.9 shows what the result should look like.

- The FILLET command terminates after working on a pair of lines. You need to use the Enter key or the Space bar to restart the command for each pair of lines, or you can choose the Multiple option by entering **M** before picking the lines.

Figure 2.9
After FILLET commands.

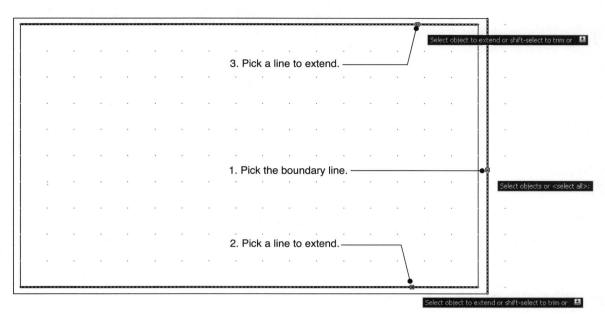

Figure 2.10
EXTEND wall lines.

Step 4: Extend the wall lines with EXTEND

As the command name suggests, the command EXTEND extends a line or other linear object toward a selected boundary object. The intention of this step is to extend the two interior horizontal wall lines to the exterior wall line on the right to make the window openings.

Click the EXTEND toolbar icon ⊟ on the
Modify toolbar.

Command: EXTEND

Current settings: Projection=UCS,
Edge=None

Select boundary edges ... **pick the vertical**   *See Figure 2.10.*
exterior wall line

Select objects: 1 found

Select objects: ↵

Select object to extend or shift-select
to trim or [Project/Edge/Undo]: **pick a**
horizontal line

Select object to extend or shift-select to
trim or [Project/Edge/Undo]: **pick a**
horizontal line

Select object to extend or shift-select to trim or   *See Figure 2.11.*
[Project/Edge/Undo]: ↵

Figure 2.11
Result of extended lines.

Step 5: Create window opening lines with OFFSET

Click the OFFSET toolbar icon 🔳 **on the Modify toolbar.**

Command: OFFSET

Specify offset distance or [Through]   *for window opening.*
<0'-8">: **24** ↵

Select object to offset or <exit>: **pick line**   *Pick original line (Figure 2.12).*

Specify point on side to offset: **pick point**   *Indicate side of offset.*

Select object to offset or <exit>: **pick line**   *Pick original line.*

Figure 2.12
Create window opening
lines.

Specify point on side to offset: **pick point**   *Indicate side of offset.*

Select object to offset or <exit>: ⏎   *Terminate the command.*

Command: ⏎

Step 6: Make the window opening with TRIM

When you have lines intersecting each other, the command TRIM allows you to trim the unwanted portion of the lines beyond the intersection. (This means that you cannot use this command if the lines do not intersect.) In this operation, one line (or a group of lines) is selected as the cutting edge(s), and you can use it (or them) to trim other lines. If the selected cutting edges intersect, they can also be used to trim each other. In this step, we will select all the lines on the right side of the floor plan as cutting edges and then cut off the portions of lines that we don't need.

Click the TRIM toolbar icon 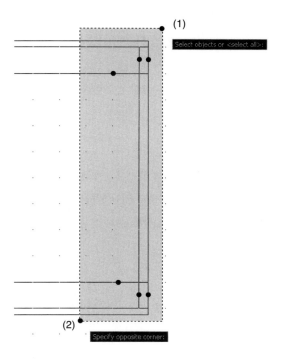 **on the Modify toolbar.**

Command: TRIM

Current settings: Projection=UCS Edge=None

Select cutting edges:

Select objects: **click point (1)** Specify opposite   *You "pull out" a "rubber band"*
corner: **drag and click point (2)** 8 found   *window (Figure 2.13).*
Select objects: ⏎   *Terminate selection.*

- In previous steps, you selected objects by clicking on each individual object. For this step, you used an **implied crossing-window** to select a group of objects all at once. When AutoCAD prompts you to select objects, you can click on an empty

Figure 2.13
Select cutting edges.

spot in the drawing area, and AutoCAD takes it as an implied request from you for a selection window to catch a group of objects and a rubber band window can be pulled out. If you pull out the window from right to left, you have a **crossing-window** that will catch and select both the objects that are entirely enclosed in the window and the objects crossed by the window frame. If you pull out the window from left to right, you have a **selection-window** that will catch only the objects that are entirely enclosed in the window. To use these selection methods, you must carefully plan the first picking point in order to drag out the type of window you need. The crossing-window is made of dotted lines and shaded with green; the selection-window is made of solid lines and shaded with blue.

Select object to trim or [Project/Edge/ Undo]: **pick line marked in Figure 2.13.**	*Pick unwanted line segment.*
Select object to trim or [Project/Edge/ Undo]: **pick line**	
Select object to trim or [Project/Edge/ Undo]: **pick line**	
Select object to trim or [Project/Edge/ Undo]: **pick line**	
Select object to trim or [Project/Edge/ Undo]: **pick line**	
Select object to trim or [Project/Edge/ Undo]: **pick line**	
Select object to trim or [Project/Edge/Undo]: ↵	*Terminate the command.*
Command:	*See Figure 2.14 for the completed result.*

Step 7: Make the door opening

To make the door opening, you need to create the lines first and then use the TRIM command to remove the portion of the wall lines in the door opening. In this step, we will use the **object tracking** technique to draw a line 3 inches from the lower left corner of the room to create the door opening line in the wall.

1 ZOOM in to look at the lower left corner of the room.

2 Look at the status line to make sure the [OTRACK] button is depressed.

3 Look at the status line to make sure the [OSNAP] button is depressed.

4 Start the LINE command.

Click the LINE toolbar icon.

Command: LINE Specify first point: **Move the cursor over the inside corner of the wall until you see a small square appear at the corner point, and DO NOT click.**

Figure 2.14
Completed window
opening.

● This is the work of the object snap (OSNAP) function. When OSNAP is on, AutoCAD will automatically snap to some particular points of an object. You may determine the types of points OSNAP catches. This will be discussed in more detail later.

Move the cursor straight up until a dotted line appears with a text box reporting the distance from the corner. See Figure 2.15. At this moment, key in 3.

Specify first point: **3⏎**   *The line starts from a point 3 inches from the corner.*

Move the cursor to the left until it touches the outside wall line.

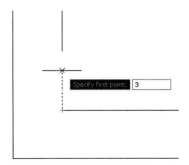

Figure 2.15
Use OTRACK.

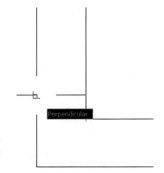

Figure 2.16
Use PERPENDICULAR
object snap.

Specify next point or
[Undo]: **PER**↵

Use the PERPENDICULAR object snap function. You should see the perpendicular symbol ⌐ appearing at the end of the rubber band line. See Figure 2.16.

Click to catch the point

Specify next point or [Undo]: ↵

End the command.

5 Use OFFSET to create the other door opening line, 36 inches away.

6 Use the TRIM command to create the opening in the wall.

See Figure 2.17.

Step 8: Save your file and end AutoCAD session

1 Save your drawing as ch02.dwg.

2 QUIT to exit AutoCAD.

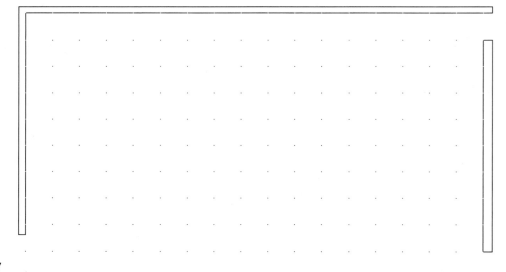

Figure 2.17
Finished wall lines.

Modify and Add to the Floor Plan

- **Create the New Walls**
- **Draw the Doors**
- **Draw the Windows**
- **Draw the Counter**

This chapter continues work on the simple floor plan from Chapter 2 by modifying and adding to it according to the designer's red-line sketch (Figure 3.1). In the process, you will continue to learn more drawing and editing commands and basic object snap functions.

Create the New Walls

In the design process, changes are inevitable. In manual drafting, making changes means erasures, dust, smudges, and repeated drafting of the same drawing elements. In CAD drafting, making changes is easy and clean. You can erase, move, rotate, scale, and stretch drawing elements easily.

1 **Start an AutoCAD session** and **OPEN** ▓ the unfinished floor plan you created in the previous tutorial.

2 **Use the SAVEAS command to save it as a new drawing and name it "Ch03" (save it to the hard disk of your computer).**

- Because the drawing settings you set in previous working sessions were saved, you don't have to set them again when you reopen an existing drawing.

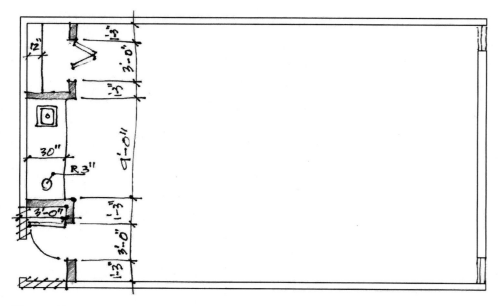

Figure 3.1
The designer's red-line markup.

Step 1: Create new walls with COPY

To make changes and additions, you need to plan your steps. Because there are already walls in the drawing, you can use the COPY command to create added walls and use modifying tools to finish them.

1   Click the COPY toolbar icon 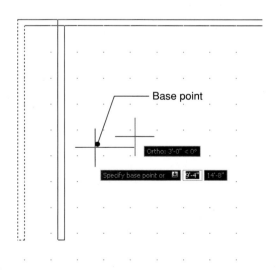 **on the Modify toolbar.**

Command: COPY

Select objects: **pick a point to pull out
a selection window**

Specify opposite corner: **pick a point
to include the wall on the left**

6 found

Select objects: **press Space bar**   *Terminate selection.*

- Pressing the Space bar while a command is being executed equals pressing the [Enter] key, which usually signals the termination of an ongoing action or the command. Because the Space bar is larger than the [Enter] key and can be easily pressed by the hand not operating the mouse, you can work faster.

Specify base point or displacement: *See Figure 3.2.*
pick a point

Specify second point of **move cursor
to the right horizontally**
or <use first point as displacement>: **36** ↵   *Enter the distance of the movement to
specify the placement of the copied wall.*

Specify second point of displacement: *Terminate command.*
press Space bar

Figure 3.2
Copy the wall.

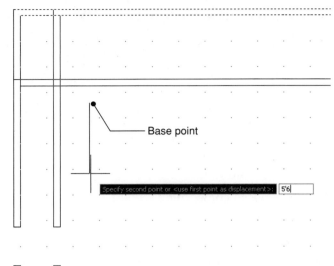

Figure 3.3
Copy the wall.

2 Use the COPY command again to create the new horizontal wall.

Command: **press Space bar**   *Repeat the last command.*

COPY

Select objects: **pick a point to pull
out a cross window**

Specify opposite corner: **pick a point
to let the window go across the top
horizontal wall** 2 found

Select objects: **press Space bar**   *Terminate selection.*

Specify base point or displacement: *See Figure 3.3.*
pick a point

Specify second point of **move cursor**   *Enter the distance of the movement to*
vertically down displacement or   *specify the placement of the copied wall.*
<use first point as displacement>: **5′6** ↵

Specify second point of displacement: *Terminate command.*
press Space bar

Step 2: Duplicate wall with MIRROR

The command MIRROR creates a flipped copy of selected objects on the other side of a Mirror Line defined by two points. You need to figure out how to locate the mirror line to make the best use of this command. You can also use this command as a flipping tool by opting to delete the old set of objects. In this step, we will use the MIRROR command to duplicate the wall on the other side of the counter because the distance between that wall and the lower horizontal wall is also 5'-6". In other words, we have a symmetrical composition.

Click the MIRROR toolbar icon 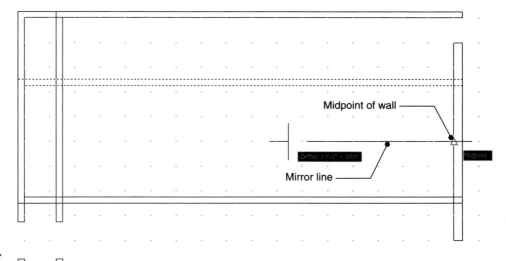 (icon) **on the Modify toolbar.**

Command: MIRROR

Select objects: **pick point to pull out a cross window to select the copied horizontal wall**

Specify opposite corner: **pick point** 2 found

Select objects: **press Space bar**   *End selection.*

Specify first point of mirror line: **MID** ↵   *Activate MIDpoint object snap mode. A small triangle will appear when the cursor is over a line.*

of **click to snap to the midpoint**

Specify second point of mirror line: **pull horizontally to the left and click**   *See Figure 3.4. Define the mirror line.*

- Tip: Turning on ORTHO mode will help to make the mirror line perfectly horizontal.

Delete source objects? [Yes/No]<N>: **press Space bar**   *Accept default value "No."*

- When you face a multiple-choice prompt like this, the item in the angular brackets <> is the default. You may simply hit the [Enter] key to accept the default choice.

- From now on, you never need to draw both sides of a symmetrical object.

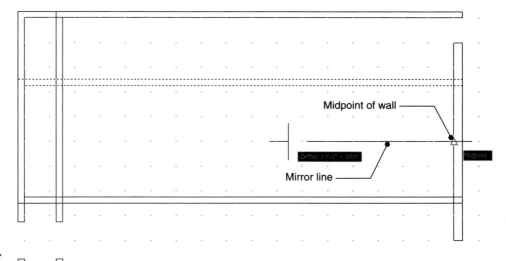

Midpoint of wall

Ortho: 13'-1" < 180°

Midpoint

Mirror line

Figure 3.4
MIRROR the wall.

Figure 3.5
Finished new walls. Dotted lines show the removed portions of the wall lines.

Step 3: Finish the new walls

Use TRIM ⊿, FILLET ▢, and ERASE ◿ to finish the new walls.   *See Figure 3.5.*

When you use the TRIM command with multiple selection of cutting edges, the order in which you pick the lines to be trimmed matters. The lines that are both cutting edges and lines to be trimmed should be trimmed last. Don't forget to ZOOM in for lines within walls.

Step 4: Adjust the location of the door with STRETCH

STRETCH is a wonderful tool to make changes in an existing drawing. After you start the command, AutoCAD will prompt you to select an object with crossing-window. As you have tried previously, you can pull out an implied crossing-window by clicking on an empty area and pulling from right to left. The selected portion of the drawing can then be stretched in a specified direction.

Click the STRETCH toolbar icon ▯ on the Modify toolbar.

Command: _stretch

Select objects to stretch by crossing-window or crossing-polygon...

Select objects: **pick point (1)** Other corner: *See Figure 3.6.*
pick point (2) 6 found

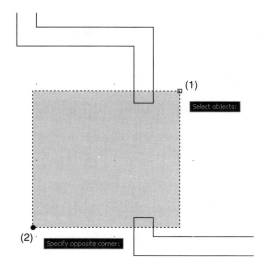

Figure 3.6
Selecting wall with implied
cross-window.

Select objects: **press Space bar**   *End selection.*

Specify base point or displacement:
0,12 ↵

- At this moment, a drastic stretch of the wall may take place in the drawing window. Don't be alarmed.

Specify second point of displacement: ↵   *The wall is stretched out 2 feet.*

Command: *The command terminates.*

- The displacement coordinates (0,12) you entered at the prompt define the movement 12″ in the direction of the y axis and 0″ in the direction of the x axis. Hitting the [Enter] key at the following prompt tells AutoCAD that the coordinates you just entered are a displacement vector, not a base point. Using the displacement input also works in other commands (such as MOVE and COPY). The reason why 12″ is used instead of 1′ is that the feet mark is farther away from the number keys on the keyboard. Entering 24 is faster than entering 2′. The difference will become more significant when both feet and inches are involved. For example, entering 30 is much faster than entering 2′6″.

- In this example, you may have noticed that the lines entirely included in the selection-window remain the same shape, and the lines crossed by the selection-window are stretched. By applying this rule when you make a selection with the crossing-window, you can predict what will be stretched and what will not.

Step 5: Make the door opening for the closet with MIRROR and TRIM

See Figure 3.7.

Figure 3.7
Finished new walls.

Draw the Doors

Step 1: Turn off object snap

Object Snap Modes help you pick particular points (such as the endpoint and mid-point of a drawing element) in the drawing area. So far, the Object Snap Mode has been on by default. When the Object Snap Mode is on, AutoCAD tries to snap to particular points automatically whenever the cursor touches an object. Sometimes, it is really convenient, and other times it is a problem because it keeps snapping points that you don't want. Object Snap can be turned off by clicking the OSNAP button on the status line or by pressing the function key [F3] to toggle it off. If you need to use a particular type of object snap once, you may enter its alias using the keyboard, as we did with PER and MID.

Step 2: Draw the entrance door

1 Zoom in to look at the door opening and leave space for the door.

See Figure 3.1 for reference.

2 Turn on ORTHO if it is not already turned on.

Use the function key [F8].

3 Draw the door with the LINE command ◰.

Command: LINE Specify first point: **END↵**

Activate one-time-only Endpoint object snap mode.

_end of **move the cursor over the corner of the door opening and click when the small square appears at the corner**

Specify next point or [Undo]: **(Move mouse to make the rubber band line go straight down) 2** ⏎

Specify next point or [Undo]: **(Move mouse to make the rubber band line go left.) 36** ⏎

Specify next point or [Close/Undo]: **(Move mouse to make the rubber band line go up.) 2** ⏎

Specify next point or [Close/Undo]: **C** ⏎   *See Figure 3.8.*

4 Turn on the OSNAP by hitting the [F3] key.

- We turn on the OSNAP because we need to snap to three endpoints in the next step.

5 Draw the door swing with the ARC command.

Click the ARC toolbar icon on the Draw toolbar.

Command: ARC Specify start point of arc or [Center]: **pick start point**   *Pick the start point of the arc (Figure 3.9).*

Specify second point of arc or [Center/End]: **C** ⏎   *"C" means Center.*

Specify center point of arc: **pick center point**   *Pick the center point of the arc.*

Specify endpoint of arc or [Angle/chord Length]: **pick end point**   *Pick the endpoint of the arc.*

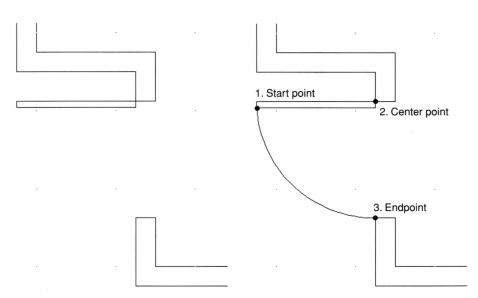

1. Start point
2. Center point
3. Endpoint

Figure 3.8
Draw the door.

Figure 3.9
Draw the door swing.

Command: *The ARC command terminates au-*
                                            tomatically.

- The ARC command generates arcs in the counterclockwise direction. For example, if you select point (3) as the starting point in the above example, and point (1) as the end, AutoCAD will not draw the arc as you expect. Instead, it will create a ¾ circle in the opposite direction. Therefore, when you use the ARC command you need to plan the sequence of the points you pick before you start to pick points.

Step 3: Draw the folding closet door

The folding closet door is made of angled lines. To draw angled lines in AutoCAD, we can use Polar Tracking to snap a rubber band line in particular angles. If we set the polar tracking angle increment to 45°, we can draw the angled lines easily and accurately.

1 Zoom in to look at the closet door opening.   *See Figure 3.1 for reference.*

2 Turn off ORTHO [F8].

3 Turn on Polar Tracking by clicking the [POLAR] button on the status line.

4 Right-click the [POLAR] button on the status line and choose Settings . . . .   *The Drafting Settings dialog box pops up (Figure 3.10).*

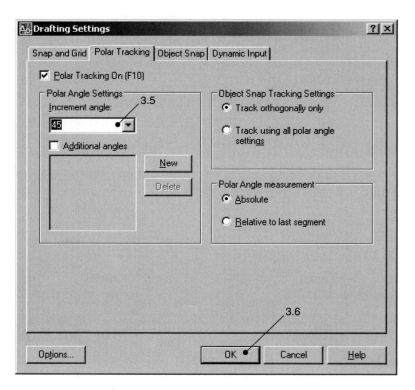

Figure 3.10
Set Polar Tracking increment angle.

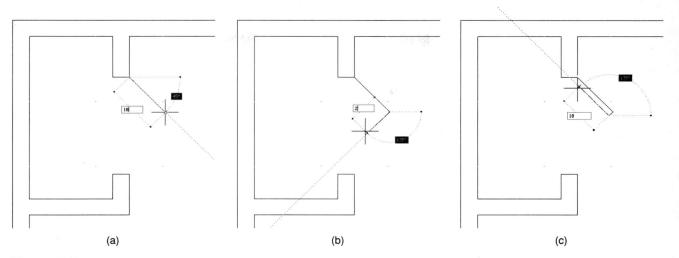

Figure 3.11
Draw the folding door using Polar Tracking.

5 Change the Increment angle value to 45.

6 Click [OK].

7 Use the LINE command 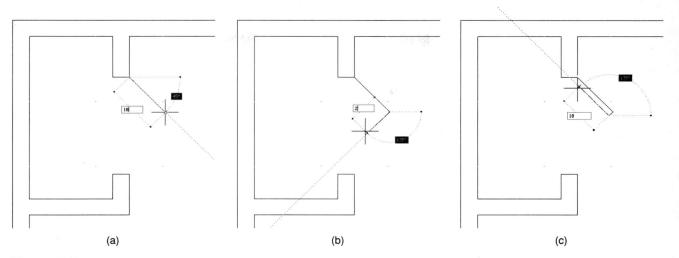 to draw the door lines.

Command: LINE Specify first point: **pick upper right corner of the closet door opening.**

Pull the rubber band toward the lower right corner tentatively until the dotted Polar Tracking line **appears. Enter the length of the line as shown below. See Figure 3.11a.**

Specify next point or [Undo]: **18** ↵

Pull the rubber band toward the lower left corner tentatively until the dotted Polar Tracking line appears. Enter the length of the line as shown below. See Figure 3.11b.

Specify next point or [Undo]: **2** ↵

Pull the rubber band toward the upper left corner tentatively until the dotted Polar Tracking line appears. Enter the length of the line as shown below. See Figure 3.11c.

Specify next point or [Close/Undo]: **18** ↵

Specify next point or [Close/Undo]: **C** ↵

8 Finish the closet door with MIRROR. See Figure 3.12.

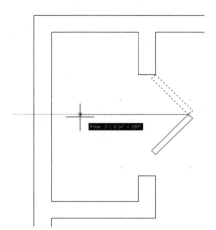

Figure 3.12
Finish the folding door
with MIRROR

Draw the Windows

Step 1: Draw the windowsill lines

1 Zoom and Pan to see the window opening in detail.

2 Draw the exterior windowsill line with the LINE command ◩.

Command: LINE Specify first point: *See Figure 3.13.*
pick point (1)

Specify next point or [Undo]: **pick point (2)**

Specify next point or [Undo]: ↵

Command:

3 Use the COPY command ◙ to create the interior sill line.

Command: COPY

Select objects: **select the first sill line** 1 found

Select objects: **press Space bar**

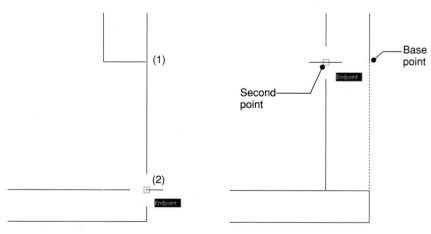

Figure 3.13
Draw the sill line.

Figure 3.14
Copy the sill line.

Specify base point or displacement: **use OSNAP to snap to the upper end of the first sill line**

Specify second point of displacement or
<use first point as displacement>: **Snap to the corner of the window opening. See Figure 3.14.**

Specify second point of displacement: ↵

Step 2: Create the window lines with OFFSET

Click the OFFSET toolbar icon ▣.

Command: OFFSET

Specify offset distance or [Through] <Through>: **2** ↵

Select object to offset or <exit>: **pick the interior sill line**   *See Figure 3.15.*

Specify point on side to offset: **Click outside the window.**

Select object to offset or <exit>: **pick newly created window line**

Specify point on side to offset: **Click outside the window.**

Select object to offset or <exit>: **pick the upper window opening line**

Specify point on side to offset: **Click below that line.**

Select object to offset or <exit>: **pick the lower window opening line**

Specify point on side to offset: **Click above that line.**

Select object to offset or <exit>: ↵

Step 3: Finish the window lines with TRIM

Finish the window lines with the TRIM command ▣.   *See Figure 3.16.*

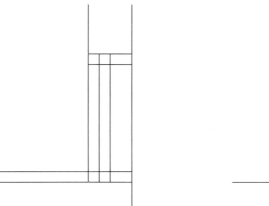
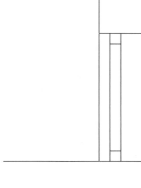

Figure 3.15
Create window lines with OFFSET.

Figure 3.16
Finished window lines.

Step 4: Duplicate the window lines with MIRROR

Use the MIRROR command 🔼 to duplicate the window lines to fill the other window opening. Use the MIDpoint OSNAP to catch the start point of the mirror line.

Draw the Counter

Step 1: Create the counter line

Use OFFSET 🔲 to create the counter line 30 inches from the wall.

See Figure 3.17.

Step 2: Draw the circular opening on the counter with CIRCLE

There are many methods to draw a circle with the CIRCLE command. The simplest one is to specify the center and radius. The challenge we have here is how to locate the center point on the counter. Let us assume that the center point is located 18″ up and 15″ to the right of the lower left corner of the counter. Although there are ways to locate a point from a reference point to start the circle, they are too complicated to use. We will first draw the circle at the corner of the counter and then use the MOVE command to move the circle to the right position.

Click the CIRCLE toolbar icon 🔲 on the Draw toolbar.

Command: CIRCLE Specify center point for
circle or [3P/2P/Ttr (tan tan radius)]:

snap to the lower left corner of the counter

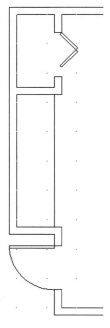

Figure 3.17
Create the counter line
using the **OFFSET** com-
mand.

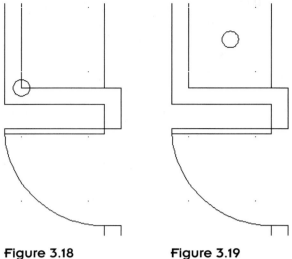

Figure 3.18
Draw the circle.

Figure 3.19
Move the circle.

Specify radius of circle or [Diameter]: **3** ↵   *Enter the radius. See Figure 3.18.*

Click the MOVE toolbar icon ⊕ **on the
Modify toolbar.**

Command: MOVE

Select objects: **pick the circle**

1 found

Select objects: ↵

Specify base point or displacement: **15,18** ↵   *Enter the displacement.*

Specify second point of displacement or <use   *See Figure 3.19.*
first point as displacement>: ↵

Step 3: Insert a sink from the AutoCAD Design Center symbol library

A symbol library can be accessed through the Design Center.

1 Click the "Design Center" button ▦   *See Figure 3.20.*
on the standard toolbar to bring up
the DESIGNCENTER palette.

2 Click the "folders" tab.

3 Click the plus sign next to the
DesignCenter folder to expand it.

4 Click the plus sign next to "Kitchens.dwg."

5 Click "Blocks."   *The blocks contained in the
drawing appear on the left.*

6 Click "Sink-single."   *A larger image of the sink pops up.*

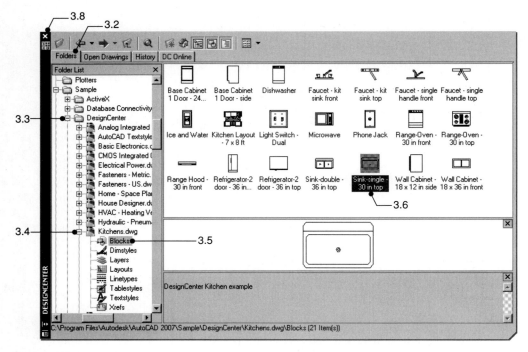

Figure 3.20
The DesignCenter palette.

7 DRAG the block (*not* the image) into the drawing window and release the mouse button to drop it.

8 Close the palette by clicking its close button ☒.

Step 4: Locate the sink

In this step, you will rotate the sink symbol and place it on the counter.

1 Use the ROTATE command to rotate the sink.

The ROTATE command rotates selected objects about a base point. You can either enter the angle of rotation or use your mouse to define the rotation angle on the screen.

Click the ROTATE toolbar icon ⟳ on the Modify toolbar.

Command: ROTATE

Current positive angle in UCS: ANGDIR=counterclockwise ANGBASE=0

Select objects: **pick the sink symbol**

1 found

Select objects: ⏎

Specify base point: **pick a point inside the symbol**

Specify rotation angle or [Reference]: **90** ↵

- You may have noticed that although the sink is made of many lines and circles, it appears to be a single object. One click picks up the sink as a whole. This type of object is called a block. How to make blocks and insert blocks will be discussed in Chapter 5.

2 MOVE ⊞ **the sink onto the countertop.**

- In this MOVE command, you will snap to the midpoint of the sink and then move it to the upper left corner of the counter to obtain a reference point. In the next step, you will move the sink 18″ down and 6″ to the right.

Command: MOVE

Select objects: **pick the sink** 1 found

Select objects: ↵

Specify base point or displacement: **MID** ↵
pick the left side of the sink   *See Figure 3.21.*

Specify second point of displacement or <use
first point as displacement>: **pick the corner of
the counter**

- This Midpoint-to-Midpoint move is an example of accurate placement of objects. For future applications, different Object Snap Modes in various combinations, such as Endpoint to Endpoint, or Endpoint to Midpoint, can be used.

3 MOVE the sink out from the corner.

Command: ↵   *Restart the MOVE command.*
MOVE

Select objects: **pick the sink** 1 found

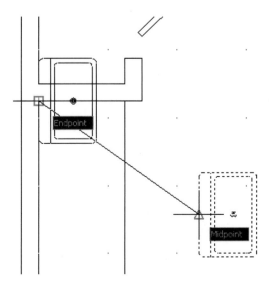

Figure 3.21
Move and align the sink.

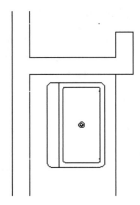

Figure 3.22
Move the sink.

Select objects: ↵   *End selection.*

Specify base point or displacement: **6,−18** ↵

Specify second point of displacement or <use   *See Figure 3.22.*
first point as displacement>: ↵

Step 5: Scale the sink block

The sink looks much wider than the one on the designer's sketch. You need to scale it to make it narrower.

1 Click the sink.

2 Right-click and choose "Properties" from   *The Properties Palette pops*
the pop-up menu.   *up. See Figure 3.23.*

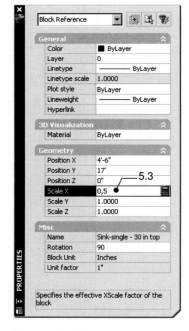

Figure 3.23
Change the scale of the block.

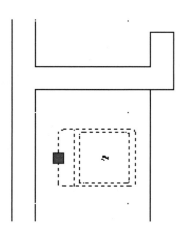

Figure 3.24
The block changes its shape.

Figure 3.25
The finished floor plan
(for Chapter 3).

3 Change value of ScaleX from 1.00 to 0.5.

The sink changes its shape. See Figure 3.24.

4 Click [Esc] to deselect the sink.

5 ZOOM out to see the whole plan.

See Figure 3.25.

6 QSAVE the drawing and QUIT AutoCAD.

Get Organized
with Layers

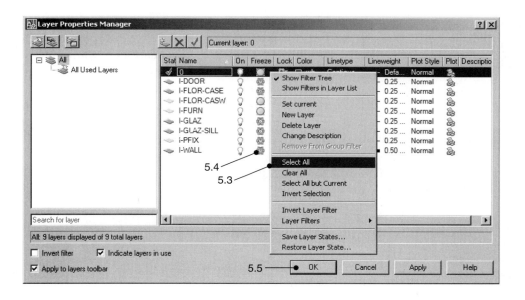

- Organize the Drawing Entities by Layers
- Make a List of Layer Names for Your Floor Plan
- Layers and Colors
- Layer and Linetype
- Layer and Lineweight
- Create and Set a Layer
- Create More Layers
- Put Drawing Entities on Their Appropriate Layers

Your drawing is becoming more and more complicated, with an increased number of objects that belong to different categories and require different representation in linetype and lineweight. You need to use layers, an important organizational device in AutoCAD, to give the drawing objects a systematic order for better management. Meanwhile, you will learn more about the properties of drawing entities.

Organize the Drawing Entities by Layers

In manual drafting, all the drawing entities you put on a sheet stay together. It will be extremely difficult to isolate any particular type of object from the rest. In AutoCAD, you can put different types of drawing entities on different layers to organize your drawing information more effectively. You may control the visibility of individual layers, you may control the activeness of layers when they are visible, and you may also use layers to control certain properties of the drawing entities, such as color and linetype. In the design profession, strict standards of layer control have been developed by individual design firms and space management departments of large institutions.

The AIA CAD Layer Guidelines

Most of the standards are based on the *CAD Layer Guidelines* developed by the American Institute of Architects (AIA) and other professional societies. According to the AIA guidelines, a layer name may be composed of four components:

1. **Discipline Code:** One character standing for major discipline groups with a dash (e.g., I- for interior).

2. **Major Group:** Four characters standing for different types of building systems (e.g., WALL for walls).

3. **Minor Group:** Four characters for further differentiation within a major group (e.g., PRHT for partial height wall in the major group walls). This modifier is optional.

4. **Status Field:** Four characters to differentiate the drawing objects by their nature, such as new construction versus existing. This modifier is also optional.

For example, the layer name **I-WALL-PRHT-NEWW** stands for Interior, Wall, Partial height, New construction.

The following is a list of the most commonly used group names related to interiors. You may use these names to compose your layer names. By combining the codes from different categories, you can create numerous layer names for your needs.

Discipline Code

A   architectural, interiors, facilities management

I   interior

E   electrical

F   fire protection

G   general

M   mechanical

P   plumbing

Q   equipment

T   telecommunications

X   others

Major Group

ANNO   annotation

WALL   wall

COLS   columns

DOOR   door

GLAZ   windows

CLNG   ceiling information

EQPM   equipment

FURN   furniture

LITE   lighting

HVAC   HVAC

FLOR   floor information

ELEV   elevation

SECT   sections

DETL   detail

Minor Group

IDEN   identification number

PRHT   partial height

FULL   full height

MOVE   movable

PATT   hatch patterns

MCUT   material cut by section

MBND	material beyond section cut
HEAD	door and window headers (shown on reflected ceiling plan)
JAMB	door and window jambs
SILL	windowsill
LEVL	level changes, ramps, etc.
STRS	stair treads
RISR	stair risers
HRAL	hand rails
SPCL	specialties (system furniture)
WDWK	woodwork (field-built)
CASE	casework (manufactured)
OVHD	overhead skylight
FILE	file cabinets (used with furniture group)
FREE	freestanding (furniture)
CHAR	chairs and seating
PNLS	panels (system furniture)
WKSF	work surface (system furniture)
STOR	storage units (system furniture)
POWR	power designations (system furniture)
PLNT	plants
GRID	ceiling grid
FNSH	finishes, woodworks, and trim
SIGN	signage
OTLN	outline
SDFF	supply diffuser
RDFF	return diffuser
PFIX	plumbing fixture
NOTE	notes
TEXT	text: general notes and specs
SYMB	symbols, bubbles, etc.
DIMS	dimensions
TTLB	title block
NPLT	nonplot information and construction lines
LEGN	legends and schedules

Status Field

EXST   existing to remain

DEMO   existing to be demolished

NEWW   new or proposed work

MOVE   items to be moved

RELO   relocated items

- This is not a complete list. For more detailed information about layer naming conventions, see *AIA CAD Layer Guidelines: U.S. national CAD standard version 2* (Washington, DC: The American Institute of Architects Press, 2002).

Make a List of Layer Names for Your Floor Plan

Using the layer name guidelines described above, you may make a list of layers for your drawing by analyzing the designer's sketch. The list may be as follows:

Drawing Object	Layer Name	Meaning
Wall	I-WALL	Interior-wall
Door	I-DOOR	Interior-door
Windows	I-GLAZ	Interior-glazing
Windowsills	I-GLAZ-SILL	Interior-glazing-sill
Counter	I-FLOR-CASE	Interior-floor information-casework
Wall cabinets	I-FLOR-CASW	Interior-floor information-casework (wall)
Sink	I-FLOR-PFIX	Interior-plumbing-fixture
Furniture	I-FURN	Interior-furniture
Floor tile	I-FLOR-PATT	Interior-floor information-pattern

- The code CASW is invented to meet our need to differentiate the objects drawn in hidden lines. The AIA guidelines allow you to invent codes at the "Minor group" level, and such codes are called "user-defined."

Layers and Colors

After we made the plan for layer names, we need to assign colors to different layers. The difference in color for different layers can help us to visually group the drawing entities, and it may also be used in plotting to control lineweights. Before we begin to assign colors to layers, we need a basic understanding of the color system in AutoCAD.

Colors in AutoCAD

AutoCAD now supports three types of color systems: indexed color, true color, and color books. As far as architectural drafting is concerned, we will use the traditional indexed color system. The AutoCAD indexed color system has a color palette of 255 colors. Each color has an index number. This number is referred to as ACI, meaning "AutoCAD Color Index." You can specify a color by its index number. The first nine colors in the index system are standard colors. Each of the first seven standard colors has both an index number and a color name. You may specify a standard color by either the color name or the index number. The color names and index numbers of the first seven standard colors are as follows:

Color	Red	Yellow	Green	Cyan	Blue	Magenta	White/black
Index	1	2	3	4	5	6	7

When you are prompted by AutoCAD to specify a color for layers or objects, the Select Color dialog box with the full color palette usually pops up. You may pick the colors you like from that palette. (You will do it later in this chapter.)

Assign Colors to Layers

In layer standards developed by individual design firms or institutions, a particular color is usually assigned to a layer. A color may also be used as a code of instruction for lineweight control in plotting when a color-dependent plot style table is used. For this tutorial, let's make the color assignment for each layer as follows:

Drawing Object	Layer Name	Color
Wall	I-WALL	1 (red)
Door	I-DOOR	2 (yellow)
Windows	I-GLAZ	3 (green)
Windowsills	I-GLAZ-SILL	4 (cyan)
Counter	I-FLOR-CASE	5 (blue)
Wall cabinets	I-FLOR-CASW	5 (blue)
Sink	I-PFIX	6 (magenta)
Furniture	I-FURN	6 (magenta)
Floor tile	I-FLOR-PATT	4 (cyan)

- This is an arbitrary assignment of colors. Standard colors are used for easy memorization. A single color is assigned to a group of layers with similar or related contents.

Layer and Linetype

Before we begin to create layers, we have to think about what type of lines should be assigned to each layer. For the floor plan you are working on, the lines you have drawn should all be continuous. When you proceed later to draw the wall cabinet above the counter, you will need the dotted line because the cabinet is above the cutting plane. In AutoCAD, there are many linetypes you can select and assign to layers and objects. We will make our selection in the process of creating individual layers.

Layer and Lineweight

In architectural drawings, lineweight is an important device to differentiate and give emphasis to certain building components. Artistically, a drawing with good lineweight control looks much better than those without lineweight differentiation. In manual drafting, lineweight can be created with different pen size and drafting techniques. In AutoCAD drafting, lineweight can be assigned directly to layers and objects. Because it would be tedious to assign lineweight to individual objects, you should assign lineweight to layers.

Create and Set a Layer

When you create a new drawing from scratch, there is only one layer: layer 0. So far, you have been drawing on that layer and, therefore, all the drawing objects are on that layer. Now you need to create more layers in order to put the drawing objects into their appropriate layers according to our layer list. After creating more layers, only one of these layers is open to receive newly created drawing elements at one time. This open layer is called the current layer. Its name and status are shown in the layer list on the properties toolbar. Up to this point, the current layer of your drawing is the layer 0. How to change the current layer will be discussed later.

Step 1: Create a new layer

1 Start AutoCAD and OPEN the drawing ch03.dwg and save it as ch04.dwg.

2 Click the LAYER toolbar icon 🗇 *The Layer Properties Manager*
on the layer toolbar. *dialog box pops up (Figure 4.1).*

- On the layer list in the dialog box, you have only the 0 layer. The layer status is shown by icons and verbal information following the layer name. They are on/off 💡 / 💡 , thaw/freeze 🔅 / ❄️ , lock/unlock 🔓 / 🔒, color ■ , linetype (shown by name), lineweight (shown by example line), plot style, and printable/nonprintable 🖨️ / 🚫. (The last two items will be discussed in Chapter 11.) You may click the icons or the item name to change the status.

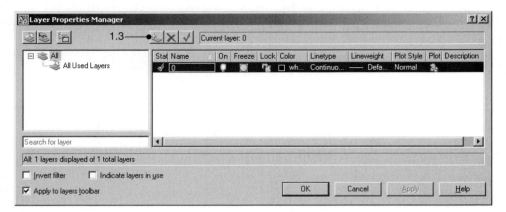

Figure 4.1
The Layer Properties
Manager dialog box.

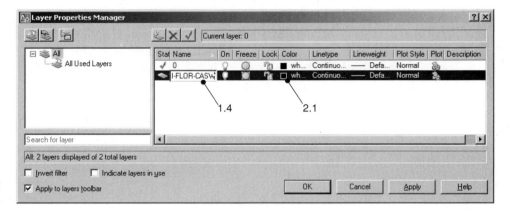

Figure 4.2
Create a new layer.

3 Click the new layer icon 🗎.

A new line appears on the list with the layer name "Layer1," and the layer name is highlighted with a rectangle over the layer name text (Figure 4.2).

- In dialog boxes, when text is highlighted, you can type a different name to replace it.

4 Type "I-FLOR-CASW" to replace "Layer1."

The layer name changes.

- On our list, the layer I-FLOR-CASW is for the wall cabinet, and it was assigned the color blue (5).

Step 2: Set layer color

When a new layer is created, it usually copies the features of the current layer (in this case, layer 0). Therefore, the new layer inherited the color white. Now you need to change it to blue.

1 Click the color icon to bring up the "Select Color" dialog box

Figure 4.3.

2 Click color blue.

The selected color shows in the field "color."

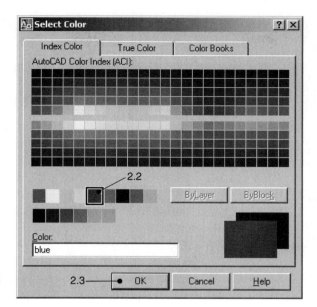

Figure 4.3
Select Color.

3 Click [OK].

The "Select Color" dialog box disappears, and the selected color appears in the layer status icon.

Step 3: Set layer linetype

When a new layer is created, it also inherits the linetype "continuous." Because the wall cabinet should be drawn with hidden lines, you need to set the linetype "Hidden" for the new layer.

Click the current linetype "continuous."

The Select Linetype dialog box pops up (Figure 4.4).

- You have only one type: continuous. Although AutoCAD has many linetypes you can select, they are stored in the AutoCAD linetype library file "acad.lin." You have to load the needed linetypes from that file into your drawing to make them available for selection.

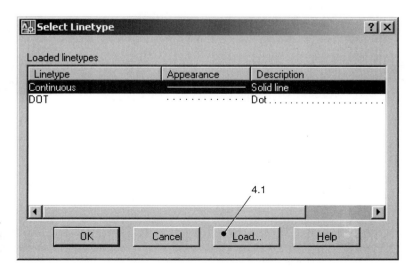

Figure 4.4
The Select Linetype dialog box.

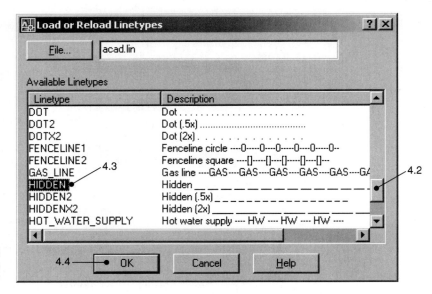

Figure 4.5
Load the linetype
"Hidden."

Step 4: Load a linetype

1 Click the button [Load...].

The Load or Reload Linetypes dialog box pops up with a long list of linetypes that are stored in the AutoCAD linetype library file (Figure 4.5).

● You may directly access the Linetype Manager and the Load or Reload Linetypes dialog boxes through the command LINETYPE or its alias LT.

2 Pull down the list to find "Hidden."

3 Click "HIDDEN" to highlight it.

4 Click [OK].

The Select Linetype dialog box comes to the front, with "Hidden" linetype added to the list (Figure 4.6).

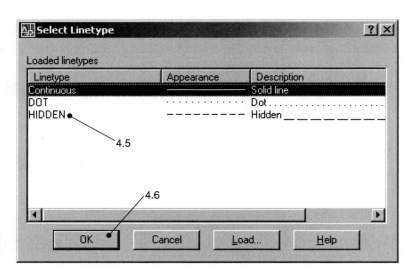

Figure 4.6
Select the linetype
"Hidden."

- You may have noticed the two linetypes "Hidden2" and "Hiddenx2" next to "Hidden." Conventionally, when the number 2 is added to a linetype, it is a half-sized version of the regular linetype (of the same name); when "x2" is added, it is a double-sized version of the regular linetype.

5 Click "Hidden" to select it.

6 Click [OK] to close the Select Linetype dialog box.

The Layer Properties Manager dialog box comes to front, and the linetype of layer "I-FLOR-CASW" has been changed to "Hidden."

- You may have noticed while loading the linetype that there are many linetypes with names starting with "ISO." These linetypes have very different scales from the non-ISO linetypes. Using the ISO linetype and the non-ISO linetype at the same time may cause difficulties in controlling the linetype scale, which will be discussed later.

Step 5: Set lineweight

1 Click "- Default" under Lineweight.

The Lineweight dialog box pops up with a long list of lineweights to choose from (Figure 4.7).

2 Choose 0.25 mm.

3 Click [OK].

4 Click [OK] to close the dialog box.

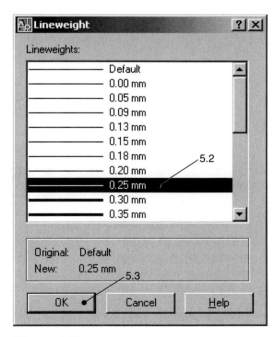

Figure 4.7
Set layer lineweight.

Create More Layers

Follow the same procedure as shown in steps 1 to 5 to create more layers according to our layer list on page 58. All new layers should have linetype Continuous. Set the lineweight of layer I-FLOR-WALL to 0.5 mm. Set the lineweight of the rest of the layers as 0.25 mm.

Put Drawing Entities on Their Appropriate Layers

If a drawing entity is created when a particular layer is the current layer, the entity is usually on that layer, unless it is a duplication of an existing entity of a different layer. Up to this point, all the drawing entities have been created in layer 0. You need to put them into appropriate layers. Now, let's try to change the layer of the door from layer 0 to layer I-DOOR.

Step 1: Put the door and swing on layer I-DOOR

1 Select the door and the door swing with an implied selection window.

- When you select drawing entities before you start a command, blue-colored boxes appear along the objects being selected. These blue boxes are called grips. How to use these grips to manipulate the objects will be discussed in later chapters. You can now see them as indicators of selection.

2 Click the layers list in the properties toolbar to unfold the layer list.

3 Click the layer "I-DOOR."   *The selected objects change color to yellow. The layer name "I-DOOR" appears in the layer list window (Figure 4.8).*

4 Hit [Esc] to cancel the selection of the door.   *The grips disappear. The layer name "0" reappears in the layer list window, and it will continue to be the current layer.*

- If the selection of the door is not cancelled by hitting the [Esc] key and a new command is launched, the previous current layer (layer 0 in this case) will not be reset as the current layer. If this happens, you can reset the current layer by clicking the layer you want to be current on the layer drop-down list.

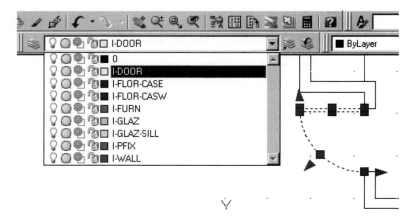

Figure 4.8
Change layers.

Step 2: Change the closet door layer

Step 3: Freeze the layer I-DOOR to simplify the view

1 Click the layer list to see the drop-down list.

2 Click the "Freeze/Thaw" icon 🔵 in front of the layer name "I-DOOR" to freeze that layer.

The icon changes into a snowflake ❄️, indicating the layer is now frozen.

3 Click the drawing area to close the layer drop-down list and to make the layer status change take effect.

The door and swing disappear.

- Freezing the layer I-DOOR means visually putting the door and swing away to simplify the drawing and to make your future selection of objects easier. We are actually taking advantage of the layer control functions of AutoCAD to make our job easier.

Step 4: Put the rest of the drawing entities onto appropriate layers

Freeze the layers you finish to simplify the task. Think about how to best use the selection-windows to catch the drawing entities you want to select.

Step 5: Thaw the frozen layers to see all the drawing entities

1 Click the layer toolbar icon ⬚ .

The Layer Properties Manager dialog box pops up.

- The key-in command for layer control is LAYER. The alias for command LAYER is LA.

2 Right-click (somewhere in the dialog box).

A menu pops up at the cursor (Figure 4.9).

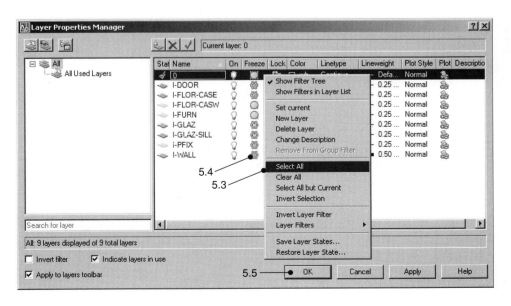

Figure 4.9
Thaw all the layers.

3 Click "Select All."   *All the layers are highlighted (selected).*

4 Click any of the snowflakes ▦.   *All the snowflakes change into a shining sun ▢.*

- Using this "select all" menu in the layer dialog box, you can also freeze all layers. There is one exception: AutoCAD does not allow you to freeze the current layer. Therefore, what you can do is to freeze all the layers but the current layer.

5 Click [OK].   *The dialog box closes and all the drawing entities appear.*

Step 6: Draw the wall cabinet and shelf

1 Use the OFFSET command to create the wall cabinet line 20″ off the wall.

2 Change the layer of the wall cabinet line to I-FLOR-CASW.

- The line does not change its appearance to show as a hidden line because the segments of dashes are too small to show. If you ZOOM in to look only at a very small portion of the line, you will find that it is dashed. To show the linetype effect in a view of the whole drawing, you need to set the linetype scale at a higher value. The linetype scale can be set at two different levels in AutoCAD: one at the object level as one of the object properties to control the linetype scale of an individual object, and one at the global level to control all the lines in the drawing. How the linetype of a line shows on the screen is determined by the linetype scale values set at both levels. The default values for line scale are 1. It is recommended that you use the global level control as much as possible. The global value of linetype scale is set through the system variable LTSCALE. In Auto-CAD, there are a lot of system variables that control how AutoCAD behaves.

3 Set the LTSCALE value.

Command: **LTSCALE** ↵
Enter new linetype scale factor <1.0000>: **48** ↵

Regenerating model.   *The linetype effect shows in the view.*

- The general rule to set the LTSCALE value is to use the scale factor of the drawing. We entered 48 because we will eventually plot the drawing at ¼″ scale. For a ¼″ scale drawing, the scale factor is 48 because 1″ on a printed ¼″ scale drawing represents 4′ or 48″ in the real world.

- This LTSCALE value is for looking at the drawing in the model space. When the drawing is later composed in the layout space (paper space), the LTSCALE value needs to be set back to 1. This will be discussed more in a later tutorial.

4 Use the OFFSET command to create the shelf in the closet 12″ off the wall.

5 Change the layer of the shelf line to I-FLOR-CASE.

Step 7: Show the lineweight on screen

At this moment, you may be wondering why the effect of lineweight does not show on the screen as the effect of the linetype does. You can simply click the [LWT] button on the status line to turn on the lineweight display.

Figure 4.10
Floor plan organized in layers.

1 Click the [LWT] button on the status line.

- The wall lines may appear to be too thick. You may adjust the lineweight display setting to make it look better. It is important to remember that this display is rather arbitrary. What you see is not what you will get in the final printout. It is for the visual effect on the computer screen only.

2 Right-click the [LWT] button and choose Settings.

3 Move the slider under Adjust Display Scale to make the line thinner or thicker.

4 Click [OK].   *The effect of the lineweight shows (Figure 4.10).*

5 Save your drawing and exit AutoCAD.

Draw the Furniture Plan

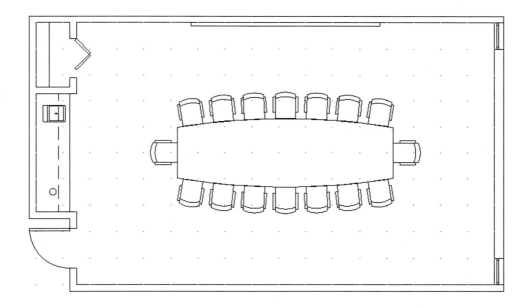

- Draw the Conference Table
- Draw a Chair
- Make the Chair a Block
- Insert the Chair Block
- Draw the Whiteboard
- Refine the Chair

In this chapter, you will draw the furniture plan according to the designer's sketch (Figure 5.1).

Draw the Conference Table

Step 1: Draw a box with the LINE command

To draw the conference table accurately, you need to first create a few auxiliary lines to define the critical points of the curve. We may call it a control box.

1 **Open your ch04.dwg drawing and**   *(command: SAVEAS)*
   save it as ch05.dwg.

2 **Use the LINE command** ▱ **to create a 16′ × 5′3″ rectangle in the middle of the space.**

3 **OFFSET** ▱ **8″ from the two**   *See Figure 5.2.*
   long sides inside the box.

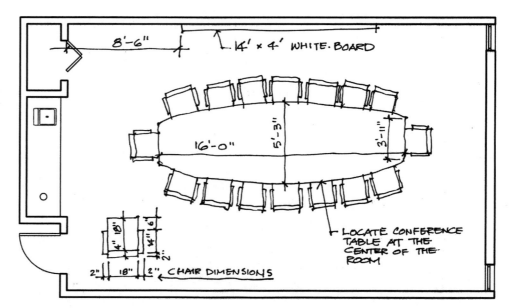

Figure 5.1
The designer's sketch.

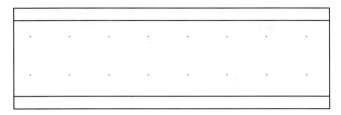

Figure 5.2
Draw the control box.

Step 2: Set running object snap for midpoint

In order to draw the curved side of the table using the ARC command, you need to catch the midpoint of the control box. Previously, we have been using the key-in method to call the midpoint object snap function whenever it is needed. This time we want to turn on the running mode for the midpoint object snap to make it automatic. This procedure can be used to set other types of object snap in the future.

1 **Right-click the [OSNAP] button in the status line and choose "Settings."**   *The Drafting Settings dialog box pops up (Figure 5.3).*

- On the Object Snap tab, all the object snap modes and their symbols are shown. You may want to examine them.

2 **Check the box before Midpoint.**

3 **Click [OK].**

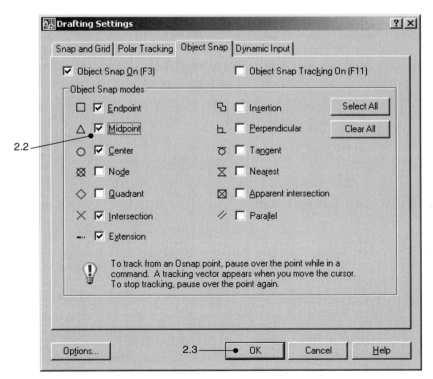

Figure 5.3
Object snap settings.

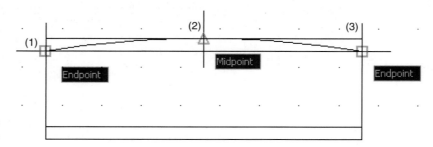

Figure 5.4
Draw the arc.

Step 3: Draw the arc

Click the ARC toolbar icon.

Command: ARC Specify start point of   *See Figure 5.4.*
arc or [Center]: **pick point 1**

Specify second point of arc or [Center/End]: **pick point 2**

Specify endpoint of arc: **pick point 3**

Step 4: Duplicate the arc with MIRROR

Use the MIRROR command to create the other side of the table.

Step 5: Clean the control box

Use the TRIM command to trim   *See Figure 5.5.*
the short sides of the table.

ERASE the horizontal lines.

Step 6: Locate the table

1 MOVE the table to   *See Figure 5.6.*
snap the midpoint of the right
side to the midpoint of the wall.

2 MOVE the table (7′6″ to the left) to the middle of the space.

Command: MOVE

Select objects: **P↵**   *Select the previously selected objects.*

4 found

Select objects: ↵

Specify base point or displacement: **-7′6,0↵**

Specify second point of displacement or <use first point as displacement>: ↵

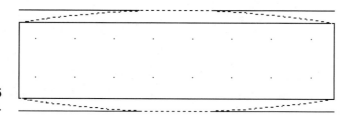

Figure 5.5
TRIM the table.

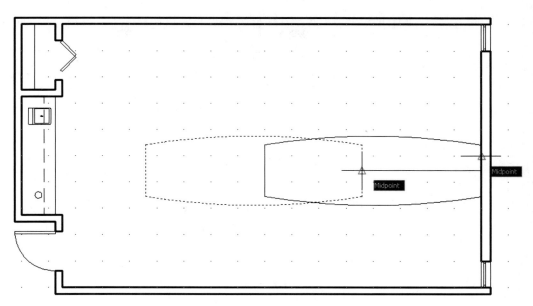

Figure 5.6
MOVE the table.

Draw a Chair

Step 1: Start with an 18 × 18 square

Draw an 18″ × 18″ square with the LINE command 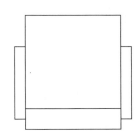.

Step 2: Use OFFSET to create lines

Use OFFSET 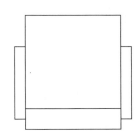 to create lines according to the dimension of the chair given in the sketch.

See Figures 5.7 and 5.8.

Step 3: Complete the chair

Use FILLET 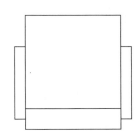 and TRIM 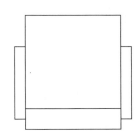 to complete the chair.

See Figure 5.9.

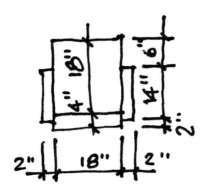

Figure 5.7
Chair dimension

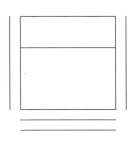

Figure 5.8
Use OFFSET to create lines.

Figure 5.9
Chair completed.

Make the Chair a Block

Because the chair will be used in different places around the table, you need to consider how to duplicate the chair and how to put the duplicates into place. Of course, you can use COPY. But after duplicating the chair with the COPY command, the many lines of all the chairs will be individual lines that will not only be difficult to handle for future revision, but also will take up a lot of disk space. Further grouping is needed. AutoCAD provides the BLOCK command for this purpose. BLOCK command makes a collection of drawing objects into an associated whole with a name; you can choose the name and insert it into the drawing with the INSERT command. In the process of inserting a block, you have control over the scale and orientation of the block. Through the DesignCenter, blocks can be shared by many drawings. As good practice, you should use blocks whenever possible. Anything that will be used repeatedly in a drawing should be converted to a block before duplication.

1 Put the chair on layer 0 if it is not drawn on layer 0.

- A block holds onto the color of the layer in which it is created and it is difficult to change it later. However, if the block is made on layer 0, the color of the block will be the same as the color of the layer in which the block is inserted, and it can be changed by the "Properties" tool. Therefore, it is a good idea to put the drawing objects on layer 0 before you make them into a block.

2 Start the BLOCK command by clicking the toolbar icon 🗔 on the Draw toolbar.

The Block Definition dialog box pops up (Figure 5.10).

3 Enter block name "CHAIR."

A descriptive name should be used for easy identification in the future.

4 Click the "Pick point" button.

The dialog box closes. You are prompted to pick the insertion base point.

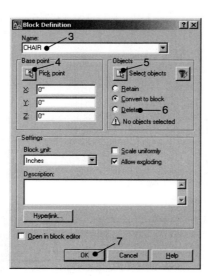

Figure 5.10
The Block Definition dialog box.

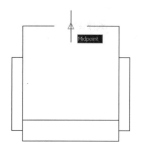

Figure 5.11
Insertion point.

Insertion base point: **pick the midpoint of the front line of the chair**	*See Figure 5.11. The dialog box returns with the point coordinates (x, y, z) fields filled in.*

● When you define the insertion base point, you need to imagine how this block will be used. If a particular point may help you to locate the block in future insertions, you should make that point the insertion base point. A well-planned insertion base point will help you to save time and make your drawing more accurate. Because this chair will be placed around the conference table, the front midpoint of the chair can be used to align the chair with the curved edges. Therefore, make the front midpoint of the chair the insertion point of the block.

5 Click the "Select Object" button.	*The dialog box closes.*
Select objects: **pick point** Specify opposite corner: **pick point** 11 found	*Use the selection-window.*
Select objects: ⏎	*End selection.*
Command:	*The dialog box returns.*

6 Check the button in front of "Delete Object."

● The three options "Retain," "Convert to block," and "Delete object" control the status of the original object. Selecting the "Delete object" option will delete the original chair made of individual lines. In this case, "Delete object" is chosen because we want to re-insert the chair block instead of moving the converted original so we can learn more about the INSERT command. In the future, you may make your own choice according to your needs.

7 Click [OK].	*The chair disappears.*

Insert the Chair Block

The INSERT command allows you to insert blocks into the drawing. The DIVIDE command allows you to divide a linear object into equal segments and insert blocks at each dividing node with the correct alignment. We will first use the INSERT command to insert a chair for the end of the conference table and then use the DIVIDE command to place chairs along the curved edge.

Step 1: INSERT a chair block

1 **Make sure layer "I-FURN" is the current layer,** so that the inserted chair will be in the right layer.

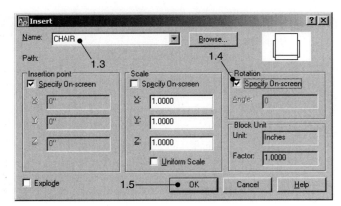

Figure 5.12
The Insert dialog box.

2 Click the INSERT toolbar icon ▣ on the Draw toolbar.

The Insert dialog box pops up (Figure 5.12).

3 Make sure the block name **CHAIR** shows in the "Name" list.

4 Check the box "Specify On-screen" under Rotation.

You need to rotate the chair at the end of the conference table.

5 Click [OK].

The dialog box closes. You are prompted to pick an insertion point.

Specify insertion point or [Scale/X/Y/Z/ Rotate/PScale/PX/PY/PZ/PRotate]: **pick the midpoint of the left end of the conference table.**

See Figure 5.13.

Specify rotation angle <0.00>: **pull the cursor straight down and click.**

See Figure 5.14. The chair is fixed in the drawing.

Command:

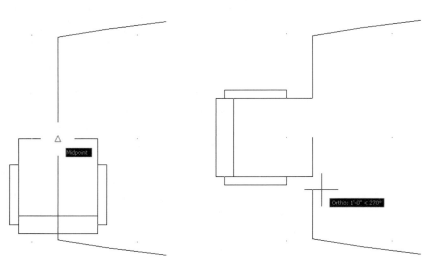

Figure 5.13
Insert the chair block.

Figure 5.14
Rotate the block during insertion.

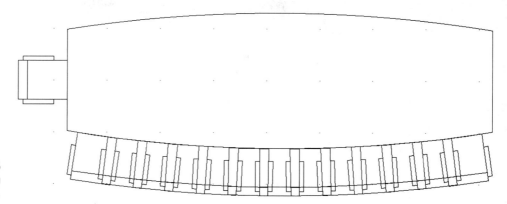

Figure 5.15
Insert chair blocks using
DIVIDE.

Step 2: Use DIVIDE to insert chairs

1 ZOOM to look at the entire conference table.

2 Enter the DIVIDE command.

Command: **DIVIDE** ↵

Select object to divide: **select the lower curved edge of the conference table**

Enter the number of segments   *B means "Block."*
or [Block]: **B** ↵

Enter name of block to insert: **CHAIR** ↵

Align block with object? [Yes/No] <Y>: ↵

Enter the number of segments: **14** ↵   *See Figure 5.15.*

- The reason for entering 14 while we need only seven chairs is to force Auto-CAD to place the first chair at the midpoint of the first one-seventh segment of the curve. We will ERASE the extra in the next step.

3 ERASE ▨ the extra chairs.   *See Figure 5.16.*

Step 3: Duplicate the chairs

Use the MIRROR command ◪ to duplicate the chairs.

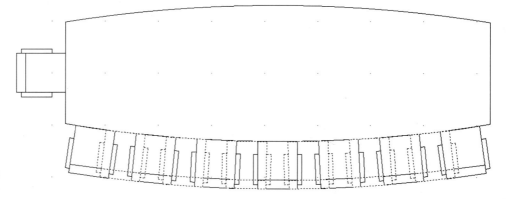

Figure 5.16
ERASE extra chairs.

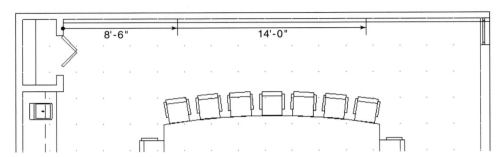

Figure 5.17
Define the whiteboard.

Draw the Whiteboard

Step 1: OFFSET from wall lines to define the whiteboard

1 Click [LWT] in the status line to turn off the lineweight display.

2 OFFSET ⬛ from wall lines to   *See Figure 5.17.*
define the whiteboard. Make the
marker tray 3 inches from the wall.

Step 2: Use the TRIM command to trim the lines

1 Use the TRIM command ⬛ to trim the lines.

2 Put the whiteboard lines into the layer I-FURN.

Refine the Chair

A block can be redefined if changes need to be made to it. If the same block name is used, all the already inserted blocks will be updated automatically. Let us assume that the designer wants to have a curved chair back replace the straight one that you drew.

Step 1: Insert a chair block

1 Set layer 0 as the current layer by clicking the layer list and choose layer 0.

2 INSERT ⬛ a chair block.

- Because we want to redefine the chair block, we need to make sure the orientation of the inserted chair is the same as the original one: front facing up.

Step 2: Explode the chair block

When individual objects are made into a block, they are "glued" together. We need to EXPLODE the block to edit its individual members. When a block is exploded, it will no long be a block.

1 ZOOM in to look at the chair.

2 Click the EXPLODE toolbar icon ⬛ on the Modify toolbar.

Command: EXPLODE

Select objects: **pick the chair block** 1 found

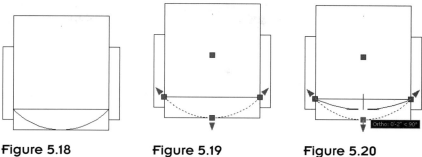

Figure 5.18
Draw an arc.

Figure 5.19
Grips appear on
the arc.

Figure 5.20
Push the arc up.

Select objects: ↵   *The chair is exploded, but there is no*
                                     obvious change.

Step 3: Draw the first arc of the curved back

1 Use the ARC command 🔲   *See Figure 5.18.*
    to draw an arc using the
    three-point method.

Step 4: Refine the arc with grips

When you are not using any command, clicking at a drawing element will cause small
blue squares to appear at control points around that element. These small blue squares
are called grips. You can use them to change the element.

1 Click the arc.   *Grips appear on the arc. See Figure 5.19.*

2 Click the grip on the middle.   *The grip turns red (hot) and it moves with*
                                      the movement of the cursor.

3 Hit the [F3] key to turn off OSNAP.

4 Move the cursor up to push the *See Figure 5.20.*
    arc to make it flatter.

5 Click to set.

6 Hit [Esc].

Step 5: Duplicate the arc

To use a command, you can either enter the command first (called a verb-noun method)
or select the object first (called a noun-verb method). The grips are still showing, which
means that the arc is selected. You can simply enter the command directly.

1 Click the COPY command toolbar icon 🔲.

Command: COPY

Select object: **pick the arc** 1 found ↵

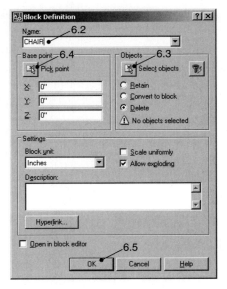

Figure 5.22
The Block Definition dialog box.

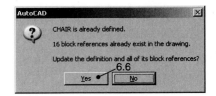

Figure 5.23
The AutoCAD warning.

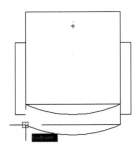

Figure 5.21
Copy the back line
of the chair.

Specify base point or displacement:
hit [F3] <Osnap on> **pick the end of
the arc**

Specify second point of displacement   *See Figure 5.21.*
or <use first point as displacement>:
pick the corner of the chair back

Specify second point of displacement: ↵

2 ERASE the original chair back lines.

Step 6: Redefine the block

1 Click the BLOCK command   *The Block Definition dialog box pops up*
toolbar icon ⬚.   *(Figure 5.22).*

2 Enter the name "chair."

3 Click [Select objects] and select
the refined chair.

4 Click [Pick point] under Base point
and select the midpoint of the
chair front.

5 Click [OK].   *An AutoCAD warning pops up*
                                          (Figure 5.23).

6 Click [Yes].   *The chair disappears.*

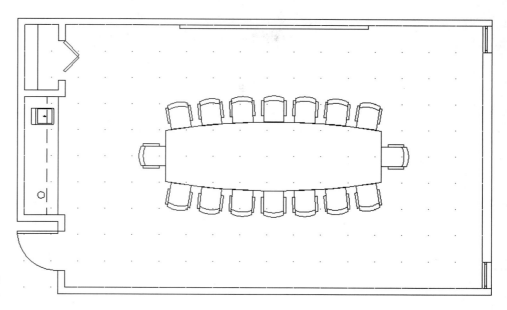

Figure 5.24
Chairs are updated.

7 ZOOM out to see the entire drawing.   *The chairs are all updated (Figure 5.24).*

8 Save the drawing and exit AutoCAD.

Draw the Reflected Ceiling Plan

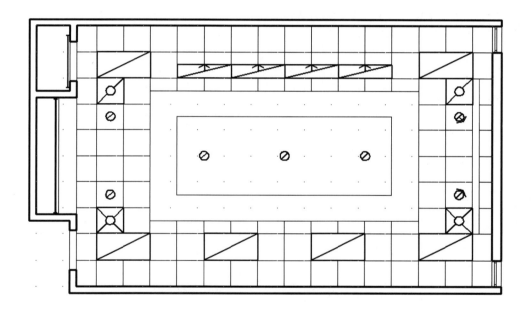

- Prepare the Drawing
- Draw the Ceiling Tile with Hatch
- Create Light Fixture Blocks
- Create the 1 × 4 Light Fixture
- Create More Light Fixtures
- Create the Air Diffusers
- Finish the Reflected Ceiling Plan

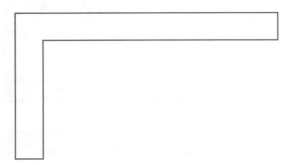

In this chapter, you will draw the reflected ceiling plan according to the designer's sketch (Figure 6.1).

Prepare the Drawing

Step 1: Turn off unneeded layers

Because the reflected ceiling plan focuses on the ceiling, we can turn off the layers that contain objects not in the scope of this drawing.

1 **Open your ch05.dwg drawing and save it as ch06.dwg.** *(command: SAVEAS)*

2 **Turn off the following layers: I-FURN, I-DOOR, I-PFIX, and I-FLOR CASE.**

- To turn off a layer, click the layer list and click the light bulb icon. When the color of the light bulb icon turns blue-gray, it is turned off.

3 **Create a new layer and name it I-CLNG.**
Set a color of your choice.

4 **Set the layer I-CLNG current.** *See Figure 6.2.*

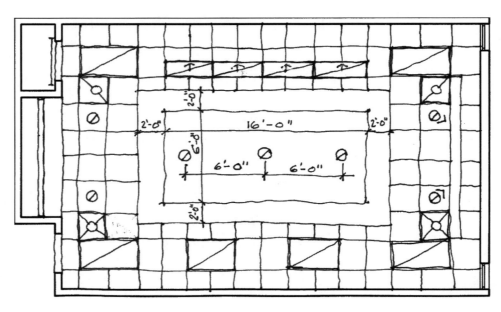

Figure 6.1
The designer's sketch of
the reflected ceiling plan.

Figure 6.2
Prepare the drawing.

Step 2: Draw wall boundary lines

In reflected ceiling plans, the object above the cutting plane can be seen through an imagined reflecting surface. Therefore, we can see the walls above door openings and the bulkhead above the counter.

1 Use the LINE command ◪ to draw lines above the doors.   *See Figure 6.3.*

2 Use the LINE command ◪ to draw a line that defines the counter area. This area has a lower ceiling.   *See Figure 6.4.*

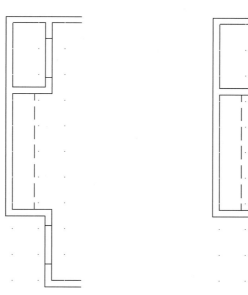

Figure 6.3
Seal the door opening.

Figure 6.4
Seal the counter area.

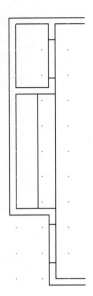

Figure 6.5
Draw the wall
cabinet line.

Step 3: Draw the wall cabinet line

In the floor plan, the wall cabinet line is above the cutting plane and it is shown in hidden line. In the reflected ceiling plan, it should be solid because it is seen directly in the reflecting surface. We cannot change the linetype because we will need the hidden line representation of the wall cabinet in the floor plan. We need to create a second representation of the wall cabinet for the reflected ceiling plan.

1 Use the LINE command ◢ to trace the hidden line wall cabinet.

2 Turn off the layer I-FLOR-CASW.   *See Figure 6.5.*

Draw the Ceiling Tile with Hatch

The HATCH command fills an enclosed area in a drawing with patterns. The command detects the enclosed area before filling it with a pattern. The User Defined pattern is simply parallel lines with direction and spacing defined by you. With the Double hatch option selected, it will generate a grid. You can use this function to draw simple ceiling tiles.

Step 1: Draw a diagonal line for the ceiling tile alignment

Before we use the HATCH command to create the ceiling tile grid, we need to find the center of the space to ensure the appropriate alignment of the tiles.

1 Use the LINE command ◢ to draw a diagonal line as shown in Figure 6.6.

Step 2: Create the ceiling grid

1 Click the HATCH toolbar icon ▨ on the Draw toolbar.   *The Hatch and Gradient dialog box pops up. See Figure 6.7.*

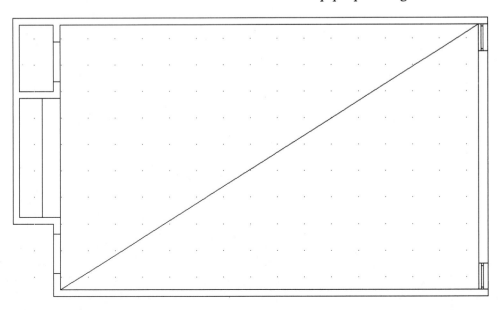

Figure 6.6
Draw a diagonal line
across the interior space.

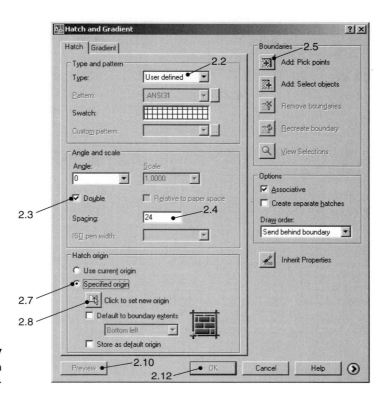

Figure 6.7
The Boundary Hatch
dialog box.

2 **Click the pull-down list** (currently showing "Predefined") **and select "User-defined."**

Some items on the dialog box turn gray.

3 **Check the box before "Double."**

4 **Double-click the field after "Spacing," and type 24** (the size of tile).

5 **Click the button "Add: Pick Points" in the Boundaries group.**

The dialog box disappears and AutoCAD prompts you to pick an internal point.

6 **Pick two points in the space on either side of diagonal line. Then hit the [Enter] key to end selection.**

The dialog box reappears.

7 **Click to check "Specify origin" in the Hatch group.**

8 **Click the button "Click to set new origin."**

The dialog box disappears and AutoCAD prompts you to pick a new origin.

9 **Use the MIDpoint object snap to catch the midpoint of the diagonal (the center point of the room).**

The dialog box returns.

10 **Click [Preview].**

The pattern appears in the space.

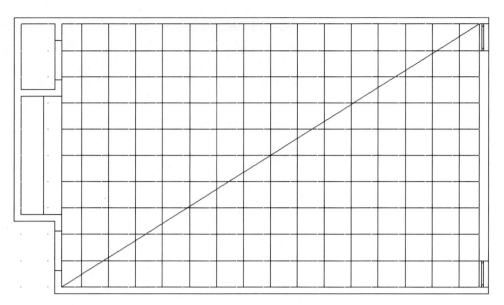

Figure 6.8
Hatch pattern applied.

11 Hit [Enter].   *The dialog box returns.*

12 Click [OK] to apply the pattern on the
drawing and end the command.   *See Figure 6.8.*

13 ERASE the diagonal line.

Step 3: Draw the cove

The designer's sketch shows that there is a lighting cove in the middle of the space above
the conference table. A 2′ wide dry wall ceiling is around its opening. You can now use
the hatch pattern to define and create the lines.

1 EXPLODE ▨ the hatch pattern.

- Hatch patterns are very much like a block. You cannot edit individual elements
  of a hatch pattern. When a patch pattern is exploded, the individual elements
  will be "freed."

2 Use the OFFSET command ▨ to create the   *See Figure 6.9.*
defining lines of the cove.

3 Use the EXTEND ▨ command and the TRIM   *See Figure 6.10.*
command ▨ to clean up the lines.

- The tiles inside the cove are left for future use to locate light fixtures.

- Hint: You may use the cross-window selection to select multiple lines that are
  to be trimmed.

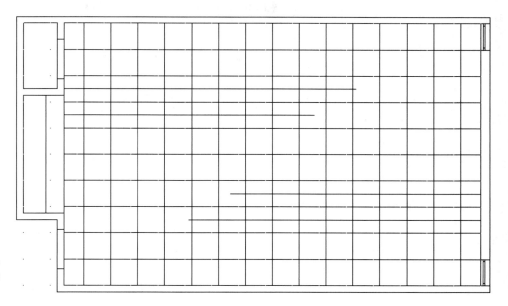

Figure 6.9
Create the defining lines
of the lighting cove.

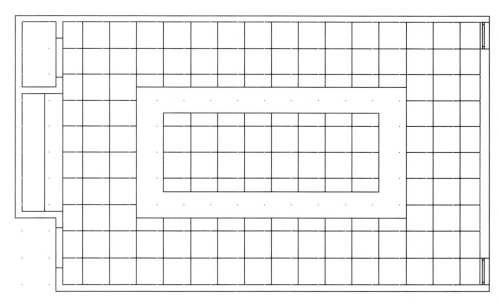

Figure 6.10
Use EXTEND and TRIM to
clean the lines of the
lighting cove.

Create Light Fixture Blocks

Lighting symbols are used in this drawing repeatedly. Therefore, you should define them as blocks. These blocks can be accessed from other drawings through the design center. Thus, you can use them in the future.

Step 1: Create the 2 × 4 fluorescent troffer block

1 Set layer 0 current.

2 ZOOM in to look at the ceiling tiles near the entrance door.

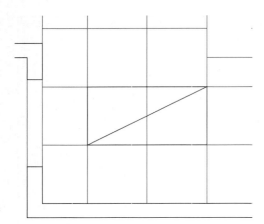

Figure 6.11
Create lines for the fluorescent troffer symbol.

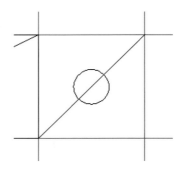

Figure 6.12
Create the recessed downlight.

3 Use the LINE command ◿ to create the
fluorescent troffer.   *See Figure 6.11.*

4 Start the BLOCK command ▣ .

5 Name it LITE2 × 4.

6 Use the lower left corner as its insertion
base point.

7 Click to check "Convert to block."   *This will convert the
                                                         selected lines into a
                                                         block and leave it on
                                                         the drawing.*

8 Click the button "Select objects" and select the lines.

9 Hit the Space bar to finish selection.

10 Click [OK].

Step 2: Create the recessed downlight block

1 Draw a diagonal line within the ceiling tile to the right of the fluorescent troffer.

2 Use the CIRCLE command ▣ to draw a circle at
the midpoint of the diagonal line. R = 4.   *See Figure 6.12.*

3 TRIM ⊬ the diagonal line outside the circle.

4 Use the BLOCK command ▣ to make it a block.
Name it LITEREC. Use the center point of the
circle as the insertion point. Check the "Delete"
option to delete the circle and the diagonal line.

5 INSERT ▣ the block above the 2 × 4 fluorescent
light fixture. See Figure 6.1 for location. Snap to the
lower left corner of the ceiling tile, and MOVE it to
the center of the tile using the displacement of 12, 12.   *See Figure 6.13.*

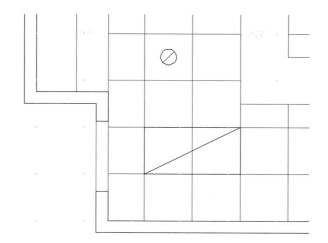

Figure 6.13
Insert the recessed
downlight block.

Create the 1 × 4 Light Fixture

With the created 2 × 4 fluorescent light fixture block, we can create the 1 × 4 light fixtures by altering its size.

Step 1: Create the tile line

1 Zoom out to look at the entire plan.

2 Use the OFFSET command 📋 to create the half tile line for the fluorescent wallwashers in front of the whiteboard.

3 TRIM 🔲 to cut off the extra portions of the line.   *See Figure 6.14.*

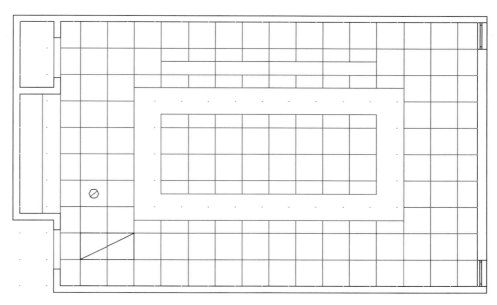

Figure 6.14
Create the half tile line for the fluorescent wallwashers.

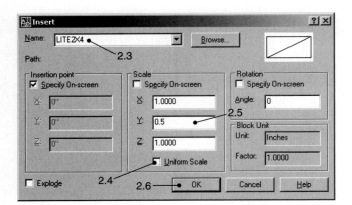

Figure 6.15
Insert LITE2×4 block with revised scale Y value.

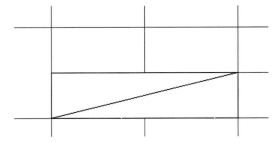

Figure 6.16
The 1 × 4 light fixture.

Step 2: INSERT the light fixture block

1 Zoom in to look at the open rectangle on the left.

2 Start the INSERT command ⬚.

The Insert dialog box pops up (see Figure 6.15).

3 Click the Name list and select LITE2×4.

4 Clear the box Uniform Scale.

5 Change the Y scale value to 0.5.

6 Click [OK] and locate the block.

See Figure 6.16.

Step 3: Use the ARRAY command to duplicate

The ARRAY command works on two types of array: polar and rectangular. The polar ARRAY function creates an array of selected objects around a center point according to your input of number and the angle in which the objects are to be evenly arranged; the rectangular ARRAY function creates an array in columns and rows. In this step, you will use the rectangular ARRAY function to duplicate the first 1 × 4 light fixture and place the duplicates evenly in a row.

1 Click the ARRAY toolbar icon ⊞ on the Modify toolbar.

The Array dialog box pops up (see Figure 6.17).

2 Set the Rows value to 1 and the Columns value to 4.

3 Change to column offset to 48.

4 Click the [Select objects] button.

5 Select the light fixture.

6 Hit the [Enter] key.

7 Click [Preview].

8 Click [Accept].

See Figure 6.18.

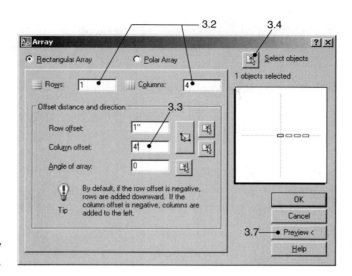

Figure 6.17
The Array dialog box.

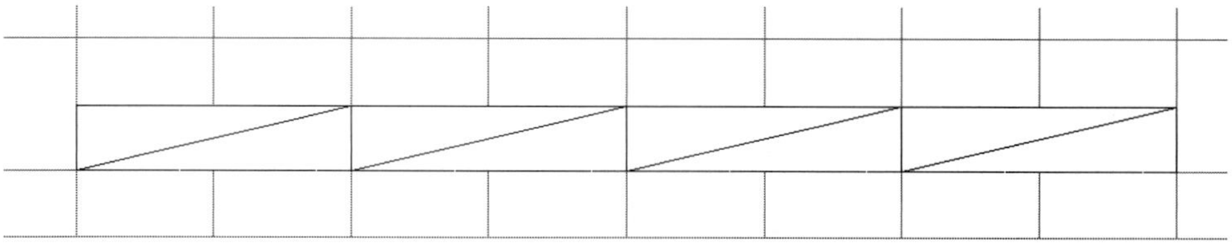

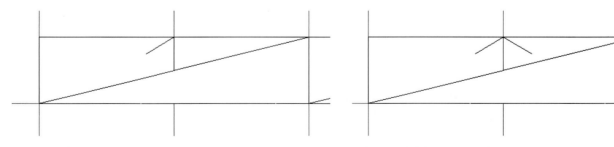

Figure 6.18
The result of the array.

Step 4: Draw the direction arrow

1 Zoom in to look at the first light fixture.

2 Use the LINE command ⬜ to draw a line from
the midpoint of the diagonal line straight up 6″
and turn to form the half of an arrowhead.   *See Figure 6.19.*

3 Use the MIRROR command ⬜ to create
the other half of the pointer.   *See Figure 6.20.*

Figure 6.19
Create the direction arrow.

Figure 6.20
Completed direction arrow.

4 Use the BLOCK command 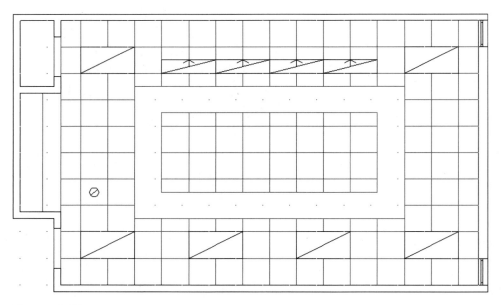 to make the arrowhead a block. Name it DIRECT. Use the midpoint of the diagonal line as its insertion point. Choose the convert to block option in the dialog box.

5 Use the ARRAY command to duplicate the arrowhead for the other three lights.

Create More Light Fixtures

Step 1: Duplicate the 2 × 4 light fixture

1 Zoom to see the entire plan.

2 Start the ARRAY command.

3 In the dialog box, set the Rows value to 2 and the Columns value to 4.

4 Set the Row offset to 14′ and Column offset to 8′.

5 Click the Select objects icon and select the 2 × 4 troffer.

6 Click OK.

7 ERASE the two extra fixtures.

8 TRIM to remove the tile line inside the 2 × 4 fixtures.   *See Figure 6.21.*

Figure 6.21
Duplicate the 2 × 4 fluorescent lights.

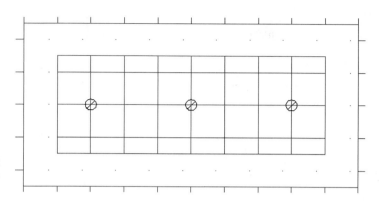

Figure 6.22
Create the downlights in
the cove area.

Step 2: Duplicate the downlights

1 INSERT one recessed downlight at the center
of the cove.

2 Use the COPY command to duplicate.   *See Figure 6.22.*

3 ERASE the grid lines inside the cove.

4 Duplicate the other downlights using the COPY command
. Use the corner of the ceiling tile as base point.   *See Figure 6.23.*

Step 3: Add a direction arrow

As shown on the sketch, the two light fixtures next to the wall on the right are recessed
directional lights. We need to add directional arrows to the recessed light symbol.

1 Zoom in to look at the two downlights on the right of the space.

2 Start the INSERT command .

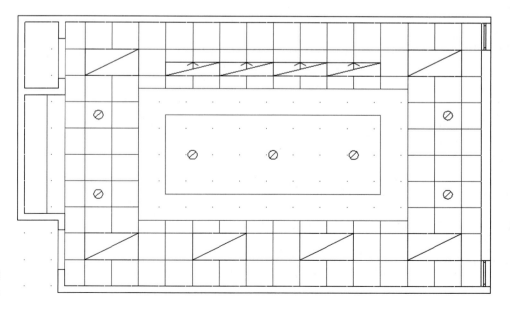

Figure 6.23
Duplicate the downlights.

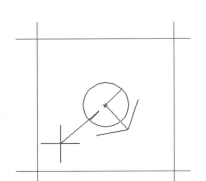

Figure 6.24
Insert the direction arrow.

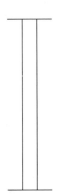

Figure 6.25
Draw the linear light symbol.

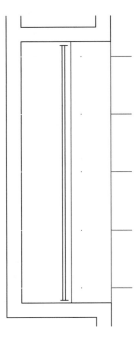

Figure 6.26
Insert the linear undercabinet light.

3 Select the pointer block "DIRECT."

4 Check the box of Specify On-screen **for Rotation.**

5 Click [OK].

6 Snap the insertion point at the center of the circle of the upper light fixture.

7 Enter −135 degrees for the rotation angle.   *See Figure 6.24.*

8 MIRROR ⬕ the arrow to the other light fixture.

Step 4: Draw the undercabinet light

1 Zoom in to look at the counter area.

2 Use the LINE command ⬕ to create a symbol for the linear lighting system as shown. The length is 1′, and the end stopper is 3″.   *See Figure 6.25.*

3 Use the BLOCK command ⬕ to make it a block. Name it LITELINEAR. Set the end point of the lower end stopper as the insertion point. Check the Retain option in the Block dialog box to keep the original objects.

- This is a unit symbol. When it is inserted, a scale factor in the Y direction can be used to make it longer or shorter.

4 INSERT ⬕ the block and set the scale Y to 8.8. Place it as   *See Figure 6.26.* shown in the sketch.

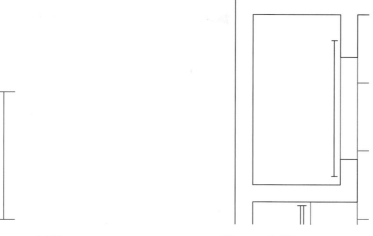

Figure 6.27
Create the fluorescent strip light.

Figure 6.28
Insert the fluorescent strip light.

Step 5: Draw the fluorescent striplight in the closet

1 Zoom to look at the original lines you used to create the linear light block.

2 TRIM ⊡ off the end stopper on one side of the symbol.

3 ERASE ✎ the vertical line on that side.   *See Figure 6.27.*

4 Use the BLOCK command ⊡ to make it a block. Name it LITESTRP. Check the Delete option in the Block dialog box to erase the original objects.

5 INSERT ⊡ the block and make it 4′ long. Place it as shown in the sketch.   *See Figure 6.28.*

Create the Air Diffusers

Step 1: Create the supply air diffuser symbol

1 ZOOM to look at a ceiling tile closely.

2 Use the LINE command ∠ to draw a 2′ × 2′ square.

3 Draw two diagonal lines.

4 Draw a circle centered at the intersection. R = 4.

5 TRIM ⊡ the diagonal lines inside the circle.   *See Figure 6.29.*

6 Use the BLOCK command ⊡ to make it a block. Name it "AIRSUPPLY." Use the corner of the ceiling tile as its insertion point. Check "Retain" to keep the original.

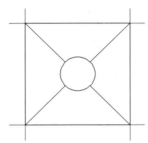

Figure 6.29
Create the air supply diffuser.

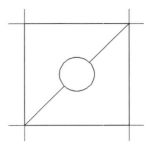

Figure 6.30
Create the air return diffuser.

Step 2: Create the return air diffuser symbol

1 ERASE ![icon] one diagonal line.   *See Figure 6.30.*

2 Use the BLOCK command ![icon] to make it a block. Name it "AIRRETURN." Use the corner of the ceiling tile as its insertion point. Check "Delete" to delete the original.

3 INSERT ![icon] the supply and return air diffuser blocks as shown in the sketch.

Finish the Reflected Ceiling Plan

Step 1: Draw the retractable projection screen

1 OFFSET ![icon] 6″ from the ceiling line to define the screen.

2 TRIM ![icon] to complete it.   *See Figure 6.31.*

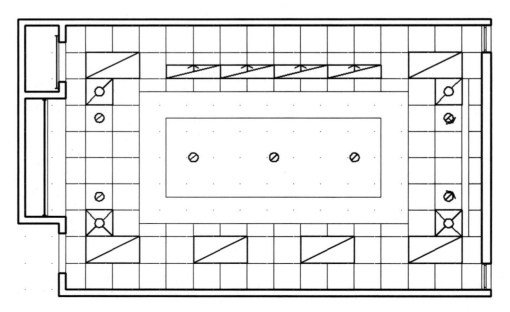

Figure 6.31
Completed reflected
ceiling plan.

Step 2: Layer management

1 Create a new layer and name it I-CLNG-LITE. Set a color of your choice. Set a lineweight of 0.4 for the layer.

2 Create a new layer and name it I-CLNG-HVAC. Set a color of your choice. Set a lineweight of 0.4 for the layer.

3 Put the light fixtures into the layer I-CLNG-LITE.

4 Put the air diffusers into the layer I-CLNG-HVAC.

5 Save the drawing and exit AutoCAD.

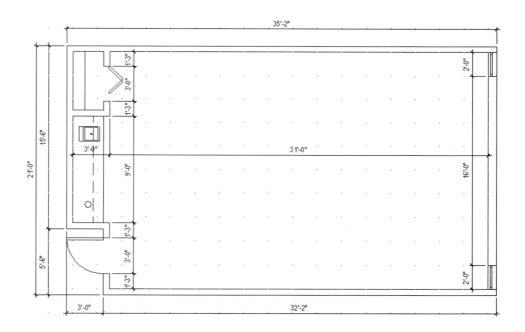

- ● Set a Dimension Style
- ● Using Dimension Commands

This chapter will guide you in dimensioning the finished floor plan. In this process, you will learn how to set up an architectural dimension style and how to use the dimension style.

Set a Dimension Style

Before you begin to dimension a drawing in AutoCAD, you need to set your dimension styles. A dimension style in AutoCAD controls all the features, from the size and format of architectural ticks to the text font. Since the "Standard" dimension style is not one used in architectural drawings, you need to define an architectural style yourself.

The terminology of dimension features used in AutoCAD is illustrated in Figure 7.1. The sizes of dimension features for a typical architectural drawing are also given in the drawing. When setting your dimension style, you may need to refer to this drawing for a better understanding of dimension settings.

- The sizes of dimension features given in the diagram below are decided by aesthetic judgment and practical concerns for visual clarity.

Step 1: Set up a text style

Before setting up a dimension style, you need to set up a text style.

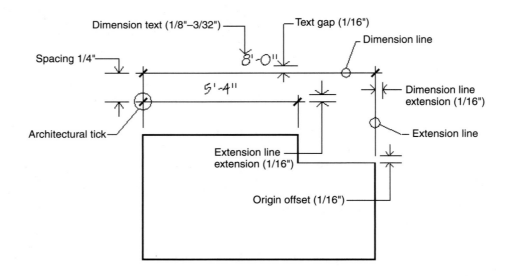

Figure 7.1
Dimension terminology and settings.

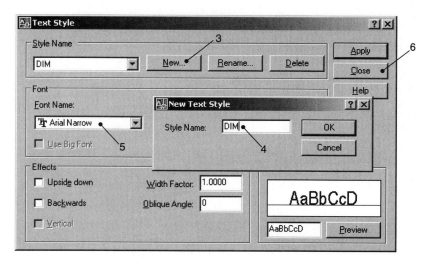

Figure 7.2
Set up a text style.

1 Open the floor plan drawing Ch06.dwg, and save it as "Ch07.dwg."

2 Click the menu item "Format" and choose "Text style."

The Text Style dialog box pops up (see Figure 7.2).

3 Click the [New] button.

The New Text Style dialog box pops up.

4 Enter DIM for Style Name, and click [OK].

5 Click the font name list and choose Arial Narrow.

6 Click [Close] and [Yes].

Step 2: Start with command DDIM

1 **Click** Dimension **on the Menu bar and choose** Dimension Style.

The Dimension Style Manager dialog box pops up (see Figure 7.3).

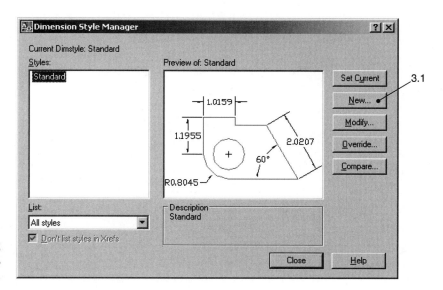

Figure 7.3
Dimension Style
Manager dialog box.

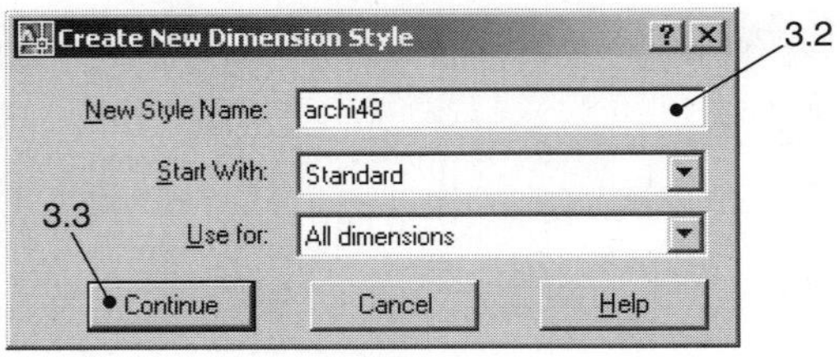

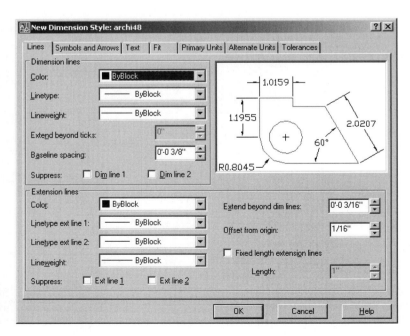

Figure 7.4
Create New Dimension
Style dialog box.

● This dialog box will lead you to more dialog boxes to set your dimension styles. At this point, there is only one existing style with the name "Standard." Similar to the "Standard" text style, it is a basic dimension style and serves as the default.

Step 3: Create and name your style

1 Click [New].

The Create New Dimension Style dialog box pops up (see Figure 7.4).

2 Type in a name (archi48) for your first architectural style.

3 Click [Continue].

The "Create New Dimension Style: ARCHI48" dialog box pops up (see Figure 7.5). AutoCAD creates a style called "archi48" based on the style "Standard."

Step 4: Set symbols and arrows

1 Click the Symbols and Arrows **tab**.

Figure 7.5
Set up a new dimension
style.

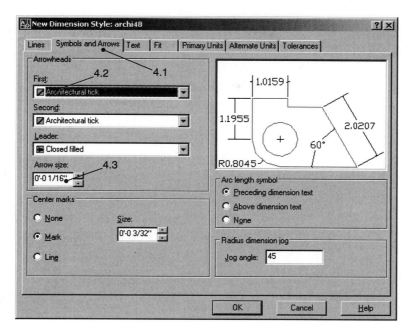

Figure 7.6
Set arrows.

2 Click the "First" list in the "Arrowheads" section and choose "architectural tick."

The second arrowhead changes automatically (see Figure 7.6).

3 Change "Arrow size" to 1/16".

Step 5: Set lines

1 Click the Lines tab.

See Figure 7.7.

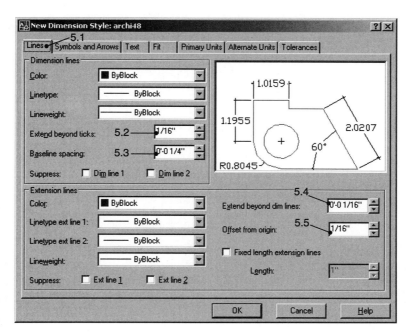

Figure 7.7
Set line features.

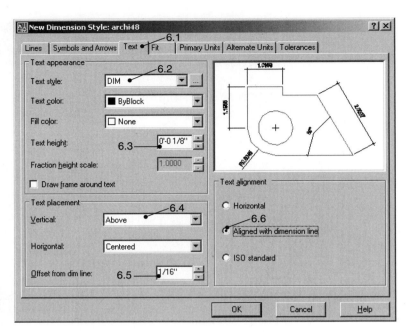

Figure 7.8
Set dimension text
features.

2 Set "Extend beyond ticks" to 1/16″.

3 Set "Baseline spacing" to ¼″.

4 Set "Extend beyond dim lines" to 1/16″.

5 Set "Offset from origin" to 1/16″.

The settings on these two tabs control the geometric features of the dimension line, extension lines, architectural ticks, and the arrowhead. All the values and settings in this dialog box are inherited from the style "Standard." The principle of setting the sizes of dimension features is to set them to their real sizes on paper. For example, if you want the arrowhead to be 1/16″, set the value for the arrowhead size as 1/16″.

Step 6: Set dimension text

1 Click the Text tab.   *The "Text" page opens (see Figure 7.8).*

2 Click the Text style **list and choose "DIM."**

3 Set "Text height" to 1/8″.

4 Set vertical text placement to "Above."

5 Set Offset from dim line to 1/16″.

6 Check "Aligned with dimension line."

Step 7: Set fit settings

1 Click the Fit **tab.**   *The "Fit" setting page opens (see Figure 7.9).*

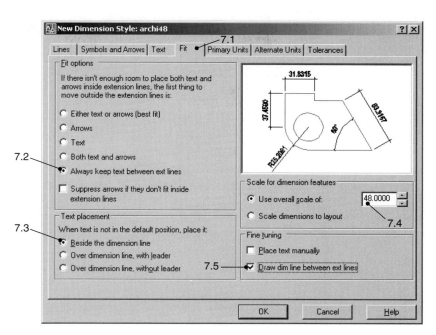

Figure 7.9
Set Fit Settings.

2 Check "Always keep text between ext lines" in "Fit Options."

3 Check "Beside the dimension line" in "Text placement."   *This ensures the dimension line runs through the space between extension lines.*

4 Change the "Scale for dimension features" to 48.

- This value has to be decided by a drawing scale in which you want to print out your drawing. Because ¼″ = 1′-0″ is a frequently used scale in this field, let us use it as the scale for the final presentation of this drawing. The value of this "Overall Scale" should equal the scale factor. Therefore, it is 48. If you need to present the drawing in a different scale, you may change this value according to the scale you will use.

5 Check "Draw dim line between ext lines" in the "Fine Tuning" section.

Step 8: Set dimension units

1 Click the "Primary Units" tab.   *The "Primary Units" page opens (see Figure 7.10). The settings on this page control the measuring unit.*

2 Click the "Units format" list and select "Architectural."

3 Click the "Fraction format" list and select "Not stacked."

4 Clear "0 Inches Suppression" check box to have 0 inch shown in dimension text.

5 Click [OK].   *The Primary Units dialog box closes.*

6 Click [Close] to close the Dimension Style Manager.

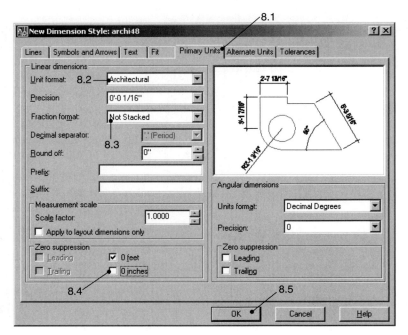

Figure 7.10
Set Primary Units.

Using Dimension Commands

In this section, you will dimension the floor plan.

Step 1: Set the dimension toolbar

The best way to use the dimension commands is through the dimension toolbar.

1 Move the cursor over a standard toolbar icon (such as ZOOM-window) and right-click.

A menu with a list of toolbars pops up.

2 Select "Dimension" from the menu.

The dimension toolbar pops up.

3 Drag the dimension toolbar by its title bar over the top frame of the AutoCAD drawing window; release it until the phantom box becomes thin near the frame.

The dimension toolbar is embedded into the frame.

Step 2: Set the running object snap

Because catching exact points is critical for accurate dimensioning, Object Snap should be used to pick every point. To avoid snapping to unwanted points, we will turn off all the Object Snap Modes except the endpoint.

1 Right-click OSNAP on the status bar and choose Settings.

The Drafting Settings dialog box pops up.

2 Click the [Clear All] button.

3 Check the box "Endpoint."

4 Click [OK].

Step 3: Prepare the drawing

1 ZOOM out to look at the whole plan (leaving space for dimensions around it).

2 Create a new layer "I-ANON-DIMS" for dimensions and set as current.
The color of the new layer should be white or yellow.

3 Turn off the layers I-CLNG, I-CLNG-LITE, and I-CLNG-HVAC to simplify
the floor plan.

4 Turn on the layers I-DOOR, I-FLOR-PFIX, I-FLOR-CASE, and I-FLOR-CASW.

- These three layers belong to the floor plan where the dimensions will be shown
  in the final presentation of the drawing. Turning them on will help you to
  determine the placement of the dimensions to avoid interference.

Step 4: Set "archi48" as the current dimension style

The concept of current dimension is similar to that of current layer or the current text
style. The dimensions you create will be in the current style. In the same way that you
can change an object's layer after its creation, you can change the style of a dimension
(that will be discussed later in this chapter). The current dimension style is shown in
the window of the drop-down list in the dimension toolbar (see Figure 7.11).

1 If you don't see "archi48" in the window, click the list and select it from the
drop-down list.

Step 5: Create your first external dimension

1 Click the linear dimension toolbar icon 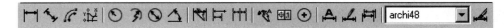 on the dimension toolbar.

Command: _dimlinear

Specify first extension line origin or   *(See Figure 7.12.)*
<select object>: **pick point (1)**

Specify second extension line origin: **pick point (2)**

Figure 7.11
The current dimension style as shown in the dimension toolbar.

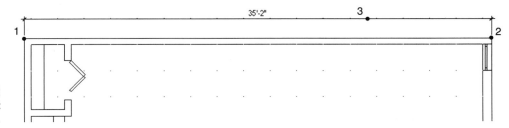

Figure 7.12
Create the first
dimension.

Specify dimension line location or

[Mtext/Text/Angle/Horizontal/Vertical/Rotated]: **pick point (3)**

- The location of point (3) defines the distance between the dimension line and the wall. You need to estimate this distance based on your experience.

Dimension text = 35'-2"   *AutoCAD reports the measured dimension.*

Command: *Command ends and the dimension is automatically entered.*

Step 6: Create continued dimensions

1 Click the linear dimension toolbar icon ▭.

2 Pick point (1), point (2).   *See Figure 7.13.*

3 Pick point (3) to locate the dimension line.

4 Click the Continue Dimension toolbar icon ▭.

Specify a second extension line origin or (Undo/<Select>): **pick point (4)**

Specify a second extension line origin or (Undo/<Select>): ↵

Select continued dimension: ↵

Command:

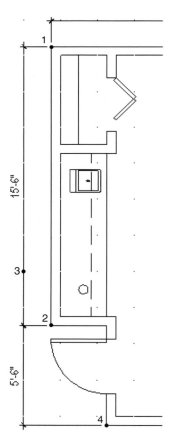

Figure 7.13
Continuous dimensioning.

Step 7: Use the baseline dimension tool to create an overall dimension

An architectural plan usually has three levels of dimensions, from the detailed dimension to the overall dimension. The Baseline Dimension tool allows you to create larger dimensions based on smaller dimensions. The new higher-level dimension is automatically placed according to the "spacing" defined in the dimension style.

1 Click the "Baseline Dimension" toolbar icon ▣.

Command: _dimbaseline

A rubber band dimension stretches out from the first point of the last dimension.

- Don't be scared by the rubber band dimension. (You did not do anything wrong!) By default, the baseline command assumes that you want to start the new baseline dimension from the first origin point of the last dimension you created. In this case, however, you want to start from the first dimension above the floor plan. Therefore, you need to choose "Select" to select it so that AutoCAD knows where to start.

Specify a second extension line origin or [Undo/Select] <Select>: ↵

For Select.

Select base dimension: **pick the end of the first extension line (point 5).**

(See Figure 7.14.)

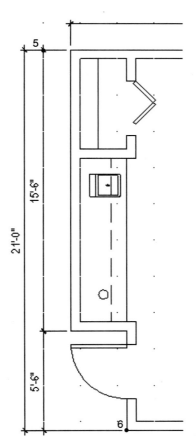

Figure 7.14
Baseline dimensioning.

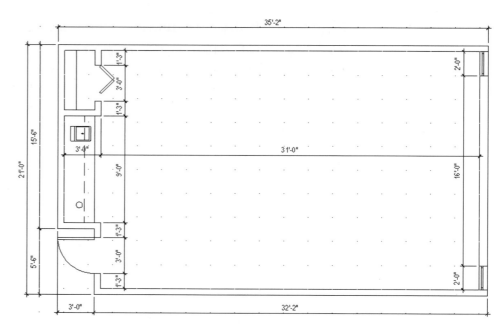

Figure 7.15
More dimensions.

Specify a second extension line origin or [Undo/Select] <Select>:
pick the corner of the wall (point 6)

Dimension text = 21'-0″

Specify a second extension line origin or [Undo/Select] <Select>: ↲

Select base dimension: ↲

Command: *Command ends.*

Step 8: Create more dimensions

1 Follow the above example and create more dimensions as shown in Figure 7.15.

2 SAVE your drawing and exit AutoCAD.

Draw an Elevation

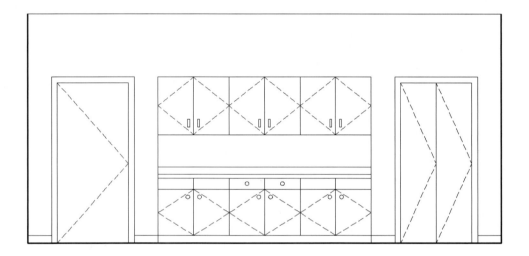

- Set up a New Drawing with MVSETUP
- Attach an External Reference File
- Draw the Elevation
- Detach the External Reference File

This chapter will show you the process of creating an interior elevation based on a floor plan. This approach is similar to what you do in manual drafting: projecting vertical lines from a floor plan. Although elevations can be generated from 3D models, this simple and straightforward approach is still widely used in the design profession and it prevents the elevations from being products of automated projection. This chapter also serves as a review session that allows you to apply some of the commonly used commands you learned in previous chapters, so that you can internalize them.

Set up a New Drawing with MVSETUP

In Chapter 2, you learned a basic procedure to set up a new drawing. In that procedure, you used the real size of the space as a clue to figure out the limits of the drawing area. This is only one of many possible situations. When you start a new drawing, you may have a sheet size and a drawing scale in mind (for example, ½″ scale on a 11″ × 17″ sheet). In such a situation, you can use the command MVSETUP (meaning Multiple View SETUP) to let AutoCAD convert the sheet size to the site size according to the print scale.

1 Start AutoCAD.

2 Start a new drawing with template "acad-Named Plot Styles.dwt."

3 Key in the command MVSETUP.

Command: **MVSETUP** ↵
Initializing. . .

Enable paper space? [No/Yes] <Y>: **N** ↵   *DON'T say "yes."*

Enter units type [Scientific/Decimal/   *A for Architectural. The AutoCAD text*
Engineering/Architectural/Metric]: **A** ↵   *window pops up with a list of scale factors.*

Architectural Scales

(480) 1/40″ = 1′

(240) 1/20″ = 1′

(192) 1/16″ = 1′

(96) 1/8″ = 1′

(48) 1/4″ = 1′

(24) 1/2″ = 1′

(16) 3/4″ = 1′

(12) 1″ = 1′

(4) 3″ = 1′

(2) 6″ = 1′

(1) FULL

Enter the scale factor: **24** ↵   *For ½″ scale.*

Enter the paper width: **17** ↵

Enter the paper height: **11** ↵

Units type (Scientific/Decimal/
Engineering/Architectural/Metric):

Command: *A rectangle paper boundary appears*
                                                    in the drawing area.

- In this step, AutoCAD set the drawing limits (34′ × 22′) for you.

4 SAVE the blank drawing as "ch08.dwg."

5 Set SNAP spacing at 1″ and turn it on.

6 Turn on ORTHO, if needed.

Attach an External Reference File

In the design process, elevations are usually drawn based on floor plans. In manual drafting, you can put a sheet of vellum or tracing paper over a floor plan, and then project lines for the elevations. Drafting with AutoCAD, you can do the same by making the floor plan an "External Reference." External Reference is a very important function that allows you to display other drawings in a drawing you are working on and use them as reference information. In this tutorial, we want to "borrow" (attach as an external reference) the floor plan and use it to generate an elevation. After we finish the elevation, we will "return" the borrowed drawing by detaching it. One of the advantages of using external reference is that it does not increase the file size of the current drawing file while obtaining information from other drawings. There are other applications for External Reference, and they will be discussed in later chapters.

1 Key in the command XREF.   *The External References palette pops up*
                                                    (see Figure 8.1).

2 Click the Attach DWG icon 🖼.   *The Select Reference File dialog box pops up*
                                                    (see Figure 8.2).

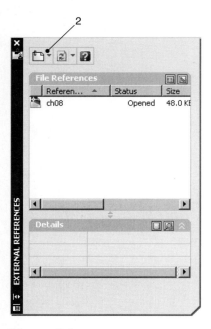

Figure 8.1
External Reference dialog box.

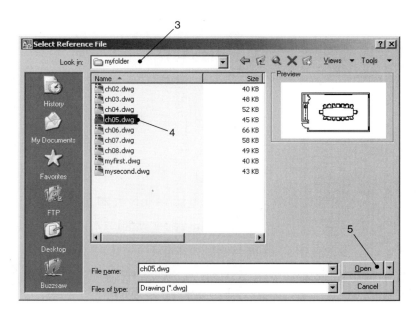

Figure 8.2
Select file to attach.

3 Click the list "**Look in:**" to open the directory in which your drawings are stored.

4 Select the drawing "**ch05**" from the list.

Your floor plan shows in the "Preview" window.

5 Click [**Open**] to attach the selected file as an external reference.

The External Reference dialog box pops up (see Figure 8.3).

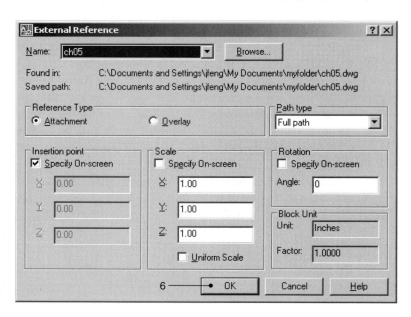

Figure 8.3
External Reference dialog box.

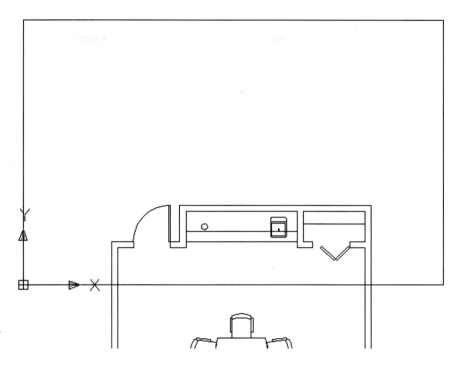

Figure 8.4
Rotate the floor plan.

6 Click [OK].   *AutoCAD prompts you for the*
                                                     insertion point.

7 Click somewhere in the drawing area   *Leave some space above the floor*
   to land the floor plan.   *plan for the elevation.*

   ● This attached Xref is very much like an inserted block.

8 Use the ROTATE command to rotate   *See Figure 8.4.*
   the floor plan by −90 degrees.

Draw the Elevation

Step 1: Freeze unwanted layers

When the floor plan is attached, all its layers can be controlled through the layer
control window in the property toolbar.

1 Click the layer list window.   *The layer list falls out.*

● You may notice that the drawing name "ch05" is added to the layer names of the
   attached file. The layer names are all grayed to indicate that you cannot make
   changes to them except freezing or thawing.

2 Freeze the layer for furniture (Ch05|I-FURN) to simplify the floor plan.

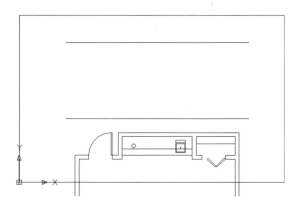

Figure 8.5
Define the floor and
ceiling.

Step 2: Define the floor and ceiling

Let's assume that the ceiling height is 10'.

1 Create a new layer "I-ELEV" and set it as current.

2 Draw a horizontal line above the floor plan as the floor line.

3 Use OFFSET to create a ceiling line 10' above the floor line.   *See Figure 8.5.*

Step 3: Draw vertical lines from the floor plan

1 ZOOM in to look at the floor plan and the floor and
ceiling lines as close as you can.

2 Use the LINE command to draw vertical lines
from the floor plan.   *See Figure 8.6.*

● The running Endpoint object snap may be very handy in this process. But you
have to be very careful to avoid unwanted snapping. If you choose to use the
running object snap, don't forget to turn it off when you finish this process.

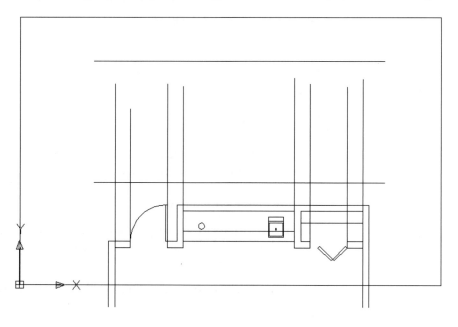

Figure 8.6
Draw vertical lines.

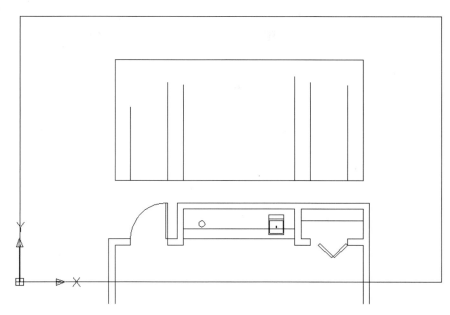

Figure 8.7
Enclose the room
boundary.

Step 4: Enclose the room elevation boundary

1 Use the FILLET command to enclose the room elevation boundary.

2 Use the TRIM command to trim off the   *See Figure 8.7.*
unwanted portions of lines.

Step 5: Draw the door and casing

To help you to visualize the elevation, the designer provides a sketch (see Figure 8.8).

1 Use OFFSET to define the top of the door (7′ above floor).

2 Use OFFSET to create the lines for a 3″ trim around the door.

3 Use FILLET to fix the corners.   *See Figure 8.9.*

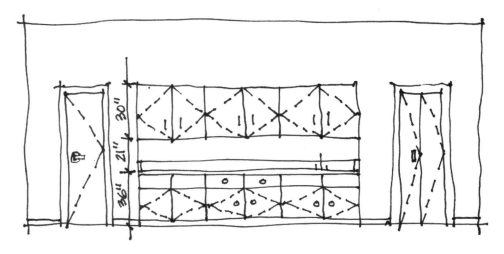

Figure 8.8
Sketch of the elevation.

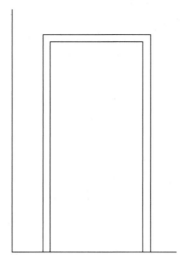

Figure 8.9
Draw the door and trim.

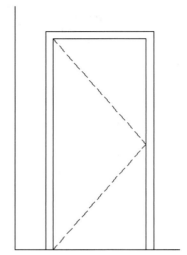

Figure 8.10
Drawing the door swing.

Step 6: Draw the door swing

In elevations, you may need to indicate the swing direction of doors and windows.

1 Create a new layer and name it "I-ELEV-DASH." Load and assign linetype "hidden2" for the layer. Make it current.

2 Turn on running Endpoint and Midpoint object snap.

3 Draw diagonal lines on the doors to indicate their swing.   *See Figure 8.10.*

4 Reset LTSCALE to show dashes properly (if necessary, new LTSCALE factor is 24).

5 Set layer "I-ELEV" as current (to draw more elevation lines).

Step 7: Draw the bifold door

1 ZOOM to look at the other side of the elevation.

2 Repeat step 5 to create the door frame.

3 Draw a line to divide the door opening into
two equal parts. (Use midpoint OSNAP.)   *See Figure 8.11.*

4 Draw door swing lines.   *See Figure 8.12.*

Step 8: Draw the counter area ceiling line

1 Use OFFSET 87″ from the floor line to create the ceiling line above the counter area.

2 Use the FILLET command to make the connections.   *See Figure 8.13.*

Step 9: Draw the counter elevation

1 Use OFFSET (4″ from the floor) to create the base cabinet door bottom line.

2 TRIM the baseline at both door openings.   *See Figure 8.14.*

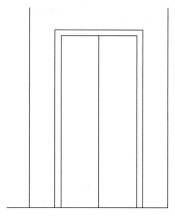

Figure 8.11
Draw the bifold door.

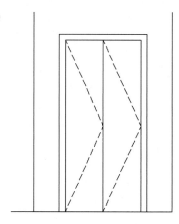

Figure 8.12
Draw the door swing.

Figure 8.13
Draw the ceiling line
above the counter area.

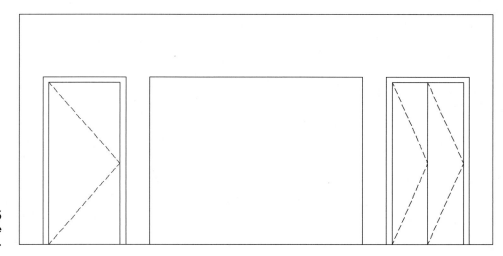

3 Use OFFSET (24″ above the baseline to create the base cabinet door top line).

4 TRIM off the extra portions. *See Figure 8.15.*

5 Use OFFSET (6″ above the base cabinet door top line) to create the bottom of the countertop. *See Figure 8.16.*

6 Use OFFSET (18″) to divide the counter into six equal segments. *See Figure 8.17.*

7 TRIM extra portions off the lines. *See Figure 8.18.*

8 OFFSET (2″ up) to create the countertop line. *See Figure 8.19.*

9 OFFSET (4″ up) to create the backsplash line.

10 OFFSET (17″ up) to create the bottom line of the wall cabinet. *See Figure 8.20.*

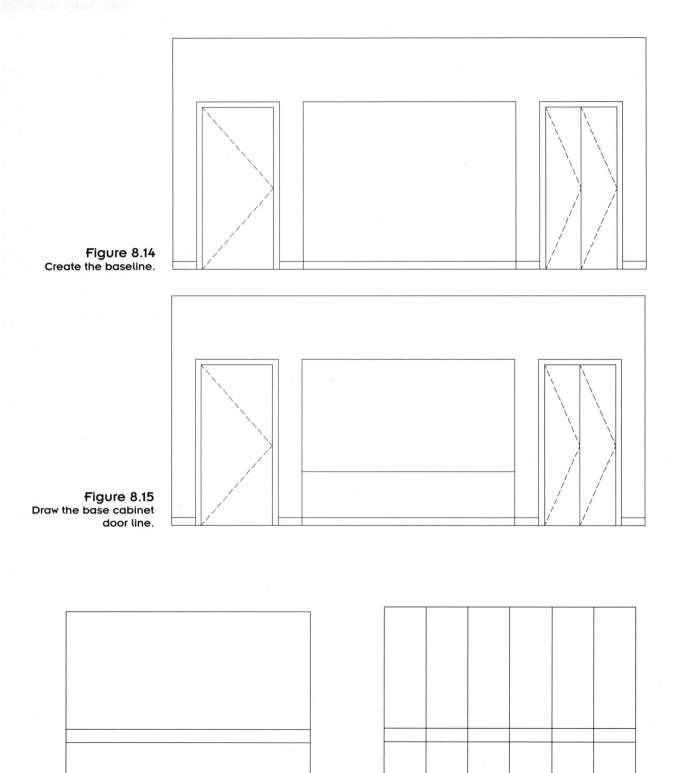

Figure 8.14
Create the baseline.

Figure 8.15
Draw the base cabinet
door line.

Figure 8.16
Draw the bottom of the countertop.

Figure 8.17
OFFSET to divide the counter.

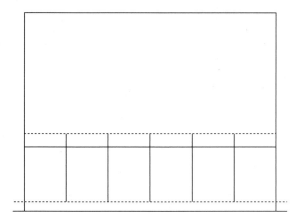

Figure 8.18
Create the doors.

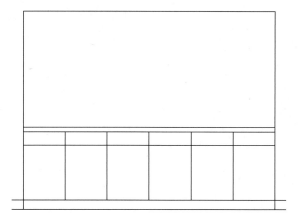

Figure 8.19
OFFSET to create the countertop line.

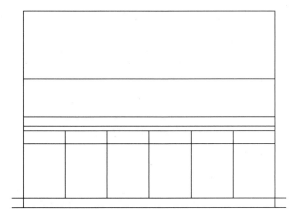

Figure 8.20
OFFSET to create more lines.

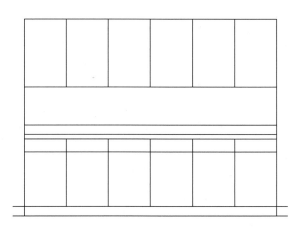

Figure 8.21
COPY the division line up to the wall cabinet.

11 COPY the vertical division lines to the wall cabinet.   *See Figure 8.21.*

12 OFFSET (12″ up from the baseline) to mark the midpoint of the base cabinet doors for the creation of the door swing lines.

13 Draw the door swing lines (using intersection OSNAP).   *See Figure 8.22.*

14 ERASE the midpoint marking line.

15 Draw the door swing lines for the wall cabinet doors. (Do the middle sections first, and then copy to the side sections. The MIRROR command may be used, too.)   *See Figure 8.23.*

16 Use the "Match Properties" tool to change the layer of the door swing lines.

 • Instead of changing the layers of all the lines, you can use the "Match Properties" tool, which allows you to change the properties of a drawing entity to match those of a "source object." In this case, the swing of the entrance door has been

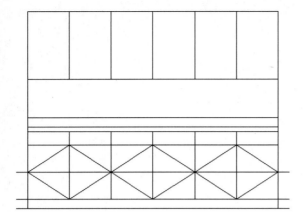

Figure 8.22
Draw the cabinet door swing lines.

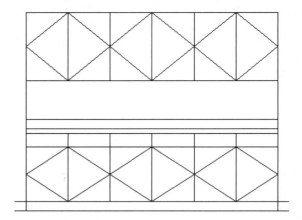

Figure 8.23
COPY the division line up to the wall cabinet.

correctly set, and you can use it as a "Source object" to let the swing of the base cabinet doors match it.

17 ZOOM out to look at the counter and the entrance door.

18 Click the "Match Properties" toolbar icon ▨ on the Standard toolbar.

Command: '_matchprop

Select source object: **pick door swing line on the entrance door**

Current active settings: Color Layer Ltype Ltscale Lineweight Thickness

PlotStyle Text Dim Hatch

Select destination object(s) or [Settings]: **pick the door swing lines on the cabinets**

· · · · · ·

Select destination object(s) or [Settings]:↵ *The lines change into dashed lines (see Figure 8.24).*

- This is a very handy tool to change object properties when you have a "source object" to match.

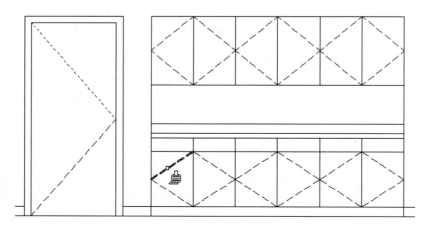

Figure 8.24
Change the layer of the door swing lines.

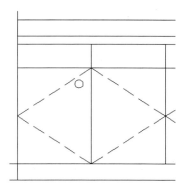

Figure 8.25
Draw the knob.

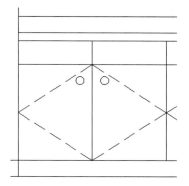

Figure 8.26
MIRROR to duplicate.

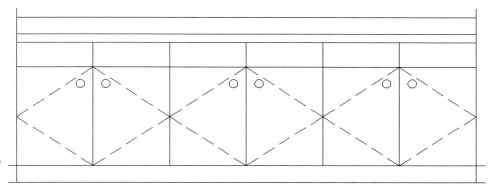

Figure 8.27
COPY to duplicate.

Step 10: Draw the cabinet knobs

1 ZOOM in to look at the first base cabinet door on the left.

2 Draw a circle (R = 1) near the upper left corner of the door.   *See Figure 8.25.*

3 MIRROR it to the opposite side.   *See Figure 8.26.*

4 COPY the knobs for other doors.   *See Figure 8.27.*

5 Draw a circle (R = 1) at the intersection of division lines.   *See Figure 8.28.*

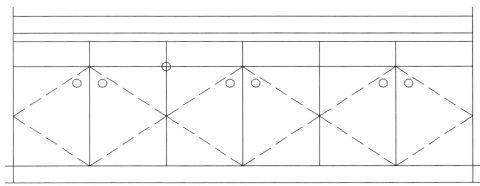

Figure 8.28
Draw a circle at the
intersection.

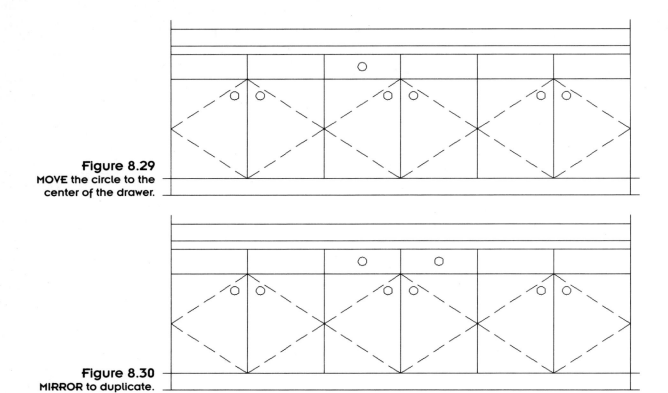

Figure 8.29
MOVE the circle to the
center of the drawer.

Figure 8.30
MIRROR to duplicate.

6 MOVE it to the center of the drawer.   *See Figure 8.29.*
   Displacement = 9,3.

7 MIRROR to duplicate.   *See Figure 8.30.*

Step 11: Draw wall cabinet door handles

1 ZOOM in to look at the first wall cabinet door on the left.

2 Draw a small rectangle (1″ × 4″) near the lower right corner.   *See Figure 8.31.*

3 MIRROR the rectangle to the opposite side.   *See Figure 8.32.*

4 COPY to duplicate.   *See Figure 8.33.*

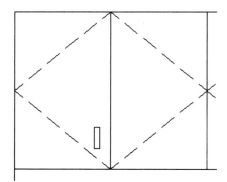

Figure 8.31
Create the wall cabinet door handle.

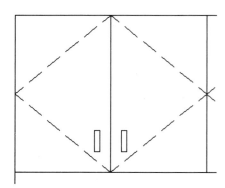

Figure 8.32
MIRROR to duplicate.

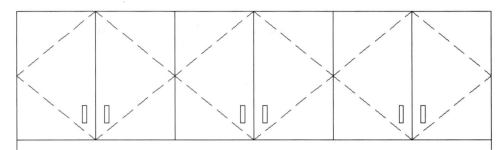

Figure 8.33
COPY to duplicate.

Step 12: Layer and lineweight control

Up to this point, you have finished all the lines. In the drawing process, lines are created by duplication, so it is difficult to keep everything in its appropriate layers. Now, it is time to get organized and to make your drawing look more beautiful by good layer and lineweight control. According to architectural drawing conventions, you may have two different lineweights: (1) the outline of the space and section profiles, and (2) visible lines. You may make a layer list as follows:

Drawing Object	Layer Name	Color
Visible lines	I-ELEV	7 (white)
Space outline	I-ELEV-OTLN	1 (red)
Door swing	I-ELEV-DASH	4 (white)

Control layers

1 Create layer "I-ELEV-OTLN."

2 Freeze the layer I-ELEV-DASH.

3 Use the "Properties" toolbar to change the layer of all the room profile lines to "I-ELEV-OTLN."

4 Change the colors of the layers according to the list (if needed).

5 Thaw all layers.

Change lineweight

1 Click the layer toolbar icon ▧ in the Properties toolbar.

2 Click the layer "I-ELEV-OTLN" in the lineweight section.

3 Select 0.50 mm.

4 Click [OK].

5 Click [OK] to close the Layer Properties Manager dialog box.

6 Click the button [LWT] in the status line.

7 Adjust the lineweight display if needed.   *See Figure 8.34.*

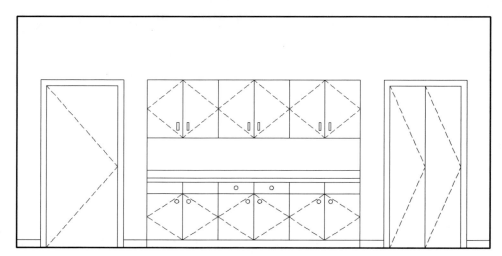

Figure 8.34
Display of lineweight.

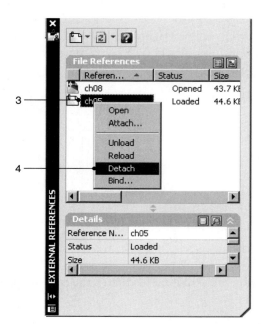

3 ———

4 ———

Figure 8.35
Detach an External
Reference.

Detach the External Reference File

Now that you have finished the elevation, you may detach the external reference file.

1 ZOOM out to see the whole drawing.

2 Use the XREF command to bring up the   *See Figure 8.35.*
External Reference dialog box.

3 Right-click the file name "ch05" on the   *A menu pops up.*
External References palette.

4 Choose Detach.   *The attached floor plan disappears.*

5 Save your drawing and exit AutoCAD.

Draw a Detail

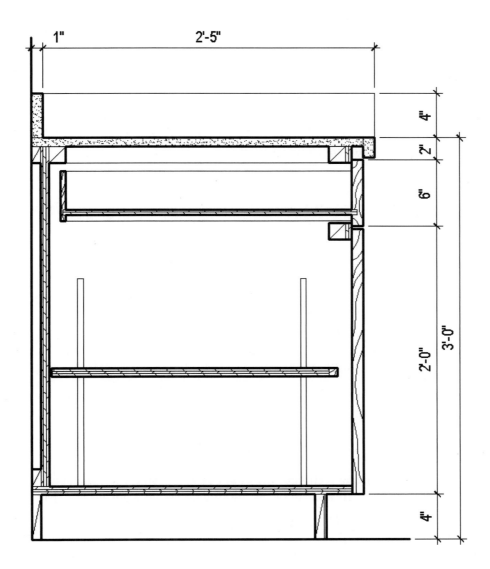

- Preparations
- Draw the Detail Lines
- Draw Material Symbols
- Create Dimensions and Notes

In this chapter, you will create a section detail of the counter. In the process, you will work more with hatch patterns.

Preparations

1 Start AutoCAD.

2 Set up a new drawing for the detail drawing, with its limits at 0,0 and 5′,5′.

3 Name the drawing ch09.dwg.

Draw the Detail Lines

Step 1: Draw the lines

1 Set SNAP spacing to ¼″.

- In a detail drawing, you need to deal with measurements in fractions of an inch.

2 Use LINE, OFFSET, FILLET, TRIM, and EXTEND to draw the lines of the detail section according to the dimensions given in Figure 9.1. (Don't draw the dimension.)

3 Create layer "I-DETL" (Interior, Detail). Make sure the lineweight is "Default."

4 Change the layer of all the lines of the detail section to "I-DETL."

Step 2: Create a profile line set

In a detail section of the cabinetry, the profile lines (the boundaries of the materials being cut) need to be enhanced with a lineweight heavier than that of visible lines. Whatever approach you take (printer pen assignment or layer lineweight), the separation of the profile lines and the visible lines is essential. In this step, let's try to create a profile line set based on the lines you just finished.

1 Create layer "I-DETL-MCUT" (Interior, Detail, Material being cut). Set the color to red for the layer, and set the lineweight to 0.5 mm.

2 Make a COPY of the detail drawing and place it in an empty space.

3 Use TRIM, FILLET, and ERASE to create the profiles, as shown in Figure 9.2.

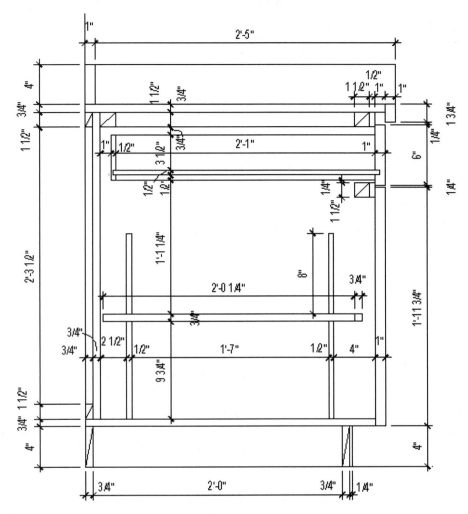

Figure 9.1
Lines of the detail
section.

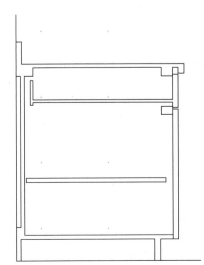

Figure 9.2
The profile line set.

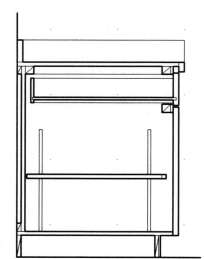

Figure 9.3
Completed heavy
profile lines.

4 Change the layer of the profiles to "I-DETL-MCUT."

5 MOVE the profile line set on top of the original line set.

● This move must be precise. Use Endpoint object snap to catch the movement defining points.

6 Click the [LWT] button to turn on the lineweight display.

The lineweight effect shows (see Figure 9.3).

Draw Material Symbols

Step 1: Change the layer for the lumber material symbols

1 Create layer "I-DETL-PATT" (Interior, Detail, Pattern) and set it as the current layer.

2 Select the diagonal lines that symbolize the unfinished lumber material, and change their layer to I-DETL-PATT.

Step 2: Draw the particleboard material symbol

The best way to draw material symbols is to use the HATCH command, especially when you can find a hatch pattern to meet your need.

1 Start the command HATCH.

The Hatch and Gradient dialog box pops up (see Figure 9.4).

2 Click the "Swatch" window.

The Hatch Pattern Palette dialog box pops up (see Figure 9.5).

3 Click the "Other Predefined" tab.

The dialog box flips a page.

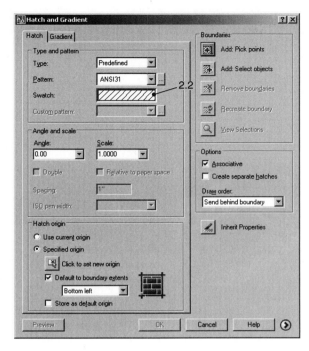

Figure 9.4
The Boundary Hatch dialog box.

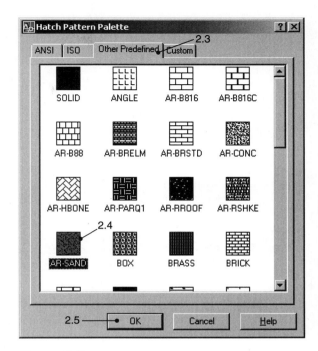

Figure 9.5
Hatch Pattern Palette.

4 Click on the sand pattern (AR-Sand).

5 Click [OK].

The Boundary Hatch dialog box reappears (see Figure 9.6). AR-Sand pattern appears in the pattern type window.

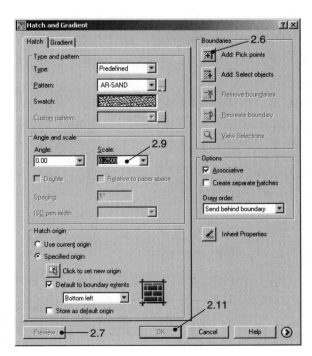

Figure 9.6
The Boundary Hatch
dialog box.

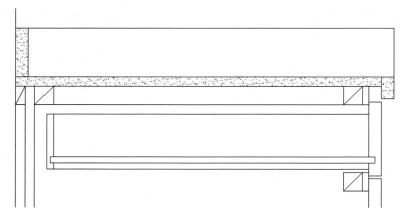

Figure 9.7
Hatch pattern
for particleboard.

6 Click Add: Pick Points **and click inside the spaces to be hatched (the backsplash board, the countertop board, and the front board). Hit the [Enter] key when you are finished.**

The Boundary Hatch dialog box reappears.

● AutoCAD will detect the hatch boundary only if the entire boundary is shown on the screen. Temporarily turning off snap may help when picking the small areas.

7 Click the [Preview] button.

The hatch pattern shown is currently set. You may feel that the density of the dots is too low, especially in small areas.

8 Hit the [Esc] key to go back to the previous dialog box.

9 Click the "Scale" list and select 0.25 to increase the density.

● The value of the scale factor is based on your visual observations of the preview.

10 Repeat 7 and 8 to reexamine the appearance of the pattern.

11 Click [OK] to finish the command.   *See Figure 9.7.*

Step 3: Draw the plywood symbol

The Hatch Pattern Palette does not have a ready-made (predefined) pattern for the plywood symbol. You need to draw it yourself combining two simple hatch patterns.

1 ZOOM in to look at the shelf as close as possible.

See Figure 9.8a.

2 Use the HATCH command to fill the core of the shelf with the "User Defined" parallel line pattern (spacing = 0.25", angle = 0).

The space is divided into three layers (see Figure 9.8b).

3 EXPLODE the hatch pattern.

● Only when a hatch pattern is exploded can the components be used as the boundaries of other hatch patterns.

4 Turn off SNAP (using the [F9] key).

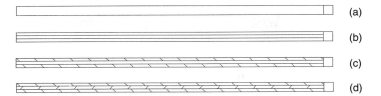

Figure 9.8
Hatch the plywood shelf.

(a)
(b)
(c)
(d)

5 Use the HATCH command to fill
the first layer and the third layer with
the "User Defined" parallel line pattern
(spacing = 1″, angle = 45).

See Figure 9.8c.

6 Use the HATCH command to fill the second
layer with the "User Defined" parallel line
pattern (spacing =1″, angle = 135).

See Figure 9.8d.

Step 4A: Hatch the wood grain (for Architectural Desktop users)

A few wood grain hatch patterns are provided in Architectural Desktop. If you have Architectural Desktop installed on your computer, you may use the ready-made wood grain hatch pattern to complete this step. If you do not have Architectural Desktop installed on your computer, you can skip the instructions shown below and following Step 4B instead.

1 ZOOM IN to look at the edge band of the shelf.

2 Start the HATCH command (H).

The Boundary Hatch and Fill dialog box pops up.

3 Click the Type list and choose Custom.

4 Click the browser button [. . .]
for Custom pattern.

The Hatch Pattern Palette pops up (see Figure 9.9).

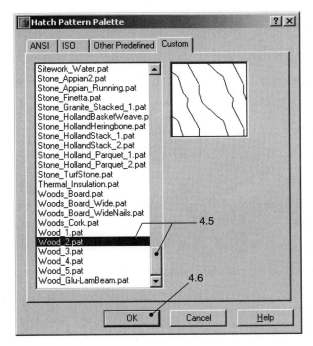

Figure 9.9
Find the wood pattern.

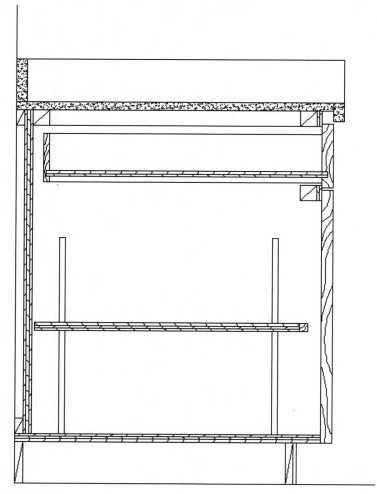

Figure 9.10
Wood grain created with the
Wood_2 hatch pattern.

Figure 9.11
Material symbols.

5 Pull the list down to the bottom and select Wood_2.pat.

6 Click [OK]. The hatch pattern is loaded into the Swatch.

7 Click Pick Points and pick a point inside the rectangle.

8 Click [Preview] to see how the pattern fits in the area.   *See Figure 9.10.*

9 Press the Space bar to continue.

10 Click [OK].

11 Hatch the wood grain pattern in the front and back of the drawer and in the door. Set scale = 2, Rotate = 15 to avoid mechanical repetition.

12 Hatch the bottom of the drawer and the counter with the plywood symbol.

13 Hatch the back and the baseboard of the counter with the plywood symbol.

- The user-defined hatch pattern for the layer of the plywood needs to be turned 90 degrees for the vertical plywood.

- See Figure 9.11 for completed material symbols.

Step 4B: Draw the wood grain (for AutoCAD users)

Because the wood grain hatch pattern is not provided in AutoCAD, you need to draw it. In this step, use the PLINE command to create polylines to make the wood grain symbol. Polyline is a special type of line. A polyline can have multiple line segments that are connected as one single object, it can have width, and it can be converted into a smooth curve or a spline curve. To connect the starting point of a polyline to the shape boundary, use the NEAR object snap to snap to the boundary line.

1 Right-click the [OSNAP] button on   *The Drafting Settings*
   the Status Line and choose Settings . . . .   *dialog box pops up.*

2 Click the [Clear All] button.

3 Check the box Nearest.

4 Click [OK].

5 ZOOM in to look at the edge band of the shelf board.

6 Click the PLINE toolbar icon on the Draw toolbar, and look at the command line.

Command: _pline

Current linewidth is 0'-0"

Specify next point or [Arc/Halfwidth/Length/   *See Figure 9.12.*
Undo/Width]: **pick point 1**

Specify next point or [Arc/Close/Halfwidth/Length/Undo/Width]: **pick point 2**

Specify next point or [Arc/Close/Halfwidth/Length/Undo/Width]: **pick point 3**

Specify next point or [Arc/Close/Halfwidth/Length/Undo/Width]: ↵

7 Restart the PLINE command and create   *See Figure 9.13.*
   another polyline.

8 Enter the command PEDIT and look at
   the command line to interact with AutoCAD.

Command: **PEDIT**↵

Select polyline or [Multiple]: **pick the first polyline.**

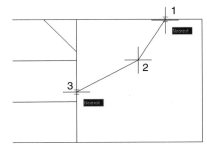

Figure 9.12
Create a polyline.

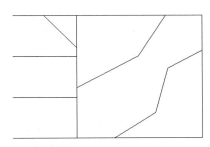

Figure 9.13
Create the second polyline.

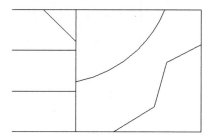

Figure 9.14
Create a smooth polyline curve.

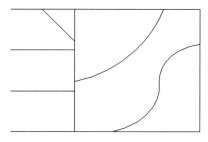

Figure 9.15
Create a smooth polyline curve.

Enter an option [Close/Join/Width/Edit vertex/Fit/Spline/Decurve/Ltype

gen/Undo]: **F**⏎

Enter an option [Close/Join/Width/Edit vertex/Fit/Spline/Decurve/Ltype

gen/Undo]: ⏎   *The first polyline turns into a*
                                            smooth curve (see Figure 9.14).

9 Restart the PEDIT command to turn   *See Figure 9.15.*
   the other polyline into a smooth curve.

10 Repeat 6 to 9 to create wood grain symbols in the front and back of the drawer
   and in the door. See Figure 9.11.

Create Dimensions and Notes

As you learned in Chapter 6, you need dimension styles and text styles to create dimensions and notes. Instead of repeating the steps as you did before to set the styles in
this drawing, you can load them from the drawing ch06.dwg using the AutoCAD
DesignCenter.

Step 1: Load a dimension style

AutoCAD DesignCenter allows you to load many drawing settings, in addition to
symbol blocks, into a drawing from other drawings. Dimension style is one of the settings you can load. Because you need to dimension this counter detail, you can load
the dimension style from ch06.dwg instead of redefining it from scratch.

1 Click the "AutoCAD DesignCenter"   *The "AutoCAD Design Center"*
   toolbar icon 🖾 in the standard   *appears as a tiled window*
   toolbar.   *(see Figure 9.16).*

2 Click the "Load" tool icon ▨.   *The Load DesignCenter Palette di-*
                                            alog box pops up (see Figure 9.16).

3 Click the "Look in" list and choose   *The list of .dwg files appears.*
   the directory where you saved the
   Chapter 6 drawing.

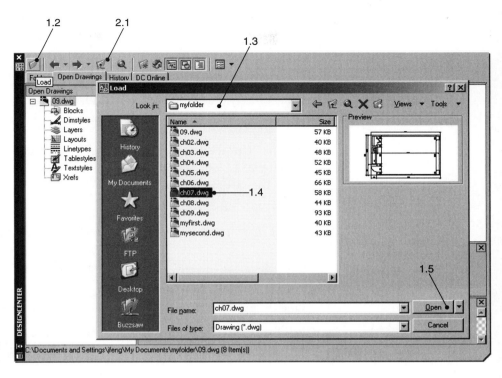

Figure 9.16
Select the file.

4 Click the Chapter 7 drawing to highlight it.

5 Click [Open].

The Load DesignCenter Palette dialog box closes. The categories of usable entities appear in the Design Center panel (see Figure 9.17).

6 Double-click "Dimstyles."

All dimension styles stored in the Chapter 7 drawing show on the panel.

7 Click the dimension style "archi48" to highlight it.

8 Drag it into the drawing window and release the held mouse button to drop it into the drawing.

AutoCAD says in the prompt area: Dimstyle(s) is added. Duplicate definitions will be ignored.

● From the "Look for" list in the "Find" dialog box, you can see that you can load blocks, dimension styles, drawings, layers, layouts, linetypes, text styles,

Figure 9.17
The DesignCenter categories.

(a)

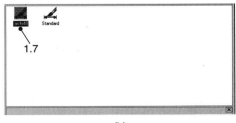

(b)

and external references through the AutoCAD DesignCenter. The procedure is similar: find it, drag it, and drop it.

Step 2: Load a text style

The dimension style archi48 uses text style DIM. We need the text style to make the dimension style work. Loading a text style is basically the same as loading a dimension style.

1 Click the "Up" toolbar icon ⬆ in the AutoCAD DesignCenter to go back to the category level.

The categories show in the panel.

2 Double-click "Textstyles."

3 Double-click "DIM."

AutoCAD says in the prompt area: Textstyle(s) added. Duplicate definitions will be ignored.

● Double-clicking an item in the DesignCenter panel equals dragging and dropping.

4 Click the "Close" box ⊠ to close the AutoCAD DesignCenter.

Step 3: Create a new dimension style for a different scale

Because the dimension style "archi48" was originally set for dimensioning the floor plan at ¼″ scale, the geometric features will be too big for the detail drawing. After loading the dimension style "archi48" from "ch06.dwg," you need to create a new dimension style based on "archi48" for 1½″ scale drawings.

1 Set the dimension toolbar.

2 Click the dimension style toolbar icon ◢ in the dimension toolbar.

The Dimension Style Manager dialog box pops up (see Figure 9.18).

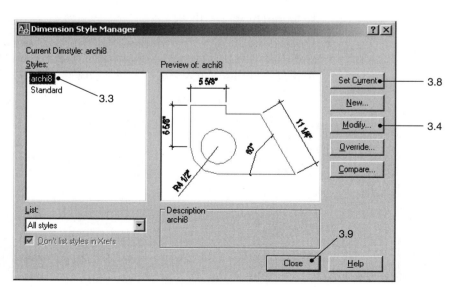

Figure 9.18
The Dimension Style Manager dialog box.

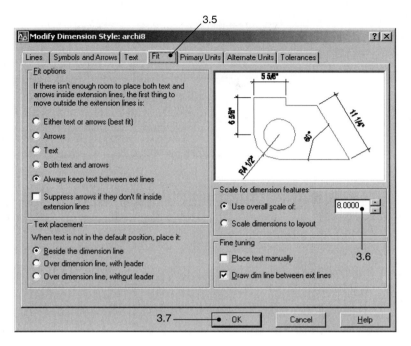

Figure 9.19
Set Overall Scale.

3 Click the style name "archi48" in the "Styles" and rename it as "archi8."

The number 8 in the name represents the scale factor for 1½″ scale.

4 Click [Modify].

The Modify Dimension Style dialog box pops up.

5 Click the "Fit" tab.

The dialog box turns to the "Fit" page (see Figure 9.19).

6 Change the value of "Use Overall Scale of" from 48 to 8.

7 Click [OK].

The Dimension Styles Manager dialog box comes back.

8 Click [Set Current] to make the style "archi8" the current dimension style.

See Figure 9.18.

9 Click [Close].

Step 4: Add dimension

1 ZOOM to look at the entire detail section. Allow some space around it for dimensioning.

2 Create a new layer "I-DETL-DIMS" (Interior, Detail, Dimension) and set it as current.

3 Use the dimension tools from the toolbar to draw dimensions as shown in Figure 9.20.

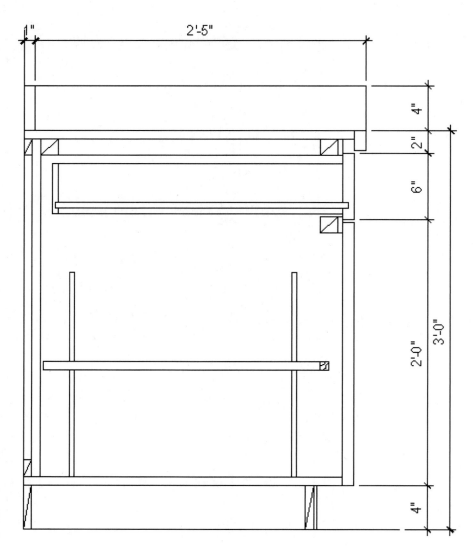

Figure 9.20
Dimensions and notes.

Step 5: Adjust the dimension text position

Sometimes, the automatically drawn dimension texts are crowded or interfere with other drawing elements. You need to adjust their position to avoid interference for better reading. In this drawing, the dimension of the backsplash thickness may need adjustment to make the text 1″ away from the wall line.

1 Click the Dimension Text Edit toolbar icon ![icon].

2 Select the dimension text and use the mouse to adjust the text position.

3 Click to set the text position.

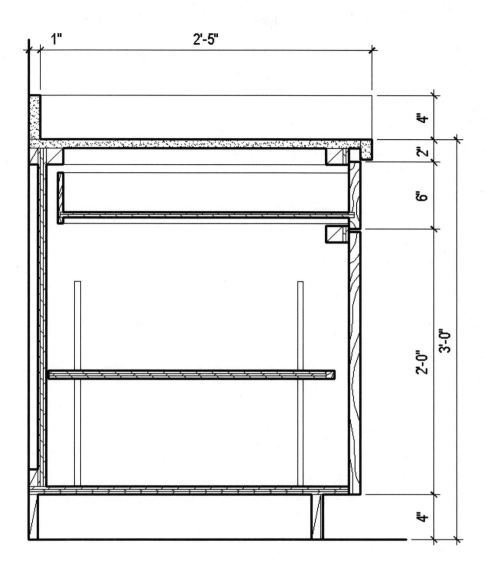

Figure 9.21
Completed detail drawing.

4 Thaw layers "I-DETL-PATT" and "I-DETL-MCUT"   *See Figure 9.21.*
to see the completed detail section.

5 Save your drawing and exit AutoCAD.

Legend and Schedule

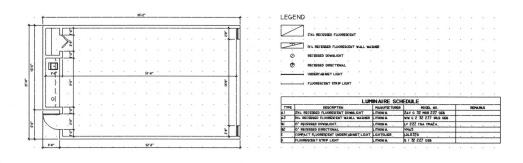

- Create the Lighting Symbol and Legend
- Create the Light Fixture Schedule

In this tutorial, you will create a legend for the lighting symbols used in the reflected ceiling plan and compile a light fixture schedule using a table.

Create the Lighting Symbol and Legend

Step 1: Preparation

1 **Open the drawing ch07.dwg.**

2 **Save it as ch10.dwg.**

3 **Reset limits to 90′,30′.**

4 **Use INSERT or COPY to create a copy of all the light fixture symbols for the legend.**   *See Figure 10.1.*

- Set the length of the symbols for the undercabinet light and the fluorescent strip 4′ to match, and align with the 4′ fluorescent downlight and wall washers.

Step 2: Define a text style for notes

1 **Click** Format **on the menu bar and choose** Text Style.   *The Text Style dialog box pops up (Figure 10.2).*

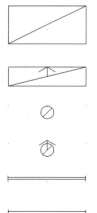

Figure 10.1
Create lighting symbols for the legend.

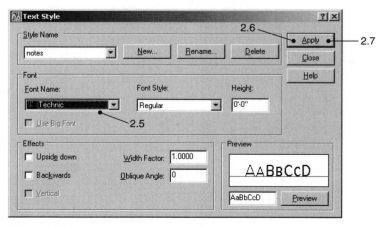

Figure 10.2
Create a text style for notes.

2 Click [New].

3 Enter name: notes.

4 Click [OK].

5 Click the font name list and select Technic.

6 Click [Apply]

7 Click [Close].   *The text style becomes the current text style, which is shown in the Styles toolbar.*

Step 3: Create texts

1 Click the MTEXT command toolbar icon **A** on the Draw toolbar.   *You are prompted to define a text box for the text to be entered.*

- Because the text box can be easily adjusted during and after the command, the initial setting for the text box can be tentative. You can always change it later.

2 Pick a point next to the 2 × 4 fluorescent light symbol. Look at the command line.

Specify opposite corner or [Height/Justify/Line spacing/Rotation/Style/Width]: **H↵**

Specify height <3/16″>: **6↵**

Specify opposite corner or [Height/Justify/Line spacing/Rotation/Style/Width]:

Pull the cursor and click a second point to define the text box.   *A ruler appears above the text box, and the Text Formatting bar pops up (see Figure 10.3).*

3 Enter text 2 × 4 RECESSED FLUORESCENT DOWNLIGHT.

4 Click [OK] on the Text Formatting bar.   *The command terminates.*

5 Copy the text and place it next to the 1 × 4 fluorescent fixture symbol.

6 Double-click the copied text.   *The ruler and the Text Formatting bar appear.*

7 Change the text to: 1 × 4 RECESSED FLUORESCENT WALLWASHER.

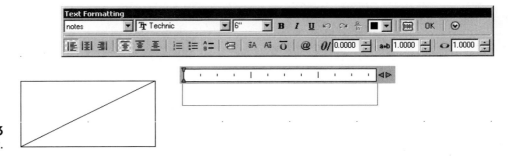

Figure 10.3
Define the text box.

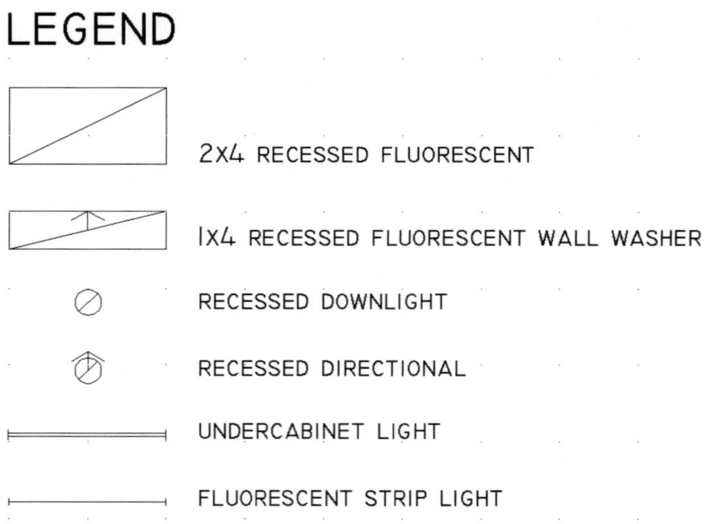

LEGEND

2X4 RECESSED FLUORESCENT

1X4 RECESSED FLUORESCENT WALL WASHER

RECESSED DOWNLIGHT

RECESSED DIRECTIONAL

UNDERCABINET LIGHT

FLUORESCENT STRIP LIGHT

Figure 10.4
The lighting legend.

8 Click [OK] on the Text Formatting bar.

9 Use the MTEXT command to create the following texts as separate entities.

RECESSED HALOGEN DOWNLIGHT⏎

RECESSED HALOGEN DIRECTIONAL⏎

UNDERCABINET LIGHT⏎

FLUORESCENT STRIP LIGHT⏎

10 Use the MTEXT command to create the title LEGEND. Text height = 12″.

11 Use the MOVE command to adjust the   *See Figure 10.4.*
alignment and spacing between lines.

● The text heights are determined according to the plotting scale of the drawing. In this case, assume that the drawing will be plotted out at ¼″ = 1′-0″ scale. If you want the title of the legend to be ¼″ high on the printed drawing, multiply ¼″ by the scale factor (that is 48). The result is 12″.

Create the Light Fixture Schedule

In lighting design, a light fixture is technically called a luminaire. We will use the term *luminaire schedule* on our drawing. A schedule is essentially a table. We will use the TABLE command to create the schedule.

Step 1: Define a table style

The format of a table is controlled by its style definition.

1 Click **Format** on the menu bar   *The Table Style dialog box pops up*
and **choose** Table Style.   *(see Figure 10.5).*

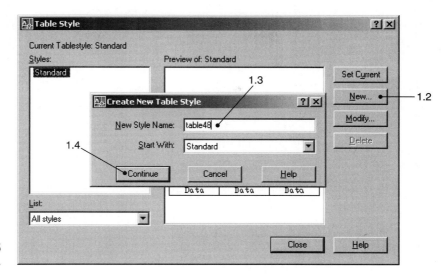

Figure 10.5
Create a new table style.

2 Click [New].

3 Enter a table name [table48].

4 Click [continue].

The New Table Style dialog box pops up (see Figure 10.6).

5 Click the Data tab.

6 Set the text style = notes.

7 Set the text height = 6.

8 Set the cell margin: vertical = 2; horizontal = 2.

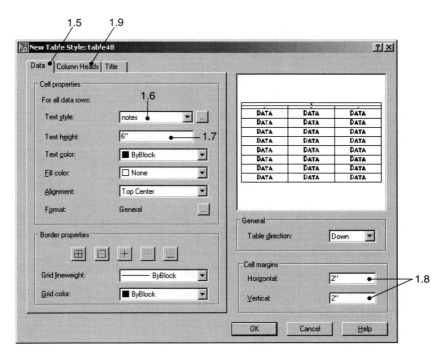

Figure 10.6
Set the data format
of the table.

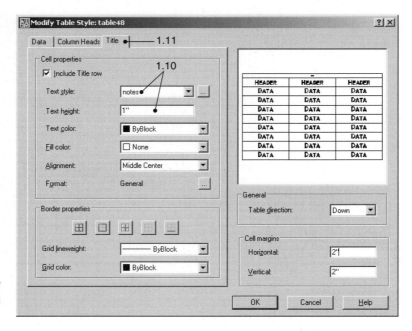

Figure 10.7
Set the column head
format of the table.

9 Click the Column Heads tab.   *See Figure 10.7.*

10 Set text style = notes, text height = 6.

11 Click the Title tab.   *See Figure 10.8.*

12 Set the text style = notes, the text height = 10.

13 Click [OK].

14 Click [Set current].

15 Click [Close].

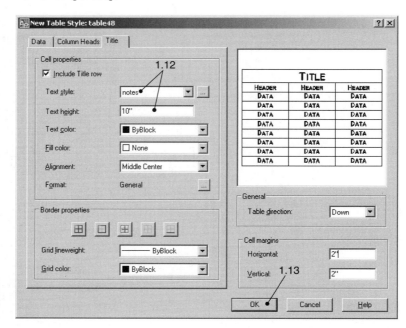

Figure 10.8
Set the title format
of the table.

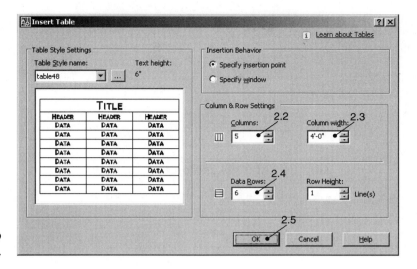

Figure 10.9
Insert a table.

Step 2: Insert a table

1 Click the table tool icon ⊞ on the Draw toolbar.

The Insert Table dialog box pops up (see Figure 10.9).

2 Set Columns = 5.

3 Set Column width = 4′.

4 Set Data Rows = 7.

5 Click [OK].

6 Click a point under the lighting legend to locate the table.

7 Enter the title: LUMINAIRE SCHEDULE.

8 Click [OK].

Step 3: Adjust the width of the table

1 Click the table.

2 Use the grip at the corner of the table to stretch the table to double the width.

See Figure 10.10.

Step 4: Adjust the column width

1 Click the grip at the top of a column line.

2 Drag the grip to adjust the width of the columns to make the table like the one shown in Figure 10.11.

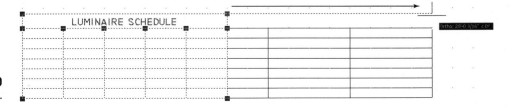

Figure 10.10
Adjust the table width.

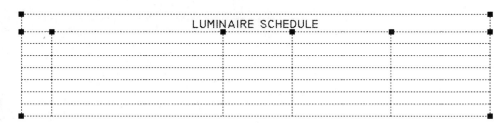

Figure 10.11
Adjust the column width.

Step 5: Enter text in a cell

1 Double-click inside the first column head cell.

2 Enter the text: TYPE.

3 Hit the [Tab] key to go to the next cell.

4 Enter DESCRIPTION.

5 Continue to enter the rest of the headings: MANUFACTURER, MODEL NO., REMARKS.

6 Double-click the cell right below TYPE to activate that particular cell.

7 Enter A1.

8 Hit the [Enter] key to go the cell below.

9 Enter text as shown in Figure 10.12.

10 Click [OK].

Step 6: Change the text style of the title

1 Double-click the title cell.   *The Text Formatting bar pops up.*

2 Highlight the text.

3 Click the bold text button.

4 Click [OK].

Step 7: Insert a row

1 Click a cell.

2 Right-click and choose Insert Row and choose Below.

- Inserting a column is similar.

Figure 10.12
Enter text as shown.

LUMINAIRE SCHEDULE				
TYPE	DESCRIPTION	MANUFACTURER	MODEL NO.	REMARKS
A1	2X4 RECESSED FLUORESCENT DOWNLIGHT	LITHONIA	2AV G 32 MDR 227 GEB	
A2	1X4 RECESSED FLUORESCENT WAWLL WASHER	LITHONIA	WW G 2 32 277 IRLS GEB	
B1	6" RECESSED DOWNLIGHT	LITHONIA	LV 227 CSA VMA2A	
B2	6" RECESSED DIRECTIONAL	LITHONIA	VMA5	
C	COMPACT FLUORESCENT UNDERCABINET LIGHT	LIGHTOLIER	LQL8376	
D	FLUORESCENT STRIP LIGHT	LITHONIA	S 1 32 227 GEB	

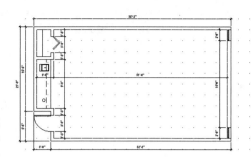

Figure 10.13
Completed Chapter 10
drawing.

Step 8: Delete a row

1 Click a cell in the newly added row.

2 Right-click and choose "delete rows."

Step 9: Change the data cell alignment of the table

1 Click Format on the menu bar and choose
Table Style.   *The Table Style dialog
                                                box pops up.*

2 Click [Modify].

3 Click the Data tab if it is not already open.

4 Change the Alignment to Top Left.

5 Click [OK].   *(See Figure 10.13.)*

6 Click [Close].

7 Save the drawing and exit AutoCAD.

Plotting

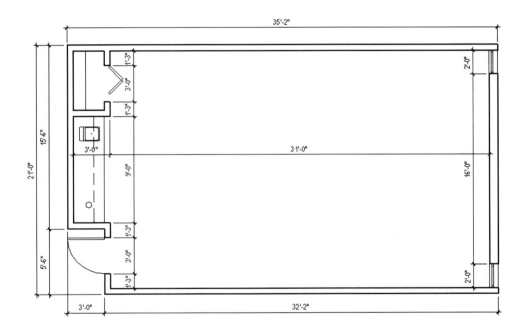

- ● Plotter Configuration
- ● Model Space and Paper Space
- ● Plotting from Model Space
- ● Plotting from a Paper Space Layout

Now that you have finished the plans, you are ready for plotting. In the process of plotting, you need to do a few things. First, you need to set up the drawing as a presentable page by setting the paper size and orientation, the area of the drawing to be printed, the drawing scale, etc.; second, you need to set the lineweight and other plot style options. Only if these things are all set up correctly can you print out the drawing as you expect. In this tutorial, you will go through these steps to print out the floor plan.

Plotter Configuration

To use a plotter, its configuration, the program that drives the plotter and the parameter settings for the program, needs to be loaded. This is usually done when the plotter is first connected to your computer, and you don't have to do it thereafter. In schools and in design firms, this is done by the IT support personnel. We assume that you already have a plotter working with your computer.

Model Space and Paper Space

In an AutoCAD drawing window, you have three tabs by default. One is the "Model" tab, and the other two are the "Layout1" and "Layout2" tabs. If a different drawing template was used to start the new drawing, you may have more or less tabs. In previous AutoCAD releases, the model tab used to be called model space, and the layout tab, the paper space. Model space is the place for you to create your drawing entities (such as lines), and paper space is the place where you assemble the drawing entities as a presentation on a drawing sheet (for plotting). Although this concept seems to be rather confusing, you have already been working in the model space in the previous chapters. Before the paper space was implemented in AutoCAD, there had been only one "world" (equivalent to the present model space) for both drawing (modeling) and presenting (plotting). The problem with this approach is that it is very confusing and difficult to have drawings of different scales on the same sheet. (You would be forced to violate the principle of always drawing at full scale.) In addition, it is impossible to present 3D views along with 2D drawings. The paper space is a solution to these problems.

Paper space is like a piece of paper placed on top of your basic drawings in model space. You can cut out holes (technically called viewports) to show, in different scales or view angles (for 3D models), the drawings in model space. The viewports can be resized and moved freely. In paper space, you also have control of layer visibility for individual viewports. You can thus create different versions of the same model space drawing. Using all these features of the paper space, you can make the task of sheet composition much easier. For this reason, you should always use the paper space for plotting. In the working process, however, plotting from model space may be a more convenient way to produce quick printouts. Therefore, you need to learn both.

Plotting from Model Space

In this section, you will make a plot of your dimensioned floor plan from model space.

Step 1: Determine the drawing scale and drawing size

In CAD drawings, you always create drawing entities in their true dimensions (or in full scale), and the drawing scale is decided by your needs for presentation. Now, it's time to make decisions on some pertinent AutoCAD settings. As a designer, you may have to follow the conventions of the profession. Because the scale $\frac{1}{4}'' = 1'$ -0$''$ is usually used for floor plans in interior design drawings, you may simply follow this convention. After the scale is determined, the question shifts to the sheet size. Similarly, you may follow the conventions of the profession, or you may have to consider available paper sizes of a certain type of printer. If you use a laser printer, your choice may be $11'' \times 8.5''$ (letter size), $14'' \times 8.5''$ (legal size), and $11'' \times 17''$ (tabloid). With a possible paper size in mind, you may then figure out whether it is large enough to hold the content. For example, we may consider a letter size sheet for our floor plan. At $\frac{1}{4}''$ scale, an $11'' \times 8.5''$ paper represents a $44' \times 34'$ space in reality [since $\frac{1}{4}'' = 1'$-0$''$ can be converted to $1'' = 4'$, $11''$ (on paper) represents $44'$ ($= 11 \times 4$).] This space seems to be large enough to hold our $35'$-2$''$ by $21'$-0$''$ room. To make sure that the sheet is indeed large enough to include the dimensions and the drawing title, you may draw a $44' \times 34'$ rectangle to do a mockup.

1 OPEN your drawing "ch10.dwg" and save it as "ch11.dwg."

- You are now in model space. This is indicated by the "Model" tab beneath the drawing area.

2 ZOOM to show the entire drawing.

3 Freeze or turn off the ceiling layers and turn on the furniture and the door layers.

Step 2: Start the PLOT command and select the right plotter

1 Click the printer icon 🖨 in the Standard toolbar.   *The Plot dialog box pops up (Figure 11.1).*

2 Click the "Printer/Plotter" name list and choose the plotter you want to use.

- The printer name shown in Figure 11.1 may not be the same as yours.

Step 3: Set the plot settings

1. Set the paper size.

1 Click the "Paper Size" list and select the correct size.

- In this example, you need a letter size sheet.
- The available paper size differs from plotter to plotter. Some plotters allow user-defined paper sizes, while others do not.

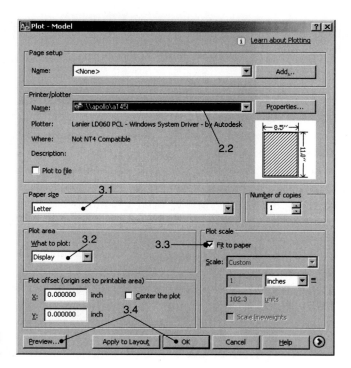

Figure 11.1
The "Plot" dialog box.

- When you select a paper size, you should remember that the "printable area" size (shown below the "Paper size" drop-down list) is always smaller than the paper size. The drawing contents must be all in the printable area in order to be plotted.

2. Define the plot area.

In AutoCAD plotting, you don't have to plot the whole drawing. There are four methods to define a particular area to plot: (1) Display: plot the area displayed on the screen, (2) Extents: plot all drawing entities on the drawing, (3) Limits: plot all drawing entities within the drawing limits, (4) Window: plot an area defined by a selection window. The last method gives you the easiest and most flexible control. It does not use a fixed proportion, as the first method does. It has better control than the second method, and it does not require a premeditated limit setting, as the third method does.

1   Check the button [Window . . .] in the "Plot area" section.

Specify window for printing

Specify first corner: **pick a point**

Specify opposite corner: **pick a second point to include all the drawing contents.**

- The lower left corner of the selection window will be placed at the lower left corner of the paper. If you want to have some space below the drawing, you may include some empty space when you pick points for the selection window. This is an easy and intuitive way of manipulating the placement of the drawing on a plot.

3. Set the scale.

1 **Clear the check box** Fit to paper.

2 **Click the** Scale **drop-down list and select** $\frac{1}{4}'' = 1'\text{-}0''$.

- If the defined plot area exceeds the paper, a red line will appear in the preview window. You may need to redefine the plot window to ensure that the drawing fits the paper.

4. Preview the plot

1 **Click [Preview . . .] button.**   *AutoCAD will show you the image on the plotting sheet that is represented by a rectangle.*

- If you need to adjust the placement of the drawing on the plot sheet, you may redefine the drawing area using the window option.

2 **Hit the [Esc] key to exit the preview.**

3 **Click [OK] to print the drawing.**

Step 4: Control lineweight and color

When you look at the printout of the drawing, you should examine the lineweight in both line thickness and color. The doors and windows may appear too light, and the wall is not dark enough, although the lineweight is correct (Figure 11.2) This problem is caused by using the object color in printing. Even when you use a black-and-white printer, the color dithering will use a gray tone to simulate the color. To solve this problem, you need to know how lineweight and colors are controlled in AutoCAD. Let us figure it out.

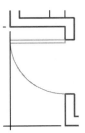

Figure 11.2
Plotted lineweight.

1 **Restart the PLOT command.**

2 **Click the** More options **button** 🔘   *The Plot dialog box is expanded* **(at the lower right corner).**   *(Figure 11.2).*

- In the **Plot options** group, you can see that the setting is **Plot with plot styles** by default. The plot style table that is being used is shown in the list at the upper right corner. In the example shown in Figure 11.3, the plot style table named **monochrome** is used. It is actually a file with the name **monochrome.stb.**

If you clear the **Plot with plot style** box, the **Plot object lineweights** box will be automatically checked. The object lineweights will be used to produce the print, but the object color will also be used for the print. The result will be the same as the previous print. One solution to this problem is to select all the objects in the drawing

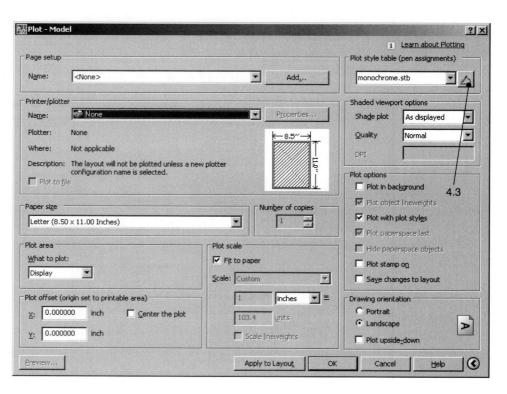

Figure 11.3
More options in the Plot
dialog.

and assign the black color to them using the Properties toolbar. This method will interfere with your previous layer color assignments, so you should avoid using it. You should use plot style table to solve this problem.

Plot style table gives you control of both color and lineweight through a plot style table. AutoCAD has a collection of plot style tables. Usually, you don't have to make your own plot style table. There are two types of plot style table: color-dependent plot style table and named plot style table. In a color-dependent plot style table, you can assign a lineweight (as well as a "pen color") to a color. All the objects of that color in a drawing will be plotted with the assigned lineweight. Using this method requires careful planning for color assignment in the drawing. In a named plot style table, you can create a named plot style that controls both the "pen color" and lineweight. The monochrome.stb is a named plot style table. But it obviously failed to produce a print with all black lines. Now, let us see why the monochrome.stb does not function as its name suggests.

3 **Click the Edit button** 🔳 **next to the plot style table list.**

The Plot Style Table Editor dialog box pops up (Figure 11.4).

The Plot Style Table Editor shows the settings of the plot styles. From the table, we can see that there are two named plot styles in this plot style table: Normal and Style 1. The style Normal is grayed. That means you cannot change it. Its setting for color is "Use object color." In comparison, Style 1 has all the same settings as Normal except the color setting that is Black. That means the objects with the plot style Style 1 will be printed in black. Now the decision is what plot style is used to produce the print. This is determined by the plot style assignment in your drawing. In your drawing, the plot style assignment for all the layers is Normal. That is why the lines are printed in color or the gray shade resulted from dithering. To make a true black-and-white print of the drawing, you need to assign Style 1 to all the layers.

Figure 11.4
Plot style settings.

4 Hit the [Esc] key twice to cancel the PLOT command.

5 Click the Layer Properties Manager toolbar **icon** ⬚.

The Layer Manager dialog box pops up.

6 Right-click at an empty spot in the dialog box, and choose Select All.

7 Click any of the "Normal" column's plot style settings.

The Select Plot Style dialog box pops up (Figure 11.5).

8 Choose Style 1 from the list.

9 Click [OK].

10 Click [OK].

11 Start the PLOT command.

12 Click the drop-down list in the Page Setup group **and select** <Previous plot>.

This will recall the settings you set for the last print.

13 Click [Preview . . .] to see the result.

See Figure 11.6.

From this example, you now know that the printed result is determined by both the plot style assignment of drawing elements and the plot style definition. Satisfactory results can be obtained only if both settings are correctly coordinated.

14 Hit the [Esc] key to end preview.

15 Click [OK] to plot.

When you start a new drawing in AutoCAD, a decision is made on the type of plot style table. In these tutorials, we have been trying to use the named plot style table because it has less restriction to color assignments. If you accidentally started a drawing with the color-dependent plot style, you need to be careful about color assignment in

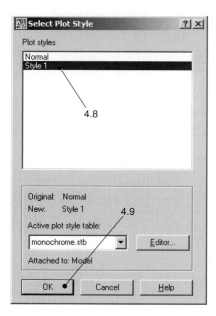

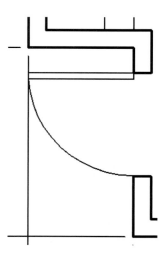

Figure 11.5
Change plot styles assignment.

Figure 11.6
The result of correct plot style
assignment in layer settings.

the drawing. If you want to use a predefined color-dependent plot style table provided
in AutoCAD, you need to know the settings and figure out how to coordinate the layer
color assignment. The color-dependent plot table is actually very similar to the named
plot style table. The major difference is that color name is used instead of the name of
a named plot style. Figure 11.7 shows a portion of the color-dependent plot style table
monochrome.ctb. You can compare it with the named plot style table.

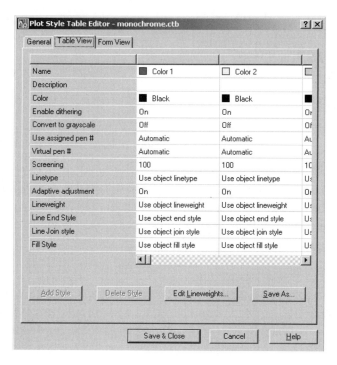

Figure 11.7
Color-dependent plot
style table
monochrome.ctb.

Step 5: Create a Plot Style Table file

Instead of using a ready-made plot style table, you can create a plot style table and use it to plot your drawing.

1 Start the PLOT command.

2 Click the More options **button** ⊚ .

3 **Click the** Plot Style table (pen
assignments) **list and choose** New. . . .

*The Add Named Plot Style Table
dialog box pops up (Figure 11.8).*

4 Check Start from scratch.

*You are requested to enter a name
for the new plot style.*

5 Click [Next >].

6 Enter a name: ch11.

7 Click [Next >].

8 Click [Plot Style Table Editor ...].

*The Plot Style Table Editor dialog box
pops up.*

9 Click [Add Style].

The Style 1 is created (Figure 11.9).

10 Click to select the name style 1 **and change it to** Thin.

11 Click to select the description 1 **and change it to** normal object line.

12 Click the color field and pick the black color.

13 Click the Lineweight field and choose 0.2500 mm.

14 Repeat 8 to 12 to create another new style:
     name = Thick
     Description = wall lines
     Color = black
     Lineweight = 0.5000 mm

15 Click [Save As ...].

The Save as dialog box pops up.

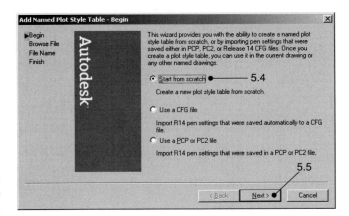

Figure 11.8
Create a new plot style
table.

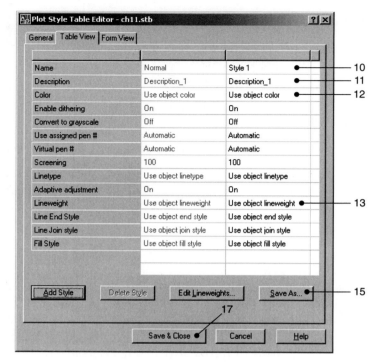

Figure 11.9
Create a plot style.

16 Click [**Save**]. The file ch11.stb is saved to the Plot Styles folder.

- The location of the folder is in C:/Document and Settings/username/Application data/Autodesk/AutoCAD 2007/enu/.

- If you want to create a backup copy to store in your own file storage, click [Save As ...] and save the file to your storage space.

17 Click [**Save & Close**].

18 Click [**Finish**].

19 Click [**Cancel**] to close the Plot-Model window.

Step 6: Assign the plot style Thin and Thick to layer settings of the drawing

1 Click the Layer toolbar icon to open the layer manager.

2 Change the plot style from Style 1 to Thin for all layers.

3 Change the plot style of layer I-WALL to Thick.

4 Start the PLOT command and see the effect in preview.

5 Plot the drawing.

Plotting from a Paper Space Layout

In the following tutorial, you will set up a paper space layout to present the floor plan you created in previous chapters.

Step 1: Start setting up a paper space layout

In the default setting of a new AutoCAD drawing, there is a tab leading to a paper space layout named "Layout1." To start setting up a paper space layout, you simply click the tab to switch to it.

1 Click the tab "Layout1."

2 **Right-click and choose** Page Setup Manager.

The Page Setup Manager dialog box pops up (Figure 11.10).

3 Click [**Modify**].

The Page Setup dialog box pops up (Figure 11.11).

4 Click the Printer/Plotter name list and choose the printer you want to use.

5 Make sure the ch11.stb is shown in the Plot style table name list.

6 Make sure letter size paper is selected.

7 Make sure the drawing orientation is "Landscape."

8 Make sure the plot scale is 1:1.

● The plot scale for paper space layout plotting should *always* be 1:1.

9 Make sure What to plot **is set to Layout.**

10 Click [**OK**].

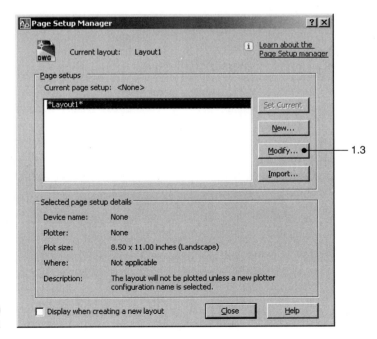

Figure 11.10
Page Setup Manager.

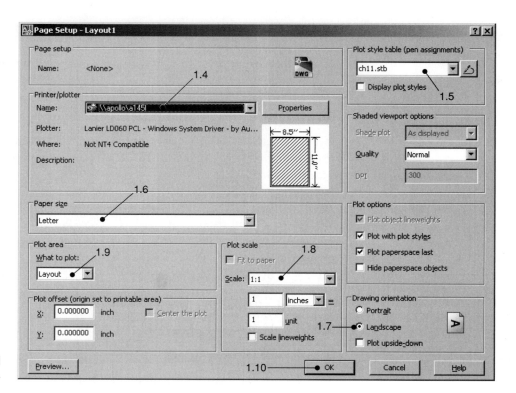

Figure 11.11
Set layout settings.

11 Click [Close].

The dialog box closes, and the paper space layout is shown (Figure 11.12).

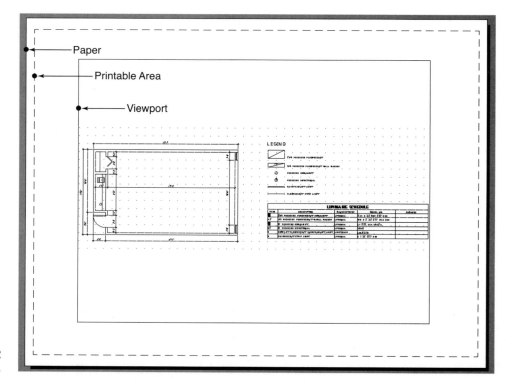

Figure 11.12
Paper space layout.

● The white colored rectangle (against the gray background) represents the paper. The dotted rectangle inside the paper boundary represents the printable area. The rectangle inside the printable area is a viewport automatically created by AutoCAD during the page setup process. The content of the model space drawing is shown inside the viewport.

Step 2: Set the drawing scale for the viewport

When a viewport is created, the drawing elements in the model space are scaled to fit the viewport. You need to reset the scale of a viewport to what you want. In this case, you want to set the scale to $\frac{1}{4}'' = 1'\text{-}0''$.

1 Click the viewport.   *The grips appear at the corners of the viewport.*

2 Click the Properties toolbar icon   *The Properties palette pops up.*
   on the Standard toolbar.

3 Set the "Standard scale"   *The scale changes in the viewport.*
   to $\frac{1}{4}'' = 1'\text{-}0''$.

Step 3: Adjust the drawing content in the viewport

In the viewport, only a portion of the plan is shown. You need to center the plan in the viewport.

1 Double-click in the viewport.   *The viewport becomes bold.*

   ● This indicates that the viewport is now in the model space mode.

2 Hold down the middle mouse button/wheel and drag to pull the floor plan to the center of the viewport. If the viewport is not large enough, show the left side of the plan. You will stretch the viewport layer.

   ● Don't roll the wheel. Zooming will change the set scale.

3 Double-click outside the viewport to make the viewport return to the paper space mode.

Step 4: Resize the viewport

After setting the scale for the viewport and moving the plan in the viewport, you need to resize the viewport to make it large enough for its content.

1 Turn off ORTHO (using the [F8] key).

   ● When ORTHO is off, you can pull the grip diagonally to change the width and length of the viewport at the same time. When ORTHO is on, you can pull the viewport in only one direction, either the *x* or the *y*.

2 Click the viewport.   *The grips appear.*

3 Click the grip at the lower right   *The grip becomes hot.*
   corner of the viewport.

4 Move the mouse to relocate the bottom and right boundaries of the viewport to show the entire floor plan, and click to set their locations. Repeat if needed.

Step 5: Move the viewport in paper space

In paper space, the viewport containing your drawing is like a picture.

1 MOVE the viewport to the center of the sheet.

Step 6: Reset the linetype scale

In the plan shown in the paper space viewport, the dashed linetypes all look solid. You need to reset the LTSCALE value for the paper space. Paper space is *always* full scale in the sense that the "paper" size is defined with its real measurement, so the LTSCALE value 48 you set previously in the model space is too big. It should be set back to 1.

Command: **LTSCALE** ↵

Enter new linetype scale factor <48.0000>: **1** ↵

Regenerating layout.

Regenerating model.   *Dashed lines show.*

- If you feel that the dashes are too big or too small, you may adjust the LTSCALE value to make them look better.

- In the AutoCAD linetype library, there is a group of linetypes whose names start with "ISO." These linetypes are much larger in unit size than other linetypes. Therefore, they require a much smaller (about ten to twenty times smaller) linetype scale factor to be shown appropriately in paper space. To avoid dealing with linetype scales individually, you should not use the "ISO" linetypes with other linetypes.

Step 7: Set the viewport layer as "non-plot"

Because the viewport frame should not be shown in your final presentation, you need to set the layer as a "non-plot" layer.

1 Create layer "I-ANON-NPLT"   *The plot icon turns into a non-plot icon.*
(interior, annotation, non-plot)
and click the plot icon to
set it as a "non-plot" layer.

- When a layer is set as a "non-plot" layer, it will not plot, although you can see it on the screen.

2 Put the viewport onto layer I-ANON-NPLT.

Step 8: Rename the layout

1 Right-click the layout1 tab and choose rename.

2 Enter "furniture plan."

3 Click [OK].

Step 9: Plot

Now you are ready to plot the drawing from the paper space layout. Before you start the following procedure, make sure the drawing is in the paper space mode (the status button shows [PAPER]). If you are still in the model space mode, you cannot plot the whole paper space layout.

1 Start the PLOT command. *The Plot dialog box pops up.*

- The plot settings for the paper space layout are very similar to model space plotting. The only significant difference is that for paper space plotting, the scale should *always* be (1″ = 1″).

2 Click the button [Preview ...] to check *See Figure 11.13.*
the plot setting.

- Now you see that the viewport boundaries disappear as a result of the "non-plot" layer setting.

3 Hit the [Esc] key to exit the preview.

4 Click [OK] to plot the drawing.

5 Save drawing and exit AutoCAD.

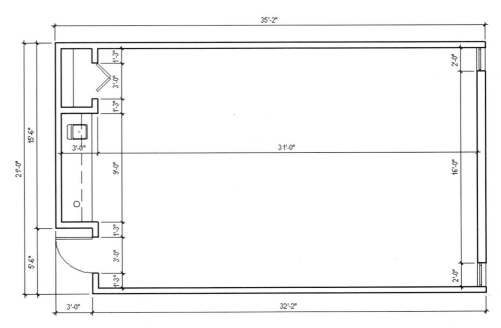

Figure 11.13
Preview of the paper space layout plot.

Assemble the Finished Drawing

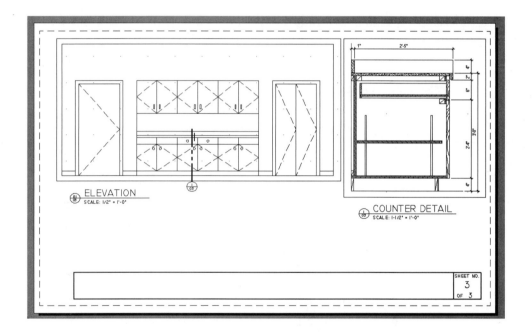

- Set up the Sheet File
- Create Annotation Markers
- Create Reference Symbols
- Create a New Viewport
- Create Drawing Titles
- Create a Drawing Title Block
- Set up the Second Sheet
- Set up the Third Layout

Up to this point, you have finished the floor plan, the reflected ceiling plan, the elevation, and the counter detail. In this tutorial, you will put these components together to make a set of finished drawings that are the drawing files ready for plot. This drawing file is also called a sheet file, as suggested in the *CAD Layer Guidelines* compiled by The American Institute of Architects. In such a file, the component drawings are linked as external reference files and shown in viewports on a paper space layout with a title block.

Set up the Sheet File

Step 1: Create a new drawing using a template

1 Start AutoCAD.

2 Create a new drawing using the acad—Named Plot Styles.dwt template.

- ADT users need to find this template file in the folder "AutoCAD Templates."

3 Set the UNITS to Architectural.

4 Set the upper right LIMITS to 100′, 60′.

5 Set SNAP grid to 1″.

6 Set Grid to 24.

7 Save the drawing as "Ch12.dwg."

Step 2: Use XREF to attach drawing files

In today's design practice, a drawing for final printing is usually made of a few interconnected files through external referencing. The file for final printing (or the sheet file) may have only the connections to other drawing files (called model files). In this step, you will assemble such a drawing with XREF and organize the components in paper space layout.

1 ZOOM-All.

2 Enter command XREF. *The External References palette pops up.*

3 Click the Attach DWG **tool icon** 🔳. *The Select Reference File dialog box pops up.*

4 Click the "Look in" list to open the directory where "Ch11.dwg" is located.

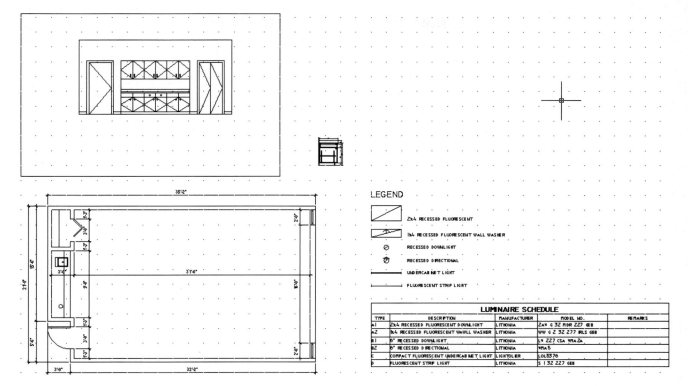

Figure 12.1
Attached drawings in model space.

5 Click to select the file "Ch11.dwg."

6 Click [Open].

7 Click [OK].

8 Pick a point somewhere near the lower left corner of the screen.

9 Use XREF to attach "Ch08.dwg" (elevation).

10 Use XREF to attach "Ch09dwg" (detail).

- As long as you can keep the XREFs from overlapping, you can place them wherever you want. Your drawing may look like Figure 12.1.

Step 3: Rename layout tab

1 Right-click the Layout1 tab and choose Rename.   *The Rename Layout dialog box pops up.*

2 Enter name: floor plans.

3 Click [OK].   *The layout name changes.*

Step 4: Create a page setup

1 Click the floor plans layout tab.   *The layout is displayed.*

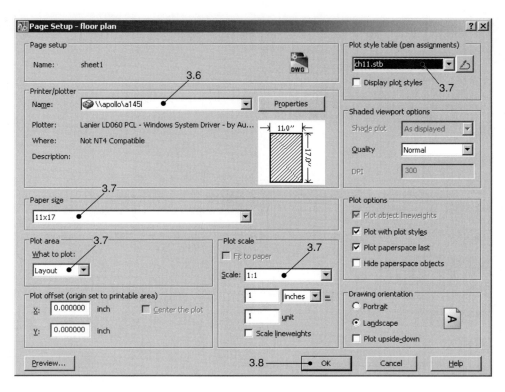

Figure 12.2
Page Setup settings.

2 **Right-click** the floor plans **layout tab and choose** Page Setup Manager.
The Page Setup Manager dialog box pops up.

3 **Click [New].**
The New Page Setup dialog box pops up.

4 **Name it as** sheet 1.

- We are now creating a named page setup. A page setup is a collection of page setup settings. It can be applied to this layout and other layouts.

5 **Click [OK].**
The Page Setup dialog box pops up (Figure 12.2).

6 **Select your printer.**

- The printer should have the capacity to print on 11 × 17 paper.

7 **Set the settings as follows:**

- Paper size: 11 × 17
- Plot area: What to plot: Layout
- Plot scale: 1:1
- Plot style table (pen assignments): ch11.stb

8 **Click [OK].**
The Page Setup Manager dialog box pops up (Figure 12.3).

9 **Click [Set Current].**
The page setup Sheet1 is applied to the layout floor plan.

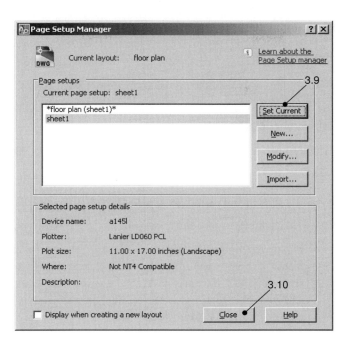

Figure 12.3
Set the Page Setup.

- The application of the page setup Sheet1 is shown as *floor plan (sheet1)* in the Page Setup Manager dialog box.

10 Click [Close]. *The layout changes (Figure 12.4).*

Step 5: Set up the first viewport

In this step, we want to use the existing viewport to show the dimensioned floor plan. We will use the ZOOM command to set the drawing scale for that viewport.

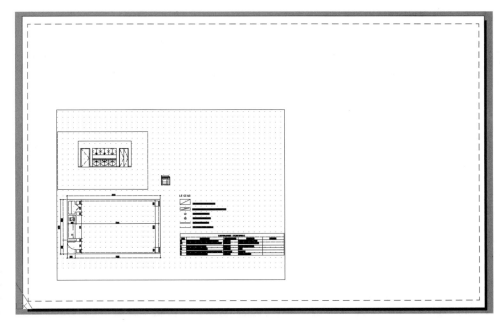

Figure 12.4
The layout after the page setup settings are applied.

1 Double-click inside the viewport.   *The status line button changes to [MODEL] to indicate the current viewport mode.*

2 Enter the ZOOM command and interact with AutoCAD through the command line.

Command: **Z⏎** ZOOM

Specify corner of window, enter a scale factor (nX or nXP), or

[All/Center/Dynamic/Extents/Previous/Scale/Window/Object] <real time>: **C⏎**

Specify center point: **click at the center of the floor plan**

Enter magnification or height <92'-11 1/4">: **1/48XP⏎**

- When setting up the scale of a viewport using the ZOOM command, the scale factor is the inverse of the drawing scale factor. In this case, you want to set the scale at $\frac{1''}{4} = 1'-0''$, and therefore, the drawing scale factor is 48, and the ZOOM scale factor is 1/48. Because you are setting the scale of a paper space viewport, add XP to indicate that.

- The advantage of using the ZOOM command to set up the viewport scale is that you can use the ZOOM-Center option to keep the wanted content visible in the viewport after the scale takes effect.

3 Double-click outside the viewport to return to the paper space mode.

4 Adjust the viewport size to make it fit the floor plan.

5 Set LTSCALE = 1 (to make the linetypes look appropriate).

6 MOVE the viewport to the upper left portion   *See Figure 12.5.*
of the layout sheet.

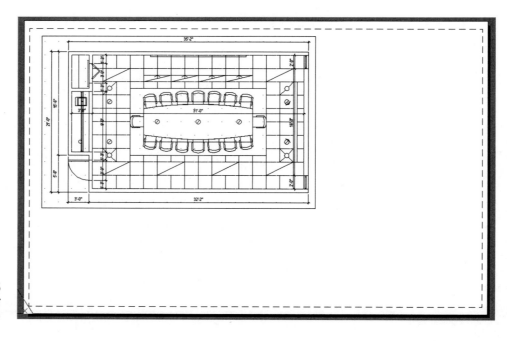

Figure 12.5
Paper space layout after
scale setting.

Create Annotation Markers

Annotation markers are used in drawings at specific reference points to refer to notes and schedule items (e.g., door numbers). They are composed of a textual identification, numbers or letters, and a graphic boundary of simple shapes. Although they are small in size, making them look good and consistent throughout your drawings can be a tedious and challenging task. Therefore, making a reusable collection of them will make your life much easier in the future.

Step 1: Import the text style

Although you have the drawings that contain text styles through external reference and they can be used to create text with the MTEXT command, you cannot use those styles in the attributes that you will create in the following steps. We need to import one through the **Design Center**.

1 Click the Design Center icon .

2 Click the Folders tab.

3 Locate and open the drawing ch11.dwg.

4 Click the category Textstyle.

5 Double-click NOTES to load it into the current drawing.   *You do not see anything happen, but the text style has actually been imported into the current drawing.*

6 Close the Design Center.

Step 2: Define an "Attribute"

Because the identification in the annotation marker is a variable, making it a simple block will not work. Instead, you need to use a special type of block associated with "Attributes." You will have a better understanding of how an attribute works after making and using it.

1 Enter the command ATTDEF (Attribute definition) to define an attribute.   *The Attribute Definition dialog box pops up (Figure 12.6).*

2 Type "ID" (identification) in the text box "Tag."

3 Type marker id: in the text box Prompt.

4 Type ? in the text box Value.

   ● Now, the value of the attribute (the number or the letter of the marker) is still empty. You will fill it in when you insert a block with this attribute.

5 Click the list Justification and choose Center.

6 Make sure style "NOTES" is the text style.

7 Change the text height to $\frac{1}{8}''$.

   ● The "Text Options" settings control the appearance of the text.

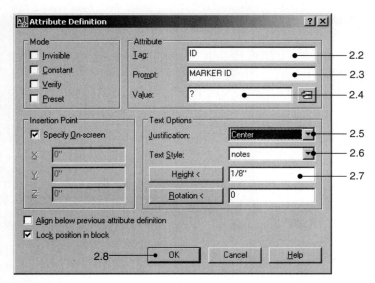

Figure 12.6
Attribute Definition dialog box.

Figure 12.7
Adjust the location of the attribute
text in the circle.

8 Click [OK].

*You will see the text "ID" on the drawing
moving with the cursor.*

9 Click at a point in an empty area.

Step 3: Make a block with attribute

1 ZOOM in to look at the created attribute closely.

2 Draw a circle ($R = \frac{1}{8}$) to enclose the text "ID."

3 Use the MOVE command to adjust the position
of the attribute in the circle (if needed).

See Figure 12.7.

4 Change the layer of the circle and the attribute text "ID" to "0."

5 Make a block including both the tag and the circle and name it "MARK." (Pick
the center of the circle as the insertion point.)

6 ZOOM out to look at the floor plan.

Step 4: Insert the block "MARK"

Inserting a block with an attribute is the best way to understand the concept. Let us
assume that we need a marker to identify the door. First, insert the block "MARK." In
the INSERT command, you will be prompted to enter the MARKER ID value. After
a value is entered, a door type marker is created.

1 Insert the block "MARK."

Command: **INSERT** ↵

The Insert dialog box pops up.

Select the block name "MARK" from the "Name" list.

Click [OK].

Specify insertion point or [Scale/X/Y/Z/Rotate/PScale/PX/PY/PZ/PRotate]:

pick a point at the door opening in the floor plan.

Enter attribute values	*AutoCAD asks you (with the prompt) to enter the value.*
MARKER ID <?>: **A** ↵	*Assume the door type is A.*
Command:	*The letter A appears in the circle (Figure 12.8).*

2 ZOOM in to look at the inserted marker.

Step 5: Change the attribute value

The value of an attribute can be changed by using the Enhanced Attribute Editor. Let us assume that you need to change the door type from A to D.

1 **Double-click the door number marker.**	*The Enhanced Attribute Editor dialog box pops up (Figure 12.9).*
2 **Type D to replace A.**	
3 **Click [OK].**	*The door type marker changes from A to D.*

- This is a simple example of using an attribute. In this example, you enjoy both the consistency of blocks and the flexibility of editable texts. There are many other applications of attributes to attach textual information to graphic entities for the purpose of management. You can associate more than one attribute to a block for more complex applications.

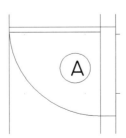

Figure 12.8
The circular annotation marker.

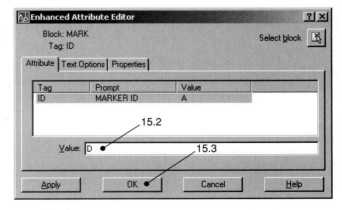

Figure 12.9
Enhanced Attribute Editor dialog box.

Create Reference Symbols

According to design drawing conventions, related drawings are symbolically linked by reference symbols such as elevation symbols and bubbles. Elevation symbols in floor plans indicate the viewing orientation and point to the sheet number and drawing numbers of the elevations. In the drawing title of an elevation, a bubble corresponding to the elevation symbol in the floor plan identifies the elevation with the drawing number and sheet number. Bubbles are also used for sections and details. The paper space is a good place for these bubbles because you can easily avoid dealing with the different scales associated with each individual drawing.

Step 1: Draw an elevation symbol

1 Set layer "0" current.   *For making blocks.*

2 Set snap spacing $\frac{1}{16}''$ and turn on SNAP and ORTHO.

3 ZOOM in to look at the floor plan.

4 Draw a circle in an empty space (R = $\frac{3}{16}$).

5 ZOOM in to look at the circle closely.

6 Use LINE to draw the pointer.   *Use Quadrant object snap if you like (see Figure 12.10a).*

7 ROTATE the pointer −45 degrees.   *See Figure 12.10b.*

Command: ROTATE

Current positive angle in UCS: ANGDIR=counterclockwise ANGBASE=0

Select objects: **pick point** Specify   *Use implied selection-window to select the*
opposite corner: **pick point** 3 found   *circle and the pointer.*

Select objects: ⏎

Specify base point: **CEN** ⏎

Of **pick the circle**

Specify rotation angle or [Reference]: **−45** ⏎

Command:

8 Start the HATCH command to   *The Boundary Hatch dialog box pops up.*
hatch the pointer with a solid pattern.

9 Click the Swatch window.

10 Click the Other Predefined **tab and click the solid pattern to select it.**

11 Click [OK].

12 Click [Pick point] and pick a point inside the pointer.

13 Hit the [Enter] key.   *The dialog box returns.*

14 Click the [Preview] button to see if it looks correct.

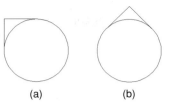

(a)   (b)

Figure 12.10
Draw the pointer.

Figure 12.11
Solid hatch the pointer.

Figure 12.12
Attribute positions in the elevation symbol.

15 Hit [Enter] to apply the pattern and end the command. *See Figure 12.11.*

16 Draw a horizontal line inside the circle. Use QUA object snap.

Step 2: Define attributes for the reference number

1 Enter the command ATTDEF.

2 Enter Tag: REF

3 Enter Prompt: Reference number

4 Enter Value: 00

5 Set Justification to Center.

6 Set Text Style to NOTES.

7 Set text Height to $\frac{3}{32}$.

8 Click [OK].

9 Snap to the midpoint of the horizontal line.

10 MOVE it up a little bit.   *See Figure 12.12 for reference.*

Step 3: Define attributes for the sheet number

1 Enter the command ATTDEF.

2 Enter Tag: SHT

3 Enter Prompt: Sheet number

4 Enter Value: 00

5 Set Justification to Center.

6 Set Text Style to NOTES.

7 Set text Height to $\frac{3}{32}$.

8 Click [OK].

9 Snap to the midpoint of the horizontal line.

10 MOVE it down.   *See Figure 12.12 for reference.*

Step 4: Create the pointer block

Because the pointer may point in different directions and the reference text always remains horizontal, you need to make two separate blocks.

1 Make sure the bubble and the pointer are all in layer 0.

2 Start the BLOCK command.

3 Enter name: POINTER.

4 Click Select objects.

5 Select the pointer using a cross window.

6 Click Pick point.

7 Pick the center point of the circle.

8 Check Delete.

9 Click [OK].

Step 5: Create the bubble block

1 Start the BLOCK command.

2 Enter name: BUBBLE.

3 Click Select objects.

4 Select the entire bubble, including the attribute texts.

5 Click Pick point.

6 Pick the center point of the circle.

7 Check Delete.

8 Click [OK].

Step 6: Insert the elevation symbol

First, insert the bubble block and fill in the reference information, then insert the pointer.

1 ZOOM to look at the floor plan.

2 Create layer "I-ANON-SYMB" and set it as the current layer.

3 Click the Insert Block toolbar icon on the *The Insert dialog box pops up.* Draw toolbar to start the INSERT command.

4 Click the Name field and choose BUBBLE.

5 Click [OK], and interact with AutoCAD through the command line.

Command: _insert

Specify insertion point or [Basepoint/Scale/X/Y/Z/Rotate]: **pick the point in front of the counter.**

Figure 12.13
The finished elevation symbol.

Specify rotation angle <0>: ↵

Enter attribute values

Sheet number <00>: **03** ↵

Reference number <00>: **E1** ↵

6 ZOOM in to look at it closely.

- If you see the circle turns into a polygon, don't worry about it. It is only Auto-CAD's way of displaying a circle quickly. If you want to see a smoother circle, you can use the REGEN command to make AutoCAD do a better job.

7 Start the INSERT command.

8 Select the block POINTER.

9 Click [OK].

10 Snap to the center point of the circle.

11 Drag the rubber band line up to make   *See Figure 12.13.*
a 90 degree rotation for the pointer.

Create a New Viewport

We want to use this viewport to show the furniture plan at a smaller scale.

Step 1: Set the Viewports toolbar

The tools to create viewports are on the Viewports toolbar. You need to set it up.

1 Right-click a toolbar icon on the Standard   *The Viewports toolbar pops up.*
toolbar and choose Viewports.

2 Drag it by the title bar to embed it into the upper frame of the drawing window.

- This toolbar works only in a horizontal position to display the scale of a selected viewport.

Step 2: Create a new viewport

1 Click the single viewport tool icon ▣.

2 Click-pull-click to define the viewport   *See Figure 12.14 for reference.*
to the right of the existing viewport.

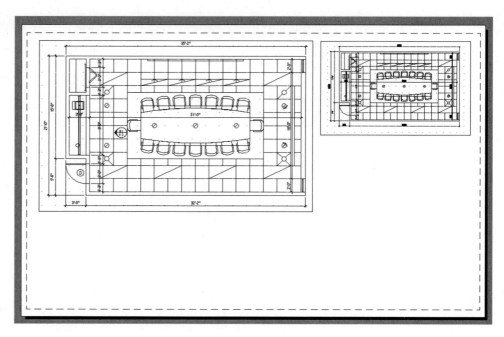

Figure 12.14
Create a new viewport.

3 Click the viewport frame of the new viewport.

The viewport scale is shown in the text window on the Viewports toolbar.

4 Click the arrow of the text window to see the roll-down list and choose 1/8″ = 1′-0″.

The content of the viewport is scaled to 1/8″ = 1′-0″.

5 Click [PAPER] on the status line to switch to model space viewport mode.

6 Hold down the middle mouse button to drag the floor plan to the center of the viewport.

7 Adjust the viewport size to fit the plan.

8 MOVE the viewport if needed.

Step 3: Differentiate the contents of the two viewports by layer control

Although the contents of both viewports are from the same drawing, you can make them look different by using layer controls.

1 Make sure all the layers are visible.

2 Double-click inside the small viewport.

3 Click the layers toolbar icon ⬙ to call up the Layer Properties Manager dialog box.

4 Click the "Freeze/Thaw in current viewport" icon ▣ in the column "Current VP Freeze" to freeze layers ch11|I-ANON-DIMS, ch11|I-CLNG, ch11|I-CLNG-LITE, **and** ch11|I-CLNG-HVAC.

See Figure 12.15.

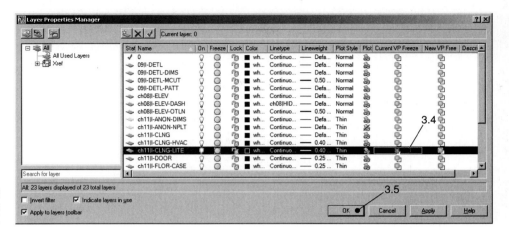

Figure 12.15
Freeze a layer in the
current viewport.

- When the layer is frozen, the shining sun icon turns into a snowflake ![snowflake icon].

5 Click [OK].

6 Click the other viewport to make it active.

7 **Freeze the layers** ch11|I-CLNG, ch11|I-CLNG-LITE, ch11|I-CLNG-HVAC,
and I-FURN **in the current viewport.**

- The floor plans in the two viewports now look different, although they actually come from the same drawing in model space.

8 **Click inside the larger viewport to activate it.**

9 Click [OK].

10 **Click [MODEL] to return to paper space layout.**   *See Figure 12.16.*

- This step shows that you can use multiple viewports and layer visibility control to
produce different representations of the same model drawing, such as the floor plan.

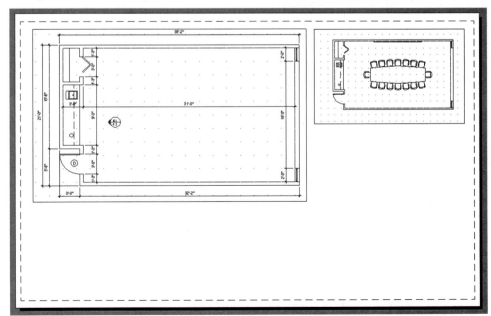

Figure 12.16
The two different repre-
sentations of the same
model in two viewports.

Step 4: Import the "non-plot" viewport layer

Layers can be imported from other drawings through the Design Center.

1 Click the Design Center icon to open the Design Center 🖳.

2 Click the Folders tab and open ch11.dwg.

3 Click the category Layers.

4 Double-click I-Anon-NPLT to load the layer into the current drawing.

5 Close the Design Center.

6 Put both viewports onto layer I-ANON-NPLT.

Create Drawing Titles

1 Make sure the text style NOTES is the current text style that is shown in the styles toolbar.

2 Use the DTEXT command to enter the drawing title text: FLOOR PLAN. Text height $= \frac{1}{4}''$.

Command: **DTEXT**↵

Current text style: "notes" Text height: 0'-0 1/8"

Specify start point of text or [Justify/Style]: **click to pick the starting point of the text string**

Specify height <0'-0 1/8">: **1/4** ↵

Specify rotation angle of text <0>: ↵ **enter the text: FLOOR PLAN**

3 Hit the [Enter] key twice to end the DTEXT command.

- DTEXT is a convenient command for typing short text. The advantage of using DTEXT over MTEXT is that it shows the text as it is in the exact position while you are typing. A major difference between the two commands is that the text lines produced by DTEXT turn into individual entities.

4 Use the LINE command to draw the underline.

5 Use the DTEXT command to enter the drawing scale note: SCALE: $\frac{1}{4}'' = 1'-0''$.

6 Use the CIRCLE command line command to draw a north arrow as shown in Figure 12.17. The radius of the circle is $\frac{1}{4}''$.

FLOOR PLAN
SCALE: 1/4" = 1'-0"

Figure 12.17
Drawing title.

7 Use the COPY command to duplicate the first drawing title for the second viewport.

8 Double-click the text to edit the text. Change FLOOR PLAN to FURNITURE PLAN, and change $\frac{1}{4}'' = 1'\text{-}0''$ to $\frac{1}{8}'' = 1'\text{-}0''$.

Create a Drawing Title Block

We need a title block for the drawing set. In the following step, you will create one as shown in Figure 12.18. Attributes will be created for the sheet number information.

Step 1: Draw the title block frame

1 Use the LINE command to create a box 15″ by 1″ starting at 0,0.

2 MOVE the box using the displacement 1.25,0.25.

3 Use the OFFSET command to create a square box at the right end.

Step 2: Create texts

1 ZOOM in to look at the square box.

2 Use the MTEXT command to enter: SHEET NO. (Text height = $\frac{1}{8}$).

3 Use the DTEXT command to enter: OF. (Text height = $\frac{1}{8}$).

4 Place the texts as shown in Figure 12.19.

Step 3: Define attributes

1 Enter the ATTDEF command.

2 Define attribute as follows:

- Tag: SHT
- Prompt: Sheet number
- Value: 00

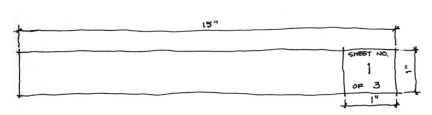

Figure 12.18
Sketch of the title block.

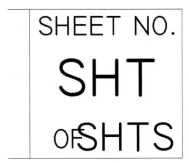

Figure 12.19
Positions of attributes.

- Justification: Center
- Text Style: NOTES
- Height: $\frac{1}{4}$

3 Click [OK] and place the attribute as shown in Figure 12.19.

4 Restart the ATTDEF command.

5 Define another attribute as follows:

- Tag: SHTS
- Prompt: Sheet count
- Value: 00
- Justification: Center
- Text Style: NOTES
- Height: $\frac{3}{16}$

6 Click [OK] and place the attribute as shown in Figure 12.19.

Step 4: Make the title block a block

1 Make sure the boxes and the text are all in the 0 layer.

2 Make them a block (Name = TITLEBLK; insertion point, 0,0; select the entire title block, including the attributes).

3 INSERT the block using 0,0 as the insertion point.

4 Enter 3 for sheet count, and enter 1 for sheet number.   *See Figure 12.20.*

5 Create a new layer and name it I-ANON-TBLK.

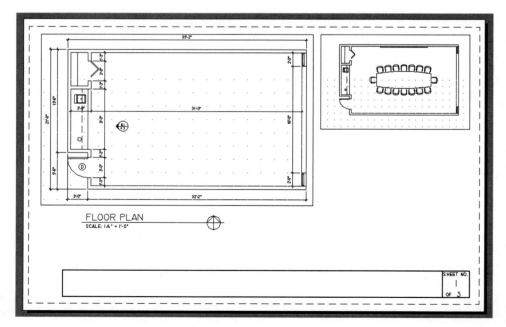

Figure 12.20
Finished layout for the
floor plans.

FLOOR PLAN
SCALE: 1/4" = 1'-0"

SHEET NO.
1
OF 3

6 Set the lineweight to 1.00 mm.

7 Put the inserted title block on the new layer.

Set up the Second Sheet

You will use this sheet to present the reflected ceiling plan.

Step 1: Rename the layout

1 Click the Layout2 tab to turn to the second layout.

2 Right-click the tab and choose Rename.

3 Rename the layout as RCP (reflected ceiling plan).

4 Click [OK].

Step 2: Page setup

1 Right-click the tab and choose Page Setup Manager.

2 Click to select the page setup named sheet1.

3 Click [Set Current] to apply that page setup to this layout.

*The name **sheet1** is added in a bracket after the layout name.*

4 Click [Close].

Step 3: Set up the viewport

1 Click the viewport frame to select the viewport.

2 Set the scale at $\frac{1}{4}'' = 1'0''$ through the Properties palette.

3 Adjust the viewport to fit the content.

4 MOVE the viewport to the upper left portion of the sheet.   *See Figure 12.21.*

Step 4: Set up a new viewport for the legend

1 Click the scale drop-down window on the Viewports toolbar and select $\frac{1}{4}'' = 1'0''$.

2 Click the Single viewport toolbar icon on the Viewports toolbar.

3 Click-pull-click to define a new viewport next to the first viewport.

See Figure 12.22 for reference.

4 Use the PAN command in the viewport to show the legend.

5 Adjust the viewport to fit the content.

6 MOVE the viewport to align it with the reflected ceiling plan.

See Figure 12.22 for reference.

- This example shows that you can define the scale before the viewport is created.

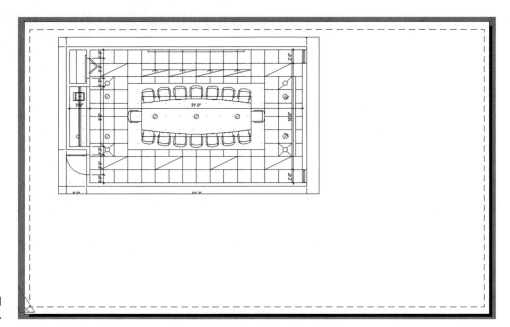

Figure 12.21
Set up viewport.

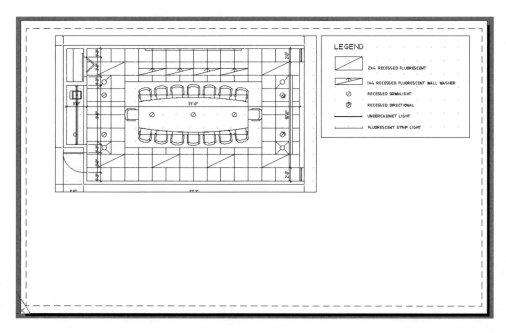

Figure 12.22
Set up the second
viewport.

Step 5: Set up a new viewport for the schedule

1 Click the Single viewport toolbar icon on the Viewports toolbar.

2 Click-pull-click to define a new   *See Figure 12.23 for reference.*
viewport next to the first viewport.

3 Use the PAN command in the viewport to show the schedule.

4 Adjust the viewport to fit the content.

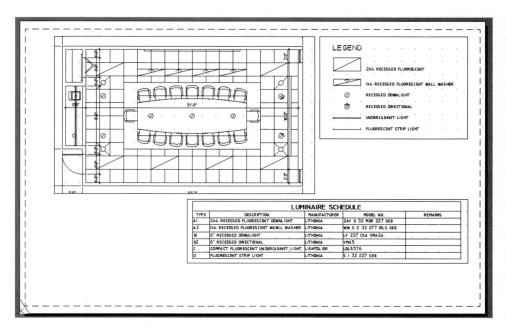

LEGEND

	2x4 RECESSED FLUORESCENT
	1x4 RECESSED FLUORESCENT WALL WASHER
⊘	RECESSED DOWNLIGHT
⊘	RECESSED DIRECTIONAL
	UNDERCABINET LIGHT
	FLUORESCENT STRIP LIGHT

LUMINAIRE SCHEDULE

TYPE	DESCRIPTION	MANUFACTURER	MODEL NO.	REMARKS
A1	2x4 RECESSED FLUORESCENT DOWNLIGHT	LITHONIA	2AV G 32 MDR 227 GEB	
A2	1x4 RECESSED FLUORESCENT WAWLL WASHER	LITHONIA	WW G 2 32 277 IRLS GEB	
B1	6" RECESSED DOWNLIGHT	LITHONIA	LV 227 CSA YMA 2A	
B2	6" RECESSED DIRECTIONAL	LITHONIA	YMA 5	
C	COMPACT FLUORESCENT UNDERCABINET LIGHT	LIGHTOLIER	LOLB376	
D	FLUORESCENT STRIP LIGHT	LITHONIA	S 1 32 227 GEB	

Figure 12.23
Set up the third viewport.

5 MOVE the viewport to align it   *See Figure 12.23 for reference.*
with the legend.

- This example shows that AutoCAD remembers the previously defined viewport scale value. The value is applied to the newly created viewport.

Step 6: Copy the drawing title

1 Click the floor plan **tab**.

2 Right-click and choose Copy.

3 Select the drawing title of the floor plan.

4 Click the RCL **tab**.

5 Right-click and choose Paste.

6 Click to set the position.

7 Enter the command DDEDIT and select the drawing title text.

8 Change it to REFLECTED CEILING PLAN.

9 Click [OK].

10 STRETCH the north arrow and   *See Figure 12.24 for reference.*
the underline.

Step 7: Insert the title block

1 Enter the INSERT command.

2 Select the block name TITLEBLK.

3 Click [OK].

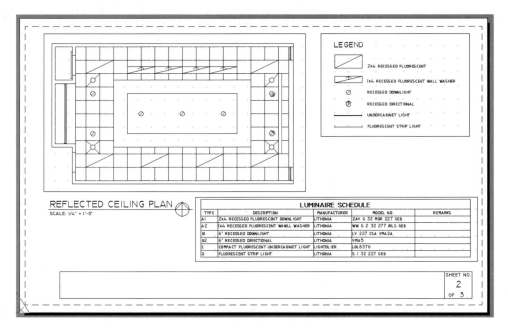

Figure 12.24
The second layout.

4 Enter 0,0 for the insertion point.

5 Enter 3 for the sheet count, and 2 for the sheet number.

Step 8: Layer management

1 Put viewport frames into layer I-ANON-NPLT.

2 Put the title block into layer I-ANON-TBLK

Step 9: Set viewport layer visibility control

1 Double-click inside the viewport for the plan.

2 Click the layers toolbar icon 🗒 to call up the Layer Properties Manager dialog box.

3 Click the "Freeze/Thaw in current viewport" icon 🔲 in the layers ch11|I-ANON-DIMS, ch11|I-DOOR, ch11|I-FLOR-CASE, ch11|I-FLOR-CASW, ch11|I-FURN, and ch11|I-PFIX to freeze them.

4 Click [OK].

5 Click [MODEL] to return to paper space layout.   *See Figure 12.24.*

Set up the Third Layout

You will create a third layout for the elevation and detail.

Step 1: Create a new layout

1 Right-click a layout tab and choose New Layout.

2 Right-click the new tab and choose Rename.

3 Rename it as elevation.

4 Click [OK].

Step 2: Page setup

1 Click the tab elevation.

2 Right-click the tab and choose Page Setup Manager.

3 Select sheet1.

4 Click [Set Current].

5 Click [Close].

Step 3: Set the viewport

1 Double-click inside the viewport to switch to the viewport model space mode.

2 Set the scale at $\frac{1}{2}'' = 1'0''$ through the Properties palette.

3 Use the PAN command in the viewport to show the elevation.

4 Adjust the viewport to fit the content.

5 MOVE the viewport to the upper left portion of the sheet.   *See Figure 12.25 for reference.*

Step 4: Set up a new viewport for the detail

1 Click the scale drop-down window on the Viewports toolbar and select $1\frac{1}{2}'' = 1'0''$.

2 Click the Single viewport toolbar icon on the Viewports toolbar.

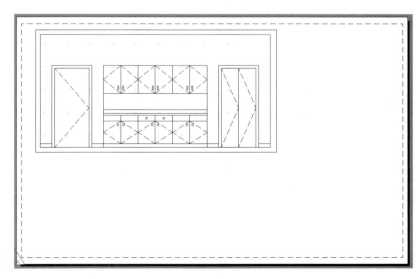

Figure 12.25
Set up the first viewport.

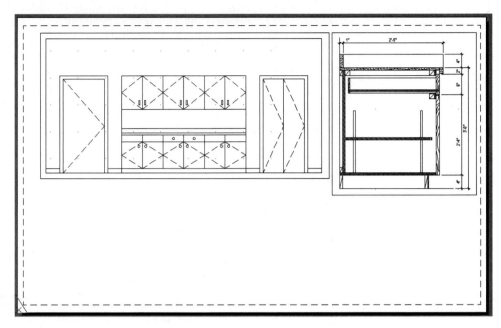

Figure 12.26
Set up the second
viewport.

3 Click-pull-click to define a new viewport   *See Figure 12.26 for reference.*
next to the first viewport.

4 Use the PAN command in the viewport to show the detail.

5 Adjust the viewport to fit the content.

6 MOVE the viewport to align it with the   *See Figure 12.26 for reference.*
reflected ceiling plan.

Step 5: Copy the drawing title

1 Click the floor plan tab.

2 Right-click and choose Copy.

3 Select the drawing title of the floor plan.

4 Click the elevation tab.

5 Right-click and choose Paste.

6 Click to set the position.

7 Enter the command DDEDIT and select the drawing title text.

8 Change it to ELEVATION.

9 Click [OK].

10 Select the scale note.

11 Change $\frac{1}{4}''$ to $\frac{1}{2}''$.

12 Click [OK].   *See Figure 12.27.*

Figure 12.27
Drawing title for the
elevation.

⊖ E1/03

ELEVATION
SCALE: 1/2" = 1'-0"

Step 6: Copy the elevation bubble

1 Click the floor plan tab.

2 Right-click and choose Copy.

3 Select the elevation symbol without the pointer.

4 Click the elevation tab.

5 Right-click and choose Paste.

6 Click to place the copy near the left end of the drawing title underline.

7 ZOOM in to look at it closely.

8 MOVE it to connect to the underline, using *See Figure 12.27.*
object snap to make a good connection.

9 ZOOM out to see the entire drawing.

Step 7: Create the detail section (cutting plane) symbol

1 COPY the elevation bubble and place it below the counter in the elevation view.

2 ZOOM in to look at the elevation.

3 Use the DDATTE command to change the reference number from "E1" to "1."

4 Use the PLINE command to draw a polyline (Width = $\frac{1}{32}$") as the cutting plane from the top of the circle up slightly beyond the countertop.

- Using Polyline to control lineweights is another approach, in addition to the ones you have learned in previous chapters. When a polyline is created, you have an option to define its width, and the lineweight shows accurately on the screen. The lineweight of a polyline will also be plotted by default. Because the heavy lineweight is required for only one object, using this approach will save you from setting color, layer, lineweight, and plot style.

Command: **PL** ↵

PLINE

Specify start point: **pick the top of the circle.**

Current line-width is 0'-0"

Specify next point or [Arc/Close/Halfwidth/   *Start setting line width.*
Length/Undo/Width]: **W** ↵

Specify starting width <0'-0">: **1/32** ↵

Specify ending width <0'-1/32">: **1/32** ↵   *Accept the default value.*

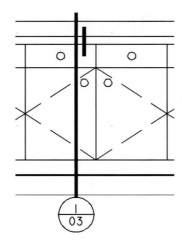

Figure 12.28
Draw a polyline cutting plane.

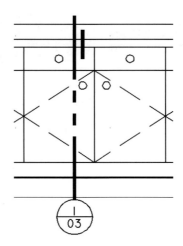

Figure 12.29
Change the linetype.

Specify next point or [Arc/Close/Halfwidth/
Length/Undo/Width]:

pick a point above the counter top

Specify next point or [Arc/Close/Halfwidth/
Length/Undo/Width]: ⏎   *No more points.*

Command:

5 Repeat the POLYLINE command to draw a short   *See Figure 12.28.*
polyline to indicate the view direction.

6 Create a new layer and name it I-ANON-CPLN.

7 Set the linetype to "Phantom2." (You need to load the linetype.)

8 Click [OK] to close the Linetype Manager dialog box.

9 Put the polyline into the new layer.   *See Figure 12.29.*

10 ZOOM-All.

Step 8: Create the drawing title for the detail drawing

1 COPY the elevation drawing title without the bubble and place the copy under
the detail drawing.

2 COPY the bubble in the section symbol to place it at the detail section drawing
title.

3 MOVE to connect the bubble to the underline of the drawing title.

4 Edit the text of the copied drawing title to change it to COUNTER DETAIL.

5 Edit the scale note to change it to $1\frac{1}{2}'' = 1'\text{-}0''$.

Figure 12.30
Drawing title for the detail.

COUNTER DETAIL
⊙ 1/03

SCALE: 1-1/2" = 1'-0"

6 Edit drawing reference number in the bubble to change E1 to 1.

See Figure 12.30.

Step 9: Insert the title block

1 Enter the INSERT command.

2 Select the block name TITLEBLK.

3 Click [OK].

4 Enter 0,0 for the insertion point.

5 Enter 3 for the sheet count, and 3 for the sheet number. *See Figure 12.31.*

Step 10: Layer management

1 Put viewport frames into layer I-ANON-NPLT.

2 Put the title block into layer I-ANON-TBLK

- If corrections need to be made to the referenced drawing, open that drawing and make the corrections because you cannot change the drawing elements of an external reference. Reload the external reference using the XREF command after the referenced drawing is updated. To reload an external reference, follow the procedure below.

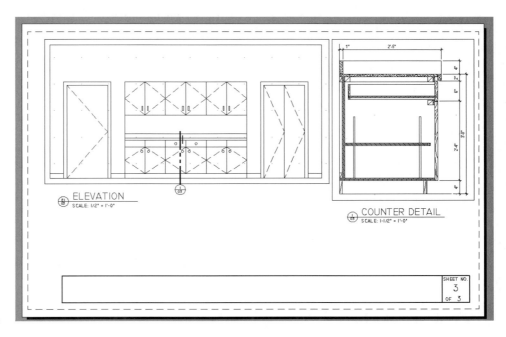

Figure 12.31
Finished sheet 3.

3 Start the XREF command to bring up the External Reference palette.

4 Click to select the updated drawing on the list.

5 Right-click and choose Reload.

6 PLOT all pages.

7 SAVE the drawing file and EXIT AutoCAD.

- In this chapter, dimensions are shown in viewports. The scale of the dimension features is predetermined in the referenced model space drawing through dimension styles. For example, we used the dimension style arch8 for the counter detail based on an anticipation that the finished drawing will be presented at $1\frac{1}{2}''$ scale. In the dimension style arch8, set the overall scale factor as 8, which is the same as the scale factor of a $1\frac{1}{2}''$ scale drawing. However, this anticipated scale may have to be changed in certain situations, such as a change in sheet size. When the viewport scale is changed, the dimension features may appear to be either too small or too large. In such a situation, you need to readjust the dimension style in the original model drawing by changing the overall scale value (on the Fit tab of the Dimension Style dialog box) to match that of the new scale factor of the viewport. You may use the following procedure.

8 Click the Dimension Style toolbar icon.

9 Select the dimension style to be adjusted.

10 Click [Modify].

11 Click the Fit tab.

12 Change the overall scale value to match the scale factor of the viewport scale.

13 Click [OK].

- After the dimension style is adjusted in the referenced model space drawing, you need to reload the external reference using the XREF command.

Build a 3D Model

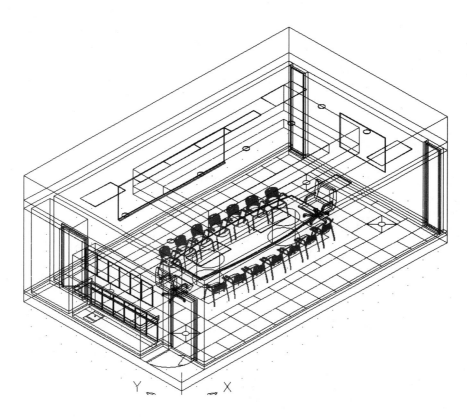

- Build the Walls
- Create the Doors
- Create the Windows
- Create the Floor
- Create the Ceiling
- Create the Counter
- Create the Whiteboard
- Create the Conference Table
- Create the Chairs
- Create a Picture
- Create the Base of the Walls
- Create Light Objects

Computer 3D modeling is usually perceived as an extremely sophisticated process. This may be true with the creation of animated dinosaurs. However, if the task is to create interior space composed primarily of simple planes, it is actually quite simple. In this chapter, you will use a simplified approach to build a 3D model of the dining space you have been drawing in previous chapters.

Build the Walls

Step 1: Prepare the floor plan

1 Start AutoCAD.

2 OPEN drawing ch06.dwg.

3 SAVEAS ch13.dwg.

4 Set the 0 layer as current and freeze all other layers except I-WALL.

Step 2: Switch to 3D Modeling workspace

Because you will make a 3D model of the designed space, you need to switch from the AutoCAD Classes user interface to 3D Modeling to take advantage of the 3D modeling tools that are already set for this kind of task. For ADT users, see the note at the end of this step.

1 Click the workspace drop-down list and choose 3D Model.   *The interface changes (Figure 13.1).*

To the right of the drawing area is the tool palette. Further to the right is the Dashboard, which has a collection of different control panels that contain groups of tools. For example, the first control panel is called 3D Make and it contains the commonly used 3D modeling tools. A click on the 3D Make control panel icon 🔲 at the upper left corner of the control panel section will expand the section with additional 3D modeling tools and at the same time change the content of the tool palette to give access to more modeling, drawing, and modifying tools in separate tabs. With the dashboard, you will have a group of dynamically organized tool palettes to support your work.

    Note for ADT users: If you try to switch to the 3D Modeling workspace, the dashboard will appear empty. To bypass this problem, you can switch back to the ADT user interface and load the dashboard from there. However, the tool palettes are not

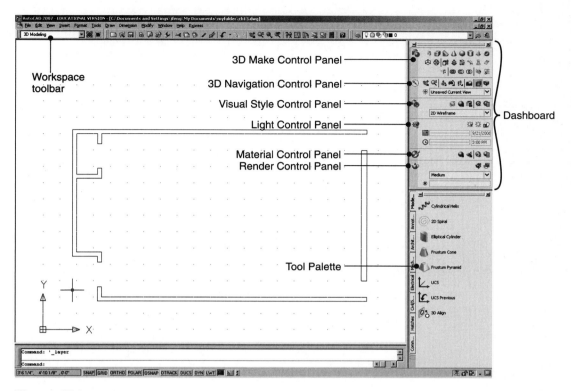

Figure 13.1
The 3D Modeling workspace interface.

associated with dashboard control panels in the same way as in AutoCAD. See Appendix B for instructions to switch to the ADT user interface.

Step 3: Set an axonometric view

An axonometric view can be set most easily through the 3D Navigation panel.

1 Click the drop-down list on the 3D Navigation control panel and select ⬛ Southeast Isometric.

The view changes (Figure 13.2).

Step 4: Pull up a wall segment

In this step, you will use the command PRESSPULL to pull the wall lines up into the third dimension.

1 Click the PRESSPULL tool icon ⬛ on the 3D Make control panel.

Command: _presspull

Click inside bounded areas to press or pull. **Pick a point inside the wall.**

You can now pull up the body of the wall from the wall line on the floor.

10'↵

Enter the height of the wall (see Figure 13.3).

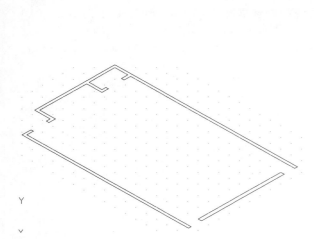

Figure 13.2
An axonometric view of the plan.

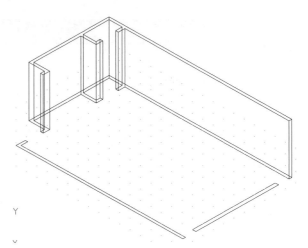

Figure 13.3
Pull up the first segment of the wall.

Step 5: Create the walls

Use the same approach to create the other two wall segments. See Figure 13.4 for the result.

Step 6: Experiment with visual styles

In AutoCAD, drawing entities can be displayed in different shading modes according to the designer's need. In the 3D Modeling workspace, the display mode of the model

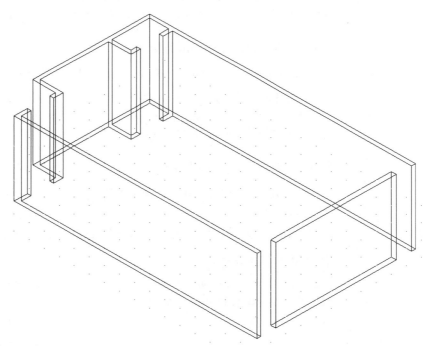

Figure 13.4
Pull up the walls.

is controlled through visual styles. We will experiment with the options provided on the Visual Style control panel to learn the various possibilities, so that you can use them in the future. The features of a visual style can be customized and saved as your own visual style for future use.

A few different shading modes in AutoCAD include wire-frame, hideline, and shaded. Up to this point, you have been using the wire-frame mode that shows a 3D model as if the model were made of wires. Although the wire-frame model allows you to see all the edges of the model, it is confusing when you try to determine the spatial relationship between wire-frame lines. A hideline view shows the solid surfaces as solid blank areas that block all the lines behind them. In a shaded view, the surfaces of solid objects are filled with different shades of the object color, assuming a generic light shining on the model from a point above your left shoulder. The shading mode can be controlled easily through the Visual Styles palette and the Visual Style control panel. Let's experiment with the visual styles. (Because the Visual Style tool palette is not available in ADT, ADT users can skip this step.)

1 Click the Visual Style Control Panel icon 🔘.

The Visual Styles tool palette is displayed.

2 Click the X-Ray Visual Style icon 🔘 on the Visual Styles tool palette.

See Figure 13.5.

This visual style shades the faces of the walls to portray the solid mass of the wall, while the semitransparency maintains the visibility of lines behind front surfaces. This may be a good shading mode to work on a 3D model.

3 Click the Sketchy Visual Style icon on 🔘 the Visual Styles tool palette.

See Figure 13.6.

- This visual style simulates the effects of hand-drawn sketches with corner crossovers, line jitters, and emphasized silhouettes. This style can be used to present a schematic design when the design should still be sketchy instead of being polished and finalized.

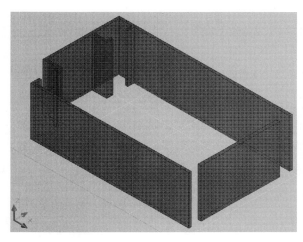

Figure 13.5
The X-Ray Visual Style.

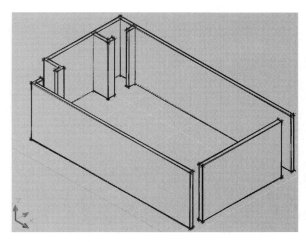

Figure 13.6
The Sketchy Visual Style.

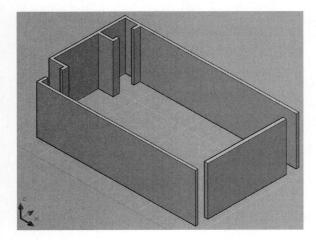

Figure 13.7
The Shades of Gray Visual Style.

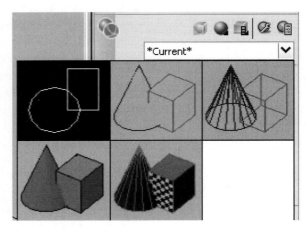

Figure 13.8
More visual styles.

4 Click the Shades of Gray icon 🎨   *See Figure 13.7.*
on the Visual Styles tool palette.

This visual style shades the model with a variety of grays to make the model solid. It is a good viewing mode to examine the formal and spatial features of the model.

5 Click the visual style list on the 3D Navigation   *See Figure 13.8.*
control panel to see more visual styles. Experiment
with them.

6 Click the visual style list and choose 2D Wireframe.

Step 7: Create the walls above door openings

In this step, we will create a solid 3D box to seal the space above the door openings.

1 ZOOM in to look at the closet door opening.

2 Click the [DUCS] (Dynamic User Coordinate System) button on the status line
to turn it off.

- When the DUCS is on, AutoCAD will automatically detect the 3D surfaces
touched by the cursor and set the user coordinate system accordingly. Turning
it off ensures the following BOX command works in the user coordinate system of the drawing to extrude the box vertically. Otherwise, you may have
unexpected results. You will use the DUCS later.

3 Click the BOX toolbar icon 📦 on the 3D Make control panel.

Command: _box

Specify corner of box or [CEnter] <0,0,0>: **pick point (1)**   *(Figure 13.9)*

Specify corner or [Cube/Length]: **pick point (2)**   *(Figure 13.10)*

Specify height: **−36** ↵

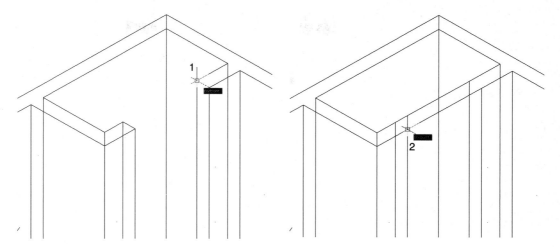

Figure 13.9
Create the box for the closet door.

Figure 13.10
Create the box for the closet door.

Command: *The box is created (Figure 13.11).*

4 ZOOM out to look at the door opening.

5 Use the BOX tool to create the
wall above the door.   *See Figure 13.12.*

6 Click the UNION toolbar icon ⬤ in the 3D Make control panel.

● The UNION command combines individual 3D solids into a single entity. It
simplifies the model.

Command: _UNION

Select objects: **pick the first box** 1 found

Select objects: **pick the second box** 1 found, 2 total

Select objects: **pick the wall** 1 found, 3 total

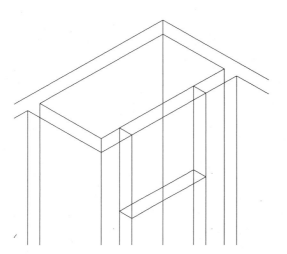

Figure 13.11
Create the box for the closet door.

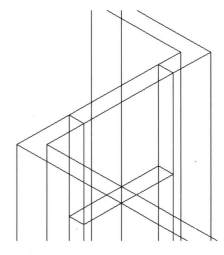

Figure 13.12
Create the box for the closet door.

Select objects: **pick the wall on the left** 1 found, 4 total

Select objects: ⏎   *See Figure 13.13.*

Step 8: Create the soffit

We can use the BOX command to create the soffit above the counter. This time, however, we will use a different approach to pick the opposite corner of a box: we will enlist the help of the dynamic user coordinate system.

1 ZOOM to look at the walls above the counter area.

2 Click the [DYN] button on the status line to turn it on.

3 Click the BOX toolbar icon ▣.

Command: _BOX

Specify corner of box or [CEnter] <0,0,0>: **move the cursor**   *(Figure 13.14)*
over the vertical surface of the wall behind the counter
to wait for the surface to be detected and highlighted
with dotted lines and pick point (1)

Specify corner or [Cube/Length]: **Move the cursor over point (2)** *(Figure 13.15)*
to let the Endpoint object snap box appear. (DO NOT click.)

Move the cursor straight down (make sure there is a vertical *(Figure 13.16)*
dotted axis line going through the corner of the wall)

Read the vertical distance reported around the cursor
while moving down the mouse.

Click when the distance reading reaches 2′9″.   *(Figure 13.16)*

4 Click the [DYN] button to turn it off.

5 UNION the soffit and the wall.

6 Put all the 3D walls on the I-WALL layer.

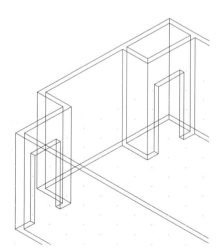

Figure 13.13
UNION the walls.

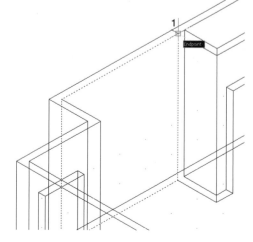

Figure 13.14
Detect the vertical surface and pick the point.

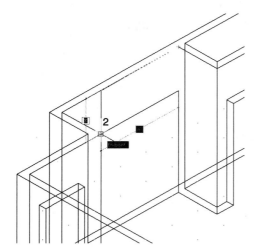

Figure 13.15
Hover over point (2) to obtain a reference point.

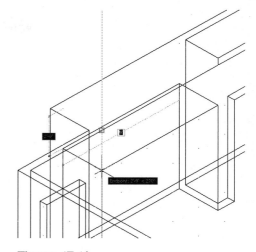

Figure 13.16
Pull down to define the corner of the box.

Create the Doors

The doors and their frames can be made of simple 3D boxes.

Step 1: Create a box for the door

1 Click the BOX toolbar icon.

Command: _BOX

Specify corner of box or [CEnter] <0,0,0>: **pick the corner**   *(Figure 13.17)*
of the door opening

Specify corner or [Cube/Length]: @–2,36,7'   *(Figure 13.18)*

- The input @–2, 367' is a 3D point relative to the last picked point. In this case, it tells AutoCAD the position of the opposite corner of the box using the previously picked corner as a reference point.

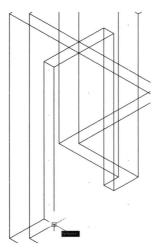

Figure 13.17
Start the box at the corner.

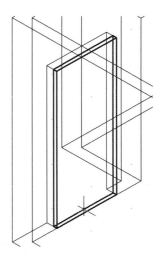

Figure 13.18
Created door.

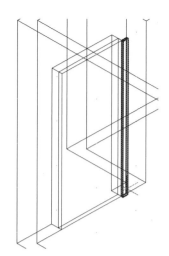

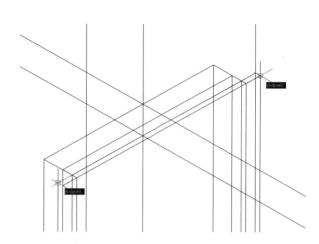

Figure 13.19
Create the door frame.

Figure 13.20
Create the horizontal frame.

Step 2: Create boxes for the door frames

1 Use the BOX command to create the door frame on the lower right corner of the door. Use @ 1,3,7' for the upper corner.

See Figure 13.19.

2 MIRROR the box to duplicate it and place it on the other side of the door.

3 Use the BOX command to create a box on top of the two door frame components. Height = 3.

See Figures 13.20 and 13.21.

4 UNION the door frame components.

Step 3: Duplicate the door

Because the purpose of this 3D model is for rendering and the folding door is likely to be in the closed position, you can simplify your task by copying the entrance door.

Step 4: Put the doors and frames in the layer I-DOOR

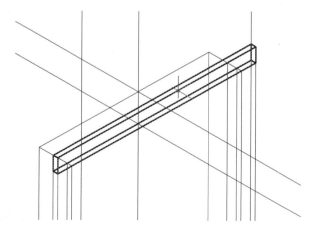

Figure 13.21
Completed door frame
components.

Create the Windows

Although you can use the same additive approach to build the window frame piece by piece and then combine the pieces with the UNION command, we will use a subtractive approach to make the window frame. In this approach, we will build a large box to represent the entire mass of the window and a smaller box to represent the void space surrounded by the frame, and then we will use the SUBTRACT command to carve out the void.

Step 1: Create the massing boxes

1 Thaw the layer I-FLOR-GLAZ.

2 ZOOM in to look at a window closely.

3 Use the BOX command to create the frame box. Height = 10'. *See Figure 13.22.*

4 Use the BOX command to create the void massing box. Height = 9'8". *See Figure 13.23.*

Step 2: Move the void massing solid up

Moving objects in the third dimension has been made easier with the new 3DMOVE command that allows you to move selected objects along the three coordinate axes.

1 Click the 3DMOVE toolbar icon ⬒ in the 3D Make control panel.

Command: _3dmove

Select objects: **click to select the void massing box** 1 found

Select objects: ↵   *The Move Grip Tool (colored tripod) appears and moves with the cursor.*

Specify base point or [Displacement] <Displacement>: **click a point in front of the window**   *The tripod is anchored (see Figure 13.24).*

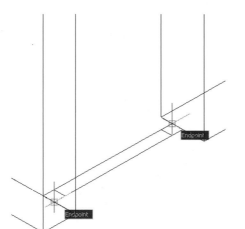

Figure 13.22
Create the frame box.

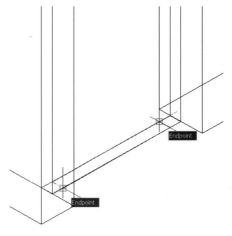

Figure 13.23
Create the void massing box.

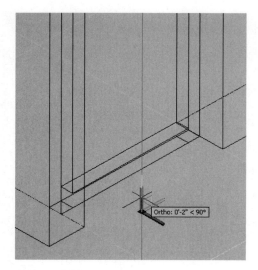

Figure 13.24
Move the void massing box up using 3DMOVE.

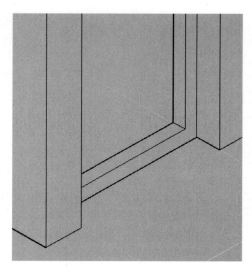

Figure 13.25
The hideline view of the frame.

Hover the cursor over the blue leg (Z) of the tripod and wait for a long blue line to appear and click the blue leg to lock the movement axis.   *The blue leg turns yellow.*

● The blue line is technically called "vector."

Pull the cursor up to indicate the upward movement direction.

Specify second point or <use first point as displacement>: **2**↵

Regenerating model.   *The box is moved up 2".*

Step 3: Subtract the interior solid from the exterior solid

In this step, you will use the SUBTRACT command to carve out the void space by subtracting the inside box from the outside box. The result will be solid walls surrounding the hollow space at the middle.

Click the SUBTRACT toolbar icon ⊚ in the 3D Make control panel.

Command: _SUBTRACT

Select solids and regions to subtract from

Select objects: **pick the frame solid** 1 found

Select objects: ↵

● It is important to remember that the object you pick first will remain.

Select solids and regions to subtract

Select objects: **pick the void massing solid** 1 found

Select objects: ↵

● The interior space is carved out, but there is no visible change in the view. You may use the hideline view to see it (Figure 13.25).

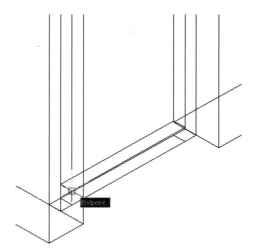

Figure 13.26
Start the glass box at the corner.

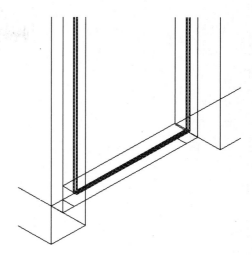

Figure 13.27
Created glass box.

Step 4: Create the glass pane

For the glass pane, you can create a box to fill the void.

1 Use the BOX command to create the box for the glass, and use OSNAP to catch the corner of the frame.   *See Figure 13.26.*

2 Enter @ 0.5,20,9'8 for the upper corner.   *See Figure 13.27.*

3 MOVE the glass box 1 inch toward the inside of the space.   *See Figure 13.28.*

4 MIRROR to duplicate the window.

Step 5: Layer management

1 Put the window frame in the layer I-GLAZ.

2 Create a layer and name it GLASS.

3 Put the glass box into the layer GLASS.

4 Freeze the layers GLASS and I-GLAZ.

Create the Floor

The floor can be a box. When you define the height of a box, a negative value will make it extrude downward.

Step 1: Create the floor

Click the BOX toolbar icon.

Command: _box

Specify corner of box or [CEnter] <0,0,0>: **pick point (1)**   *(Figure 13.29)*

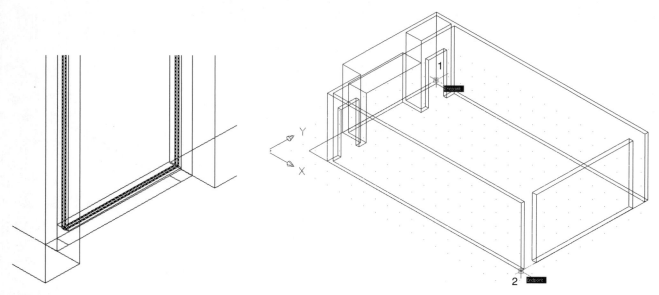

Figure 13.28
The glass box moved into the frame.

Figure 13.29
Create the floor.

Specify corner or [Cube/Length]: **pick point (2)**

Specify height: **–12**↵   *(Figure 13.30)*

Step 2: Layer management

1 Create a new layer and name it FLOOR.

2 Put the new floor into the layer FLOOR.

3 Freeze the layer FLOOR.

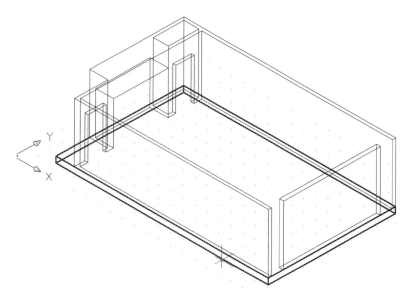

Figure 13.30
Finished floor.

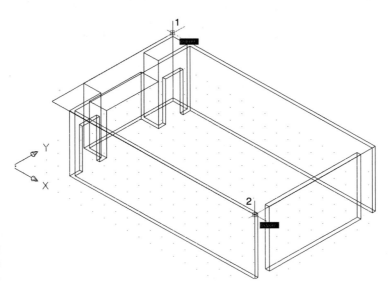

Figure 13.31
Create the main space
ceiling.

Create the Ceiling

Step 1: Create the ceiling of the main space

1 Click the BOX toolbar icon.

Command: _box

Specify corner of box or [CEnter] <0,0,0>: **pick point 1**   *(Figure 13.31)*

Specify corner or [Cube/Length]: **pick point 2**

Specify height: **12** ↵   *(Figure 13.32)*

Step 2: Create the cove opening

1 Thaw the layer I-CLNG and set the layer as the current layer.

2 Freeze the layer I-WALL.

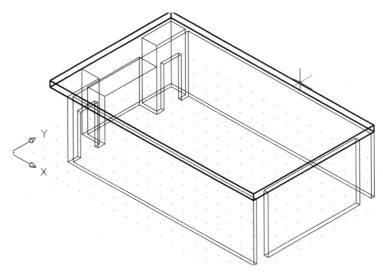

Figure 13.32
Created ceiling.

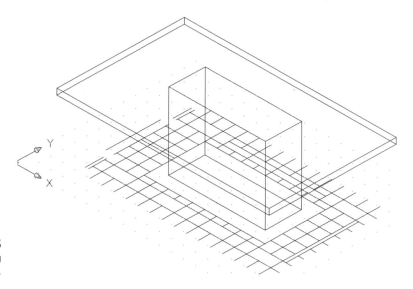

Figure 13.33
Create the void massing
solid.

3 Use the BOX command to create a 15′ tall cove
opening void massing solid.   *See Figure 13.33.*

4 SUBTRACT the void massing solid from the ceiling solid.   *See Figure 13.34.*

Step 3: Create the drywall ceiling around the opening

1 Use the BOX command to create a massing
solid for the drywall ceiling. Height = 13′.   *See Figure 13.35.*

2 Click the 3D Make control panel icon to expand it.

3 Click the Interference tool icon ▦.

4 Look at the command line.

Command: _interfere

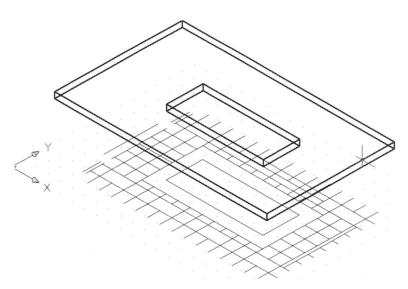

Figure 13.34
Subtract the massing solid.

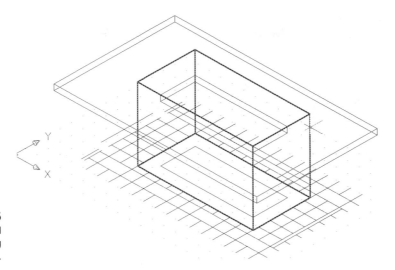

Figure 13.35
Create the massing solid
for the drywall ceiling
around the opening.

Select first set of objects or [Nested selection/Settings]: **pick the ceiling** 1 found

Select first set of objects or [Nested selection/Settings]: ↵

Select second set of objects or [Nested selection/checK first set] <checK>: **pick the massing solid**

1 found

Select second set of objects or [Nested selection/checK first set] <checK>: ↵

Regenerating model.   *The form of interference is shown*
in red (Figure 13.36).

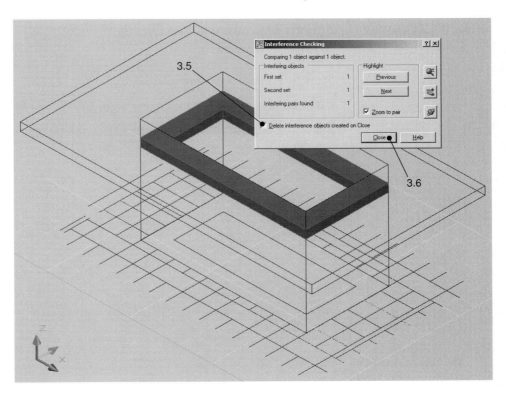

Figure 13.36
Create the interference
object around the opening.

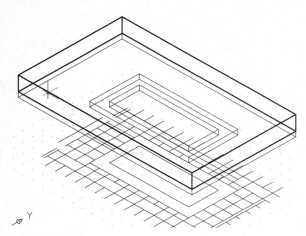

Figure 13.37
Create the upper ceiling massing solid.

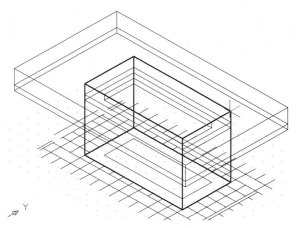

Figure 13.38
Create the cove void massing solid.

5 Clear the check box "Delete Interference Objects on Close."

6 Click [Close].

7 SUBTRACT the massing solid from the ceiling.

Step 4: Create the upper ceiling

1 Use the BOX command to create a massing solid for the upper ceiling. Height = 3′.   *See Figure 13.37.*

2 Use the BOX command to create a void massing solid for the cove space. Height = 13′.   *See Figure 13.38.*

3 SUBTRACT the void solid from the 3′ thick upper ceiling solid.   *See Figure 13.39.*

Step 5: Layer management

1 Create two new layers and name them COVE and DRYWALL, respectively.

2 Put the upper ceiling into layer COVE, and put the drywall object into layer DRYWALL.

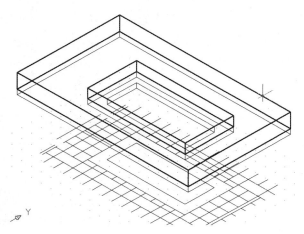

Figure 13.39
Subtract the void from
the solid.

3 Put the ceiling objects into layer I-CLNG

4 Freeze the I-CLNG, COVE, and DRYWALL layers.

Create the Counter

Step 1: Preparation

1 Thaw the layers I-FLOR-CASE, I-FLOR-CASW, and I-WALL.

2 ZOOM in to look at the counter area.

- The modify tools can be found on the Tool pallette.

3 OFFSET 4″ from the counter line toward the wall to define the base position.

4 OFFSET 2″ from the counter line toward the wall to define the base cabinet body.

Step 2: Create the base

Use the BOX command to create the base. Height = 4   *(Figure 13.40)*

Step 3: Layer management

1 Create a new layer and name it BASE.

2 Put the base into the layer BASE.

3 Freeze the layer BASE.

4 ERASE the base definition line on the floor.

Step 4: Create the base cabinet body

1 Use the BOX command to create the box as   *See Figure 13.41.*
the base cabinet body. Height = 30″.

2 3DMOVE the box up 4″.

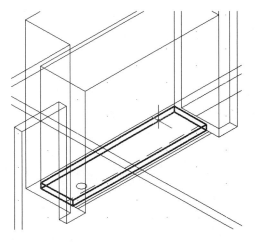

Figure 13.40
Create the base.

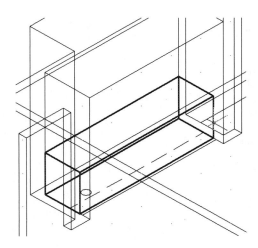

Figure 13.41
Create the base cabinet body.

Step 5: Layer management

1 Create a new layer and name it COUNTER.

2 Put the base cabinet body into the layer COUNTER.

3 Freeze the layer COUNTER.

4 ERASE the counter body definition line on the floor.

Step 6: Create the countertop with backsplash

1 Use the BOX command to create a massing solid for the countertop including the backsplash. Height = 6.   *See Figure 13.42.*

2 Create a void massing box.

Command: _box

Specify corner of box or [CEnter] <0,0,0>: **pick the corner of the box**   *(Figure 13.43)*

Specify corner or [Cube/Length]: **@-29,8'10,4** ↵

3 MOVE the void massing box up and to the right.

Command: **M** ↵

MOVE

Select objects: **pick the void massing solid** 1 found

Select objects: ↵

Specify base point or [Displacement] <Displacement>: **0,1,2** ↵

Specify second point or <use first point as displacement>: ↵

- In this MOVE command, you typed in the command alias M to start the command. Many AutoCAD commands have alias shortcuts. When a command

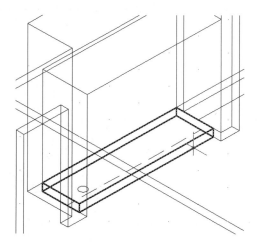

Figure 13.42
Create the countertop.

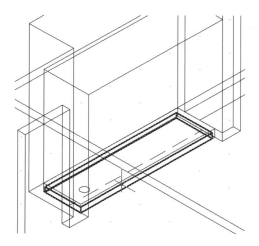

Figure 13.43
Create the void massing solid.

toolbar icon is not on the desktop, using the alias is quick and convenient, as long as you can remember the command alias.

● In this MOVE command, you also used the displacement to move an object up. The displacement input 0,1,2 simply means the displacement in the *x*, *y*, and *z* directions.

4 SUBTRACT the void massing solid from the countertop massing box.

5 MOVE the countertop up 34″.   *See Figure 13.44.*

Step 7: Layer management

1 Create a new layer and name it COUNTERTOP.

2 Put the countertop into the layer COUNTERTOP.

3 Freeze the layer COUNTERTOP.

4 ERASE the countertop line on the floor.

Step 8: Create the wall cabinet body

1 Use the BOX command to create a box based on   *See Figure 13.45.*
the floor plan. Height = 30″.

2 Move the box up 57″ (using 3DMOVE or MOVE).

Step 9: Layer management

1 Thaw the layer COUNTER.

2 Put the wall cabinet body into the layer COUNTER.

3 Freeze the layer I-WALL.

4 ERASE the wall cabinet line on the floor.

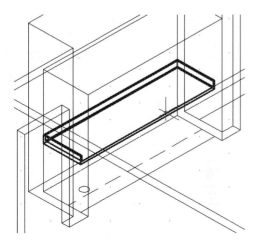

Figure 13.44
Countertop with backsplash.

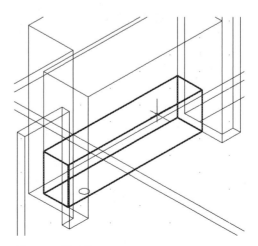

Figure 13.45
Create the wall cabinet body.

Step 10: Create a base cabinet door

After some careful planning, we figured out that the first cabinet door should be located 1.25″ from the corner. Instead of creating the door at the corner and moving it 1.25″, we can use the object snap tracking function to locate the start point of the 3D solid box. Using the object snap tracking is a very delicate act. You must be patient and careful to make it work.

1 ZOOM in to look at the lower left corner of the base cabinet body.

2 Make sure the OTRACK button is depressed on the status line.

3 Click the BOX toolbar icon.

Command: _box

Specify corner of box or [CEnter] <0,0,0>:

    a Hover over the lower left corner of the base cabinet body to wait for the Endpoint object snap box to appear at the corner.

    b Move the cursor to the right tentatively to trigger the object snap tracking line to appear.

       The tracking line is a dotted line running in the direction of the movement (Figure 13.46).

    c Key in the distance of offset: 1.25

    d Continue with the BOX command.

Specify corner or [Cube/Length]: **@1,17,23**↵   *See Figure 13.47.*

Step 11: Create a drawer front board

1 Create a box on top of the first cabinet door. Height = 6.

2 Move the box up 1″.   *See Figure 13.48.*

Step 12: Duplicate the boxes

1 COPY both boxes and place them 17.5″ to the right.

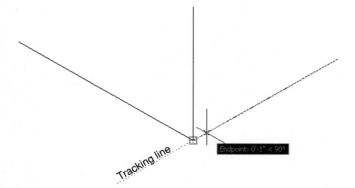

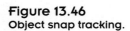

Figure 13.46
Object snap tracking.

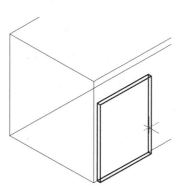

Figure 13.47
Create the cabinet door.

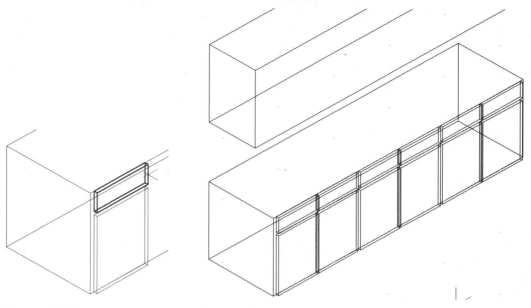

Figure 13.48
Create the drawer front.

Figure 13.49
Duplicate the doors.

2 COPY all four door and drawer pieces and place them 35.5″ and 71″ to the right.

See Figure 13.49.

Step 13: Create the wall cabinet doors

1 COPY all the cabinet doors and place them on the wall cabinets.

See Figure 13.50.

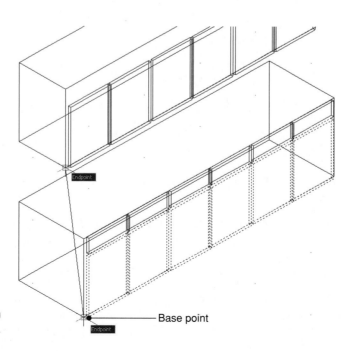

Endpoint

Endpoint

Base point

Figure 13.50
Copy the cabinet doors.

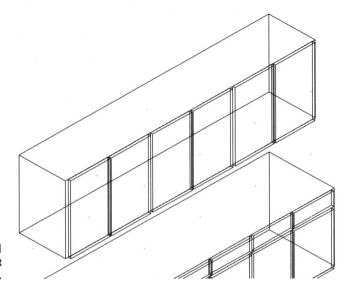

Figure 13.51
Union the wall cabinet
doors.

2 COPY all the newly created wall cabinet doors and place them 7″ above their original position. Displacement = 0,0,7.

3 UNION the overlapping boxes.   *See Figure 13.51.*

Step 14: Layer management

1 Put the cabinet doors into the layer COUNTER.

2 Freeze the layers COUNTER, I-FLOR-CASW, and I-FLOR-CASE.

3 Thaw the layer I-FURN.

4 ZOOM out to look at the entire drawing.

Create the Whiteboard

The whiteboard can be made of two boxes, one for the board and one for the marker tray.

Step 1: Create the board and the marker tray

1 Measure the length of the whiteboard.

Command: **DI** ↵

DIST Specify first point: **pick the end point of the long marker tray line on the floor**

Specify second point: **pick the other end of the long line**

Distance = 14′-0″, Angle in XY Plane = 0.00, Angle from XY Plane = 0.00

Delta X = 14′-0″, Delta Y = 0′-0″, Delta Z = 0′-0″

● The command DIST (DI) allows you to measure the distance between two selected points. Because you cannot remember all the dimensions of the objects you create, this command is often very useful. In this case, you now know the board should be 14′ long, and you will use this information to create the board.

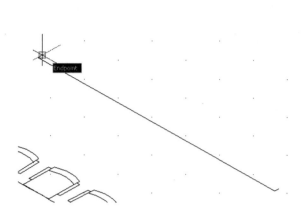

Figure 13.52
Start point of the box for the whiteboard.

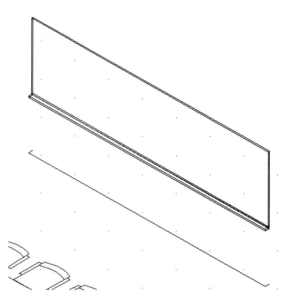

Figure 13.53
Finished whiteboard.

2 Create the box for the board.

Command: **BOX** ↵

Specify corner of box or [CEnter] <0,0,0>: **pick point**   *See Figure 13.52.*

Specify corner or [Cube/Length]: @ **14′, −1,4′** ↵

3 Move the box up 3′.

4 Create the box for the marker tray, using the lines on the floor as guide. Height = 1.

5 MOVE the box up 35″.   *See Figure 13.53.*

Step 2: Layer management

1 Create a layer and name it BOARD.

2 Create a layer and name it TRAY.

3 Put the box for the whiteboard into the layer BOARD.

4 Put the box for the marker tray into the layer TRAY.

5 Freeze the layers BOARD and TRAY.

6 ERASE the lines on the floor.

Create the Conference Table

Step 1: Create the tabletop

1 Use the PRESSPULL command to create the tabletop. Height = 2″.

2 MOVE the tabletop up 28″.

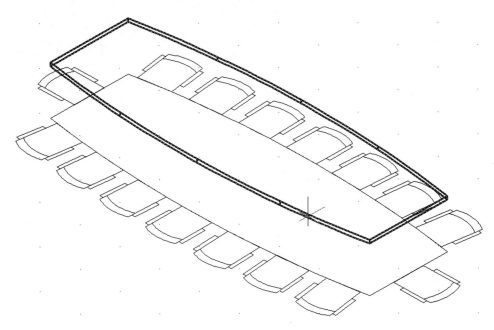

Figure 13.54
Select the top edges
of the tabletop.

Step 2: Round the edge

You used the FILLET command in the previous chapters to join lines. You can use the same command to round the edges of 3D solid forms.

Command: **F** ↵   *Use the command alias to start the FILLET command.*

FILLET

Current settings: Mode = TRIM, Radius = 0'-0"

Select first object or [Polyline/Radius/   *(See Figure 13.54.)*
Trim/mUltiple]: **pick an edge of the tabletop**

Enter fillet radius: **1** ↵

Select an edge or [Chain/Radius]: **pick the second edge**

Select an edge or [Chain/Radius]: **pick the third edge**

Select an edge or [Chain/Radius]: **pick the fourth edge**

Select an edge or [Chain/Radius]: ↵

4 edge(s) selected for fillet.   *(See Figure 13.55.)*

Step 3: Create the support

1 Create a 3D solid cylinder centered at the midpoint of the narrow end.

Click the cylinder tool icon 🛢 in the 3D Make control panel.

Command: _cylinder

Current wire frame density: ISOLINES = 4

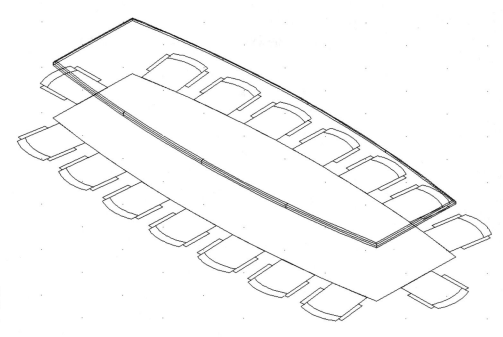

Figure 13.55
Tabletop with rounded
edges.

Specify center point for base of cylinder or [Elliptical] <0,0,0>: **MID**⏎

Of **pick the midpoint of the short end of the table**   *(See Figure 13.56.)*

Specify radius for base of cylinder or [Diameter]: **18**⏎

Specify height of cylinder or [Center of other end]: **28**⏎

2 MOVE the cylinder 3′ to the left.

3 MIRROR to create a cylinder on the other side of the table.

Step 4: Layer management

1 Create a layer and name it TABLETOP.

2 Create a layer and name it SUPPORT.

3 Put the tabletop into the layer TABLETOP.

4 Put the supports into the layer SUPPORT.

5 Freeze the layers TABLETOP and SUPPORT.

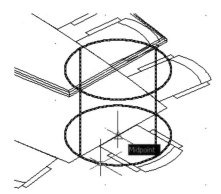

Figure 13.56
Create the support.

Create the Chairs

Furniture is important for interiors. Creating a good detailed model of a piece of furniture may be time consuming and challenging. Because ready-made 3D models are available in many different places on the Internet, we will try to find our pieces and import them into the drawing.

Step 1: Import a chair from DesignCenter Online

1 Click the Design Center toolbar icon ▦.

2 Click the DC Online tab.   *See Figure 13.57.*

3 Click 3D Architectural in Standard Parts.

4 Click Furniture.

5 Click Chairs.

6 Click Executive Chair 1.

● A dropper ⬇ appears when the cursor moves on top of the image. This is the so-called i-drop indicator. It means that you can drag and drop the model into your drawing.

7 Drag and drop the chair into your drawing.

8 Click to put the chair somewhere.

9 Close the Design Center window.

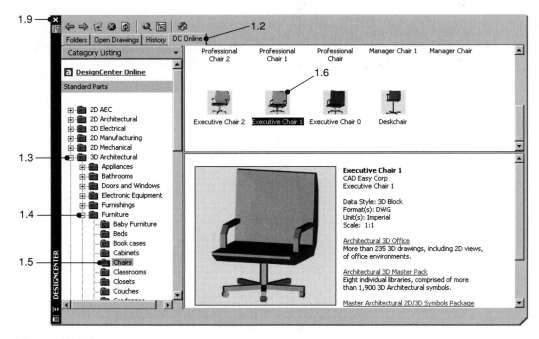

Figure 13.57
Chair models in DC Online.

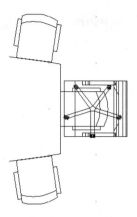

Figure 13.58
Place the chair at the short end of the table.

Step 2: Locate the chair

The chair is large in size. We will place it at the short ends of the table.

1 Turn off OSNAP on the status line.

2 Click the top view icon in the View toolbar to switch to plan view.

3 ROTATE the chair. (Use alias RO.)

4 MOVE the chair to the end of the table. (Use alias M.)   *See Figure 13.58.*

5 MIRROR to duplicate. (Use alias MI.)

6 ERASE the chair under the new 3D chairs. (Use alias E.)

7 Put the chairs into the layer I-FURN.

Step 3: Import a chair from a manufacturer's website

1 Click the Design Center toolbar icon ▦.

2 Click the DC Online tab.

3 Click 3D Architectural under Manufacturers.

4 Click Interiors.

5 Click Furnishings.

6 Click Herman Miller.

7 Click the HermanMiller logo.

8 Click the 3D Models category list and choose Stacking Chairs.

9 Use the i-drop tool to import the Caper Stacking Chair.

  ● The address for the Herman Miller website may change. You can make your own decision on furniture selection.

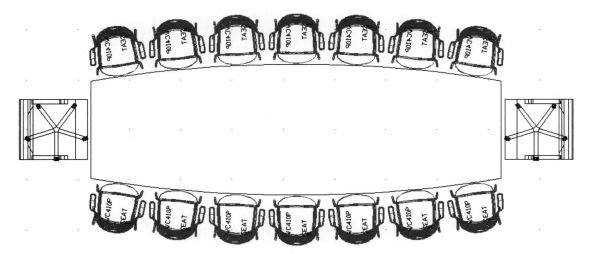

Figure 13.59
The 3D chairs replaced the 2D chairs.

10 Click to put the chair somewhere in the drawing.

11 Close the Design Center window.

Step 4: Locate the chair

The imported chair is a block. We will explode the block and use it to redefine the chair block so that we can replace the 2D chair blocks in their current positions with the 3D chair.

1 ROTATE (RO) the chair to make the front of the chair face the white board.

2 MOVE (M) the chair to an empty spot.

3 EXPLODE (X) the chair.

4 Make it a block, using the name CHAIR. The insertion point should be the point on the floor right below the midpoint of the front edge of the seat. (Hit the [F3] key to turn off the object snap to avoid snapping to the seat.)

The 3D chair replaces the 2D chairs (see Figure 13.59).

5 Enter the command ATTDISP to turn off the attributes of the chairs.

Command: **ATTDISP**⏎

Enter attribute visibility setting [Normal/ON/OFF] <Normal>: **OFF**⏎

Regenerating model.

The text under the 3D chairs disappears.

● The command ATTDISP means Attribute Display. It controls the visibility of the attributes. This command will become very useful when you import system furniture from manufacturers' websites or 3D model libraries.

Figure 13.60
Create a picture
on the wall.

Create a Picture

We need a picture on the wall on the left to serve as a focal point.

Step 1: Create a box

1 Thaw the layer I-WALL.

2 Click the southwest view icon ⬙ to switch to an axonometric view.

3 ZOOM in to look at the wall facing the counter.

4 Create a box starting at the midpoint of the wall, using @ −1, 6′, 4′ to define the corner.

5 Move the box 3′ to the right to center it.

6 Move the box 4′ up.   *See Figure 13.60.*

Step 2: Layer management

1 Create a layer and name it PICTURE.

2 Put the picture into the layer PICTURE.

3 Thaw the layer BASE.

Create the Base of the Walls

1 Hit the [F3] key to turn on the OSNAP.

2 Click the 3D Make control panel icon and click the SLICE command icon ⬙.

Command: _slice

Select objects: **select the wall** 1 found

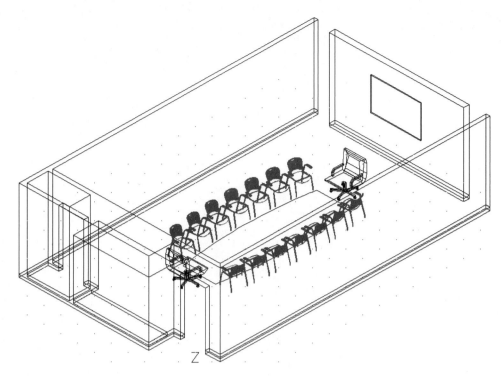

Figure 13.61
Slice the wall to create
the base.

Select objects: **select the wall between windows** 1 found, 2 total

Select objects: ⏎

Specify first point on slicing plane by [Object/Zaxis/View/XY/YZ/ZX/3points]

<3points>: **XY**⏎

Specify a point on the XY-plane <0,0,0>: **pick the upper corner of the cabinet base**

Specify a point on desired side of the plane or [keep Both sides]: **B**⏎   *The walls are sliced into the upper portion and the lower portion (Figure 13.61).*

3 Put the lower portion of the walls into the layer BASE.

4 Freeze the layers BASE, I-WALL, PICTURE, and I-FURN.

Create Light Objects

To prepare your model for rendering in the next chapter, you need to create an object to represent light fixtures that glow on the ceiling because the light created in AutoCAD gives light but the light itself cannot be seen. You need to assign a self-illuminating material to the light objects to make them look like glowing lights.

Step 1: Redefine the fluorescent light block

1 Thaw the layer I-CLNG-LITE.

2 ZOOM to look at a 2 × 4 fluorescent light fixture symbol.

3 Create a box using the light fixture symbol as a guide. Height = 0.5".

4 Use the BLOCK command (alias: B) to redefine the block "lite 2 × 4." Insertion point = lower left corner.

Step 2: Redefine the recessed can block

1 ZOOM in to look at a recessed can symbol.

2 Use the CYLINDER tool to create a thin disc. Radius = 4". Height = 0.5".

3 Use the BLOCK command (B) to redefine the block "literec." Insertion point = center of cylinder on the floor.

Step 3: Move the light objects up

1 ERASE (E) the direction pointer and the linear fluorescent light symbols.

2 Use the 3DMOVE command to move all the light objects up 9'11.5".

3 Use the 3DMOVE command to move the three light objects in the cove area up 3'.

4 Thaw all the layers.   *See Figure 13.62.*

5 Save the file and exit AutoCAD.

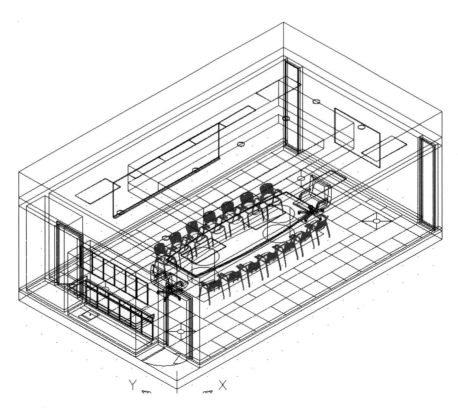

Figure 13.62
Finished 3D model.

Chapter **14**

Rendering

- Clean up the Model
- Set the Perspective Views
- Set up Lighting
- Select and Apply Materials
- Set Background Image
- Render and Fine-Tune an Image
- Final Rendering

In this chapter, you will learn the basics of rendering in AutoCAD to generate a real-istic view of a space.

Clean up the Model

It is a good habit to clean up your model before rendering. Because the model was built based on a 2D drawing, some 2D elements left in the drawing must be cleaned up.

Step 1: Preparation

1 Start AutoCAD.

2 Switch to the 3D Modeling workspace if needed.

3 Open the ch13.dwg drawing and save it as ch14.dwg.

4 Thaw and turn on all layers.

Step 2: ERASE the 2D components

1 Click the view list on the 3D Navigation control panel and choose Left to switch to the left-side view.

2 Start the ERASE command (E) and use a selection-window (*not* a crossing-window) to select all the 2D elements on the floor and erase them.

See Figure 14.1.

Step 3: Purge unused styles and layers

1 Enter the command PURGE.

The Purge dialog box pops up (see Figure 14.2).

2 Click [Purge All].

The Confirm Purge dialog box pops up (see Figure 14.3).

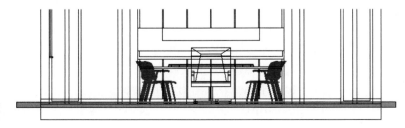

Figure 14.1
Select the 2D elements to erase.

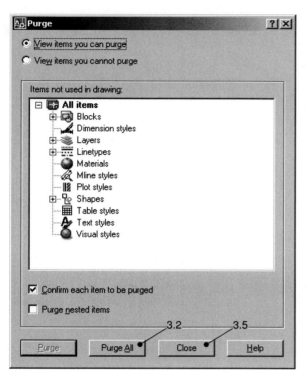

Figure 14.2
Purge dialog box.

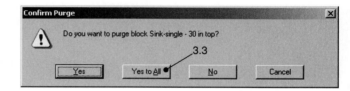

Figure 14.3
Confirm purge.

3 Click [Yes to All].

4 Repeat this until you don't see any [+] sign in front of the item list.

5 Click [Close].

Set the Perspective Views

Setting a perspective is similar to taking a photograph in an interior space. When you take the photograph, you hold a camera and aim at a certain point; you move back and forth or you adjust the zoom lens to change the scope of the view. In AutoCAD, you need to define a target point and a camera point, and you change the zoom value to change the scope of the view. You may also move the camera or the target point to change the view. When the view is set, you can save it as a named view that can be called out whenever you need it.

Step 1: Set up a one-point perspective

1 Click the Visual Style list to select 2D Wireframe.

2 Switch to Top View through the view list on the dashboard.

3 ZOOM to look at the floor plan and turn off the OSNAP.

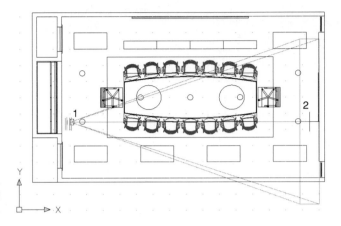

Figure 14.4
Set the target and
camera points.

4 **Click the Create Camera tool icon ▦.**

The CAMERA command starts.
See the command line and
interact with AutoCAD.

Command: _camera

Current camera settings: Height=0″ Lens Length=50.0000 mm

Specify camera location: **pick point 1**   *See Figure 14.4.*

- At this point, AutoCAD wants a 3D point. You may enter the coordinates
  (*x*, *y*, *z*) if you know them, but you usually don't. Because picking a 3D point
  directly from the drawing area is very difficult, you need to use .XY (called a
  point filter). The point filter .XY allows you to pick the location of a point on
  the floor and enter how far you want it to be above (or below) the picked
  point. AutoCAD takes the *x* and *y* coordinates from the point you pick. Entering the *z* coordinate makes it a 3D point coordinate. The 5′5 you enter is the
  normal eye level.

Specify target location:. **.XY↵**

of **try your best to keep the rubber band line level and pick point 2** (need Z):
5′5↵

Enter an option [?/Name/LOcation/Height/Target/LEns/Clipping/View/eXit]<eXit>:
H↵

Specify camera height <5′>: **5′5↵**

Enter an option [?/Name/LOcation/Height/Target/LEns/Clipping/View/eXit]<eXit>:
LE↵

Specify lens length in mm <50.0000>: **24↵**

Enter an option [?/Name/LOcation/Height/Target/LEns/Clipping/View/eXit]<eXit>: **N↵**

Enter name for new camera <Camera1>: **onepoint↵**

Enter an option [?/Name/LOcation/Height/Target/LEns/Clipping/View/eXit]<eXit>: **V**↵

Switch to camera view? [Yes/No] <No>: **Y**↵   *The result is shown in Figure 14.5.*

- You are now in a perspective view. If you don't like it, you can repeat step 1 to reset it with different camera and target points.

Step 2: Set a two-point perspective

Setting a two-point perspective is basically the same as setting a one-point perspective, which you did in Step 2. The only difference is that the direction from the camera to the target is not parallel to any walls.

1 Click the Visual Style list to select 2D Wireframe.

2 Switch to Top View through the view list on the dashboard.

3 Click the Create Camera tool icon .   *The CAMERA command starts. See the command line and interact with AutoCAD.*

Command: _camera

Current camera settings: Height=0″ Lens Length=50.0000 mm

Specify camera location: **pick point 1**   *See Figure 14.6.*

Specify target location: **.XY**↵

of **pick point 2** (need Z): **5′5**↵

Enter an option [?/Name/LOcation/Height/Target/LEns/Clipping/View/eXit]<eXit>: **H**↵

Specify camera height <5′-5″>: **5′5**↵   *See the note below.*

Enter an option [?/Name/LOcation/Height/Target/LEns/Clipping/View/eXit]<eXit>: **LE**↵

Figure 14.5
The resulting perspective view.

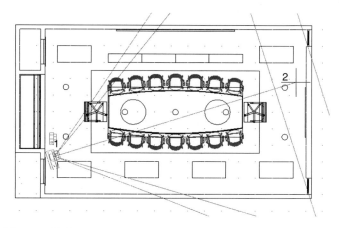

Figure 14.6
Set a two-point perspective view.

Figure 14.7
A two-point perspective
view.

Specify lens length in mm <24.0000>: **24**↵   *See the note below.*

Enter an option [?/Name/LOcation/Height/Target/LEns/Clipping/View/eXit]<eXit>: **N**↵

Enter name for new camera <Camera1>: **twopoint**↵

Enter an option [?/Name/LOcation/Height/Target/LEns/Clipping/View/eXit]<eXit>: **V**↵

Switch to camera view? [Yes/No] <No>: **Y**↵   *The result is shown in Figure 14.7.*

- AutoCAD remembers the camera height and lens length values in the previous step when you set up the one-point perspective. You may simply hit [Enter] to accept the value in the brackets. If the values are not 5′-5″ and 24, you still need to enter those values, as shown above.

Step 3: Restore a saved view

1 Enter command "VIEW."   *The View dialog box pops up (Figure 14.8).*

2 Select "one point."

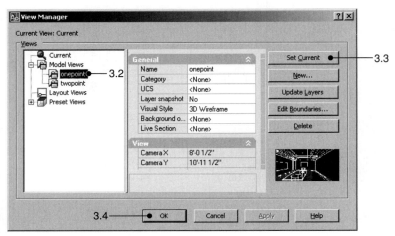

Figure 14.8
Restore a named view.

3 Click [Set current].

4 Click [OK].   *The saved view "onepoint" is*
                                                      shown.

Step 4: Plot a hideline perspective view

Sometimes you may need to plot a perspective view so that you can render it by hand.

1 Set a visual hideline style, such as 3D Hidden or Sketchy, through the Visual Style Control Panel.

2 Start the PLOT command.

3 Set the Shade plot option under Shaded viewport options to As displayed.

4 Preview the plot and click [OK] to plot.

Set up Lighting

Light is essential to vision in the real world, and virtual lights are critical in computer visualization. Only under appropriate lighting will the materials show properly in an AutoCAD rendering. Lights in this release of AutoCAD simulate lights in the real world. In general, we can set up the lights based on the ceiling plan.

In AutoCAD, there are three types of lights: point light, spotlight, and distance light. A point light works like a bare bulb that emits light in all directions equally. The point light is easy to set up, but the light effect is uneven. The surfaces close to it usually have hot spots. For this reason, you should avoid using it unless hot spots are the desired lighting effect. A spotlight in AutoCAD is defined by a target point and the light position point. You can set the beam spread up to 160°. Although it is difficult to set up and to adjust, the lighting effect is well controlled. A distant light is a kind of parallel light similar to sunshine. The uniformity of intensity makes it hard to use in interiors, but it is the tool to simulate sunshine in sun-pattern studies.

Step 1: Create a top view

When placing lights in the model, you need to switch between the top view in 2D wireframe visual style and a perspective view in 3D wireframe visual style. To avoid switching visual styles, create a named top view so that you can switch to it at any time because a visual style can be associated with a named view.

1 Click the Visual Style list to select 2D Wireframe.

2 Switch to Top View through the view list on the dashboard.

3 Start the VIEW command (V).

4 Click [New].

5 Enter name "lightplan."

6 Click [OK].

7 Click [OK].

Step 2: Create downlights in the cove area

The beam spread of the recessed cans in the cove area is similar to a spotlight. You will eventually use spotlights to simulate the recessed cans. Because the creation of a spotlight requires both a camera point and a target point, you will create a point light first and change it to a spotlight.

1 Click the Light Control Panel icon ⬛ .   *The light tools fill the tool palette.*

2 Click the Create a Point Light tool   *The Viewport Lighting Mode*
  icon ⬛ on the Light control panel.   *dialog box pops up.*

3 Click [Yes].

4 Look at the command line.

Specify source location <0,0,0>: **.XY** ↵

of **pick a point at the center of a recessed can symbol over the conference table** (need Z): **12'11** ↵

Enter an option to change [Name/Intensity/Status/shadoW/Attenuation/Color/eXit] <eXit>: **N**↵

Enter light name <Pointlight1>: **cove**↵

Enter an option to change [Name/Intensity/Status/shadoW/Attenuation/Color/eXit] <eXit>: ↵

5 Click the just-created light, right-click,   *The Properties palette pops up*
  and choose Properties.   *(Figure 14.9).*

6 Change the type to "spotlight."

7 Change the hotspot angle to 0.

8 Change the Target Z to 6' and close the Properties palette.

9 Duplicate the light with the COPY command for the other two lights in the cove area.

Step 3: Render the scene to examine the lighting effect

1 Click the view list of the 3D Navigation control panel on the dashboard and choose "twopoint."

2 Click the render toolbar icon ⬛ .   *The tabletop is satisfactorily lighted (Figure 14.10).*

Step 4: Create a spotlight to highlight the picture

1 Switch to the plan view "lightplan" through the view list on the 3D Navigation control panel.

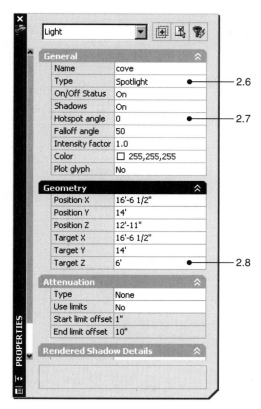

Figure 14.9
Change the light parameters.

Figure 14.10
Rendered scene.

2 Click the Create a point light icon ▣ and use the point filter .xy to locate the light between the two recessed lights in front of the picture. Z = 9′11″. Hit [Enter].

  ● In real lighting design, two spotlights may have a better lighting effect on the highlighted picture, but we are not doing a realistic lighting simulation. Therefore, we use one spotlight on the picture to show that the picture is highlighted. That may be adequate to convey the designer's intention. Lighting calculation is rather intensive, and you need to try to reduce the number of lights and thus reduce the time spent on rendering. This computational economy will become more significant when your model becomes more and more complex.

3 Click to select the newly created light and right-click to choose Properties.

4 Change the name of the light to picture in the Properties palette.

5 Change the type to spotlight.

6 Change the hotspot angle to 0.

7 Change the target Z to 6′ and close the Properties palette.

8 Switch to a front (elevation) view through the view list on the dashboard.

9 Click the light in front of the picture.   *The cone shows (Figure 14.11).*

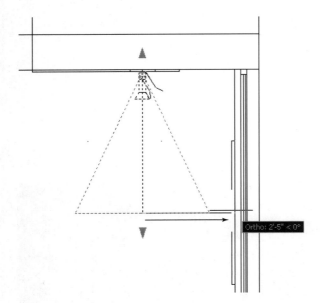

Figure 14.11
Aim the spotlight at the picture.

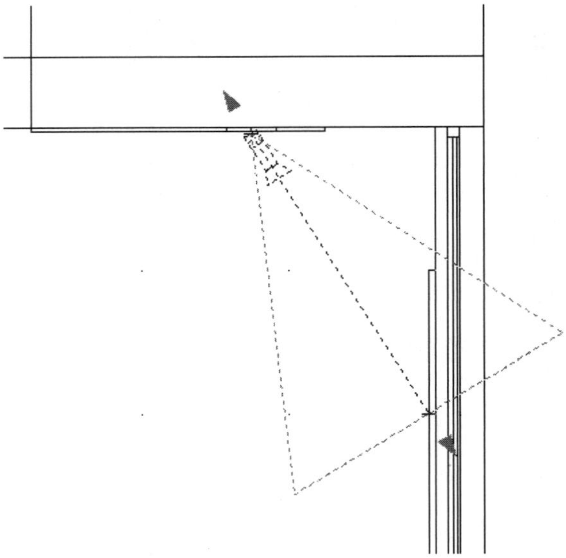

Figure 14.12
Spotlight is aimed at the picture.

10 Click to pick the target.

11 Pull it to the picture and click to set.   *See Figure 14.12.*

- ORTHO should be off to complete this step.

Step 5: Render the scene to check the lighting effect

1 Switch to the two-point perspective view.

2 Test render the scene.   *See Figure 14.13.*

Step 6: Create spotlights to light the whiteboard

1 Switch to the light plan view.

Figure 14.13
Check the lighting effect
of the spotlight on the
picture.

2 Create a point light in front of the whiteboard. Use the .xy point filter to locate the light 9′11″ above the floor.

3 Select the light and change the name of the light to "board."

4 Change the light type to spotlight.

5 Change the hotspot to 0.

6 Change the target Z to 6′.

7 Switch to the right view (elevation).

8 Move the target to the board.

9 Switch to the top view.

10 Use the COPY command to duplicate the light.   *See Figure 14.14.*

Step 7: Render the scene to check the lighting effect

1 Switch to the two-point perspective view.

2 Test render the scene.   *See Figure 14.15.*

Step 8: Create a spotlight for the 2 × 4 fluorescent lights

1 Switch to the plan view.

2 Create a point light at the center of a 2 × 4 light fixture, using the .xy point filter to set the Z at 9′11″ from the floor.

3 Select the light from the Light List palette and change the name to "2 × 4."

4 Change the light type to spotlight.

5 Change the hotspot to 0.

6 Change the falloff to 90.

Figure 14.15
Rendered lighting effect.

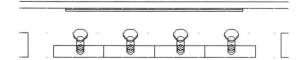

Figure 14.14
Copy the lights.

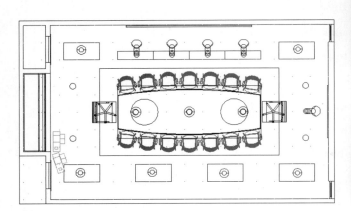

Figure 14.16
Copy the lights.

Figure 14.17
Test render the scene.

7 Use the COPY command to duplicate the lights.   *See Figure 14.16.*

8 Switch to the perspective view and test render.   *See Figure 14.17.*

Select and Apply Materials

Step 1A: Select and import materials from the materials library (for AutoCAD users)

AutoCAD has a materials library with some ready-made materials. The materials in the materials library need to be imported first from the library to your drawing before you can apply them to your model. For Architectural Desktop, the render materials are supposed to be handled in VIZ Render, and therefore the materials library is not as readily available as in AutoCAD. Architectural Desktop users need to skip this step and use the instructions in Step 1B to import materials from the Catalog Library through the Content Browser.

1 Click the Materials control panel icon .   *The materials fill the tool palette (Figure 14.18).*

2 Click the Materials tool icon 🔘 .   *The Material Editor palette pops up (Figure 14.19).*

3 Click the "Woods and Plastics" tab on the Materials palette.

4 Drag "Woods-Plastics. Finish Carpentry.   *The material appears in the*
Wood. Cherry." and drop into the top   *window (Figure 14.20).*
window of the Materials palette.

5 Repeat 4 to import the following materials:

Doors and Windows—Materials Sample (tab)

Doors—Windows. Metal Doors & Frames. Aluminum Windows. Painted. White.

Figure 14.18
Materials palette.

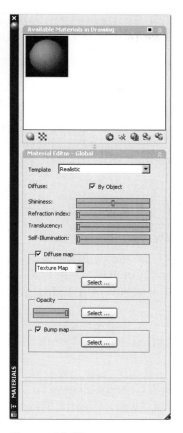

Figure 14.19
Material Editor palette.

Figure 14.20
Import material into the drawing.

Doors—Windows. Door Hardware. Chrome. Satin.
Doors & Windows. Glazing. Glass. Clear.

Fabric—Materials Sample (tab)

Furnishings. Fabrics. Leather. Black.

Finishes—Materials Sample (tab)

Finishes. Ceilings. Acoustical Tile. Exposed Grid. 2 × 2. Fissured. White.
Finishes. Gypsum Board. Painted. White.

Flooring—Materials Sample (tab)

Finishes. Flooring. Cork.

Masonry—Materials Sample (tab)

Masonry. Unit Masonry. Brick. Modular. Common.

Step 1B: Select and import materials from the materials library (for ADT users)

In ADT, you can access the render materials catalog through the Content Browser. You then need to drop the materials into the drawing and make them available for your model.

1 Click the Content Browser toolbar icon 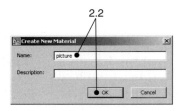.   *The Catalog Library pops up.*

2 Click Render Materials Catalog.

3 Click the <u>Woods and Plastics</u> and then <u>Finish Carpentry</u>.

4 Use the i-drop tool to drag "Woods-Plastics. Finish Carpentry. Wood. Cherry." and drop them into the drawing.   *The Create AEC Materials dialog box pops up.*

5 Click [OK].

Repeat the above steps to import the following materials:

Doors and Windows

> Doors—Windows. Metal doors & Frames. Aluminum Windows. Painted. White.
> Doors—Windows. Door Hardware. Chrome. Satin.
> Doors & Windows. Glazing. Glass. Clear.

Fabric

> Furnishings. Fabrics. Leather. Black.

Finishes

> Finishes. Ceilings. Acoustical Tile. Exposed Grid. 2 × 2. Fissured. White.
> Finishes. Gypsum Board. Painted. White.

Flooring

> Finishes. Flooring. Cork.

Masonry

> Masonry. Unit Masonry. Brick. Modular. Common.

Step 2: Create a new material for the picture

In addition to the ready-made materials, you can create your own materials. In this step, you will create a material for the picture on the wall from an image file stored in your computer. In the future, you can follow this procedure to create your own materials using image files scanned from your interior materials.

1 Click the Create New Material tool icon on the Material Editor.   *The Create New Material dialog box pops up (Figure 14.21).*

Figure 14.21
Name the new material.

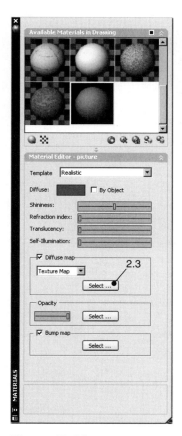

Figure 14.22
Create a new material.

Figure 14.23
Set the diffuse map.

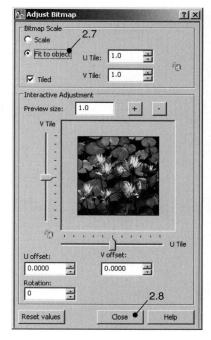

Figure 14.24
Adjust the mapping scale.

2 Enter the name "picture" for the new material and click [OK].

The new material shows in the Material Editor. The color is gray. (See Figure 14.22.)

3 Click [Select. . .] under Diffuse map.

The Select Image File dialog box pops up.

4 Find the image file water lilies.jpg provided with Microsoft Windows. The typical location of the file is in C:\Documents and Settings\All Users\Documents\My Pictures\Sample Pictures.

5 Double-click the file name to open it.

The image is mapped on the sphere (Figure 14.23).

6 Click the Adjust scale/tiling . . . icon 🖼 under Diffuse map.

The Adjust Bitmap dialog box pops up (Figure 14.24).

7 Check "Fit to Object" in the "Bitmap Scale" group.

8 Click [Close].

Step 3: Create a new solid color material for the wall

1 Click the Create New Material tool icon 🔵 on the Material Editor.

The Create New Material dialog box pops up.

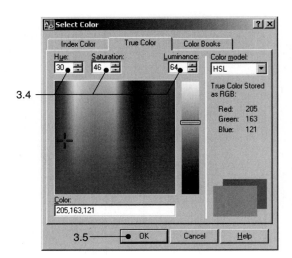

Figure 14.25
Select a diffuse color.

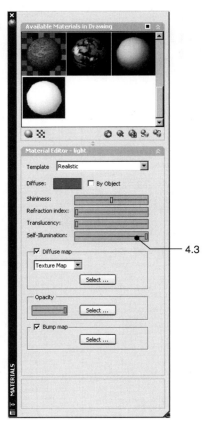

Figure 14.26
Set the Self-Illumination.

2 Enter the name "wall" for the new material and click [OK].

The new material shows in the Material Editor. The color is gray.

3 Click the diffuse color swatch.

The Select Color dialog box pops up (Figure 14.25).

4 Select a beige color using the HSL color model (Hue = 34, Saturation = 46, Luminance = 64).

5 Click [OK].

Step 4: Create a self-illuminating material for the light fixtures

1 Click the Create New Material tool icon 🔘 on the Material Editor.

The Create New Material dialog box pops up.

2 Enter the name "light" for the new material and click [OK].

The new material shows in the Material Editor.

3 Drag the Self-Illumination slider to the right end.

See Figure 14.26.

Step 5: Create a self-illuminating material for the cove

1 Click the Create New Material tool icon ⚙ on the Material Editor.

The Create New Material dialog box pops up.

2 Enter the name "cove" for the new material and click [OK].

The new material shows in the Material Editor.

3 Drag the Self-Illumination slider to the right and stop when you reach 80(%).

Step 6: Attach materials to objects by layers

1 Click the Attach By Layer tool icon ⚙ on the Materials Control Panel on the dashboard.

The Material Attachment Options dialog box pops up (Figure 14.27).

2 Drag the material "wall" to the right and drop it over the layer I-WALL.

3 Attach materials to layers as shown in the following list.

Material	Layer
Woods & Plastics. Finish Carpentry. Wood. Cherry.	tabletop, support
Doors & Windows. Metal Doors & Frames. Aluminum Windows. Painted. White.	I-GLAZ board
Doors & Windows. Door Hardware. Chrome. Satin.	SEAT-BASE
Doors & Windows. Glazing. Glass. Clear.	GLASS
Furnishings. Fabrics. Leather. Black.	I-FURN
	SEAT-BACK
	SEAT-ARMPADS
	SEAT-FABRIC
	BASE
Finishes. Ceilings. Acoustical Tile. Exposed Grid. 2 × 2. Fissured. White.	I-CLNG
Finishes. Gypsum Board. Painted. White.	DRYWALL
Finishes. Flooring. Cork.	floor
Cove	cove
Light	I-CLNG-LITE
Picture	picture

● This list of materials assignments does *not* include the layers that are not in the perspective view.

4 Click [Close].

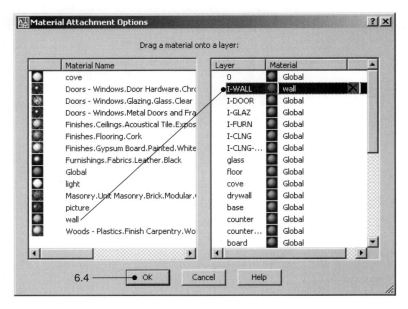

Figure 14.27
Attach materials
by layers.

Set Background Image

The background in AutoCAD rendering is like a backdrop on a stage. You can put up
a landscape image so that you can see it through the windows, for example.

1 Start the VIEW command.

*The View Manager dialog box pops up
(Figure 14.28).*

2 Click twopoint to select the view.

3 Click <None> to the right of
Background override and choose
Image from the drop-down list.

*The Background dialog box pops up
(Figure 14.29).*

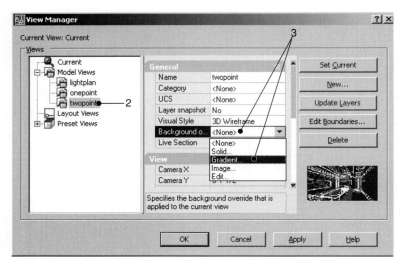

Figure 14.28
Set up a background image.

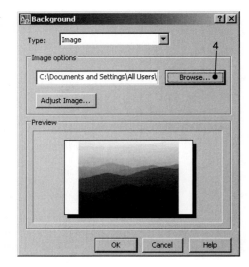

Figure 14.29
Select the background image.

4 Click [Browse. . .].

5 Find the file "Blue hills.jpg" from the Sample Pictures directory. [Change the file type to JFIF (jpeg) to display the image file name if needed.]

6 Double-click the file name to open it.

7 Click [OK] twice.

8 Click the view list on the Visual Style control panel and choose twopoint.

The background image appears and the background of the view turns black.

Render and Fine-Tune an Image

Step 1: View the model in the Realistic visual style

1 Click the visual style list on the dashboard.

2 Choose Realistic 🖼.

The materials show in the model (Figure 14.30).

Step 2: Render the view

1 Click the Render toolbar icon 🖼. *See Figure 14.31.*

The rendered image looks good, but it has a few problems that need adjustment:

1. The floor is too bright; we need to make it darker.

2. The background image does not show through the window glass.

3. The ceiling tile alignment is not correct.

4. We may want to see more wood grain on the tabletop.

Figure 14.30
View the model in Realistic visual style.

Figure 14.31
Rendered view.

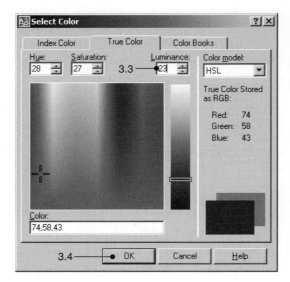

Figure 14.32
Reduce the luminance.

Figure 14.33
Darkened floor.

5. The wall surfaces may be enriched by using brick on the end wall of the space.

6. The whiteboard looks black.

We will try to solve these problems one by one.

Step 3: Adjust cork floor material

1 Click the cork floor materials on the Material Editor.

2 Click the diffuse color swatch.   *The Select Color dialog box pops up (Figure 14.32).*

3 Make it darker by setting the luminance to 23.

4 Click [OK] to close the Select Color dialog box.

5 Adjust the Opacity slider to about 50.

- This setting will allow the texture bitmap to blend with a dark background color to reduce the brightness of the floor.

6 Render to see the result.   *See Figure 14.33.*

Step 4: Adjust the material mapping scale to show wood grain

1 Click the wood material on the Material Editor.

2 Click the Adjust scale/tiling . . . icon 🖼️.   *The Adjust Bitmap dialog box pops up (Figure 14.34).*

3 Change the unit from Inch to Feet.

4 Click [Close].

5 Render to see the effect.   *See Figure 14.35.*

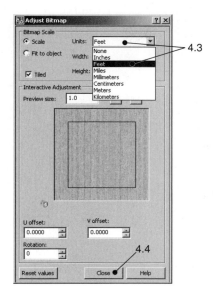

Figure 14.34
Adjust mapping scale.

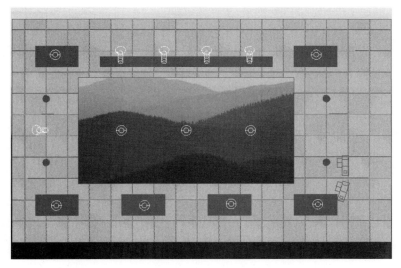

Figure 14.35
Make wood grain more visible.

Step 5: Adjust the ceiling tile alignment

1 Switch to a bottom view through the view list on the dashboard.

2 Freeze all layers except I-CLNG and I-CLNG-LITE.

3 Make sure the visual style is Realistic.

4 Click the Viewport Light Mode tool icon on the Light control panel to turn off the user-defined lighting.

The ceiling tile grid shows (Figure 14.36).

Figure 14.36
The bottom view of the ceiling in the Realistic visual style.

Figure 14.37
Launch the Box Mapping tool.

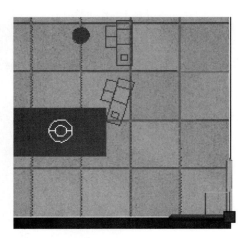

Figure 14.38
Use the tripod to move the ceiling grid.

5 Click and hold the Planar
Mapping tool icon ![icon].

*Four mapping tool icons
pop up.*

6 Pick the Box Mapping tool icon ![icon]. *See Figure 14.37.*

7 Click to select the ceiling tile
and hit the [Enter] key.

*The colored tripod appears at the corner of
the ceiling (Figure 14.38).*

8 Hover the cursor over the red leg of the tripod and click when the red line appears.

9 Move the grid with the cursor to align it with the lights.

10 Click to set.

11 Hover the cursor over the green leg of the tripod and click when the green line
appears.

12 Move the grid with the cursor to align it with the lights.

13 Click to set.

14 Hit the [Enter] key to accept
the adjustment.

See Figure 14.39.

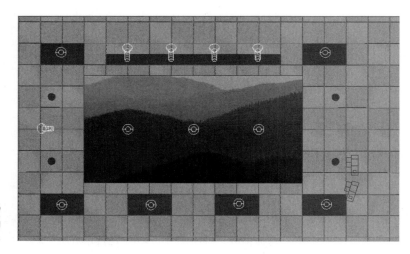

Figure 14.39
The aligned ceiling
tile grid.

Figure 14.40
Assign material directly to an object.

Step 6: Change the material of the end wall

We assigned materials by layer. Therefore, all the walls have the same color. Now, we want to assign bricks to one wall. We can assign the material directly to that particular object. This assignment overrides the assignment by layer.

1 Switch back to the two-point perspective view.

2 Make sure the view is in the Realistic visual style.

3 Hover the cursor over the wall and click when it is highlighted.

4 Click the brick material on the Material Editor to select it.

5 Click the Apply Material to Objects tool icon ![icon] on the Material Editor.   *The brick material shows on the wall (Figure 14.40).*

Step 7: Find a material from the materials library

The material samples we had on the palette are very limited in number, but more materials are available in a materials library. We will find a better white material for the whiteboard.

1 Right-click the title bar of the tool palette and choose Materials Library.   *More materials fill the tool palette.*

2 Find the Woods-Plastics. Plastics. PVC. White on the Woods and Plastics tab.

3 Click the material.   *The cursor turns into a paintbrush in the drawing area. You are prompted to select the object to apply the material.*

4 Pick the whiteboard and hit the [Enter] key.   *The whiteboard changes color.*

Final Rendering

Now you are ready to create a high-quality image of your model.

Step 1: Render the reflected light

Before you start the final rendering, you need to decide how to render the reflected illumination. In this release of AutoCAD, the reflected illumination can be rendered with two different methods known as global illumination (GI) and Final Gather. These methods are advanced physics–based lighting simulations that require intensive computation, which means prolonged rendering time for us. On a well-equipped notebook computer, a large, high-quality image may need hours of rendering time. Therefore, we will use a different approach to "fake" the lighting effect of reflected illuminations.

1 Switch to the "lightplan" view.

2 Create a point light using the .xy filter to place it at the middle of the space 20′ below the floor (Z = −20′).

3 Select the light from the light list.

4 Change the light parameters through the Properties palette as follows:

Name:	reflect
Shadow:	OFF
Intensity factor:	0.25

5 Click the color parameter and click the arrow to see the list.

6 Choose Select Color.   *The Select Color dialog box pops up.*

7 Select a warm color (Hue = 34, Saturation = 91, Luminance = 83 or R = 251, G = 217, B = 173).

8 Click [OK].

9 Switch to the two-point perspective   *See Figure 14.41.*
view and render to see the effect.

Step 2: Set the output image quality

Preset quality-control settings in AutoCAD are ranked as follows:

Draft

Low

Figure 14.41
Check the effect of
reflected light.

Medium

High

Presentation

The default setting is Medium, and we have been using it with previous test render-ings. When you are ready for the final rendering, use a higher-quality setting. It will take a longer time to render a higher-quality image.

1 Click the Render control panel icon 🌐.

2 Click the Render Preset list and select High.   *See Figure 14.42.*

Step 3: Render to a file

1 Click the Render to a File tool   *The icon turns into a yellow-orange color.*
icon 🔳 on the dashboard
to turn it on.

2 Click the browse button [. . .].   *The Render Output File dialog box pops up.*

3 Find the file storage directory where you want to save the rendered image file.

4 Click the file type list and select TIF(*.tif).

5 Enter a name for the file (finalrender).

6 Click [Save].   *The TIFF Image Options dialog box pops up.*

7 Click [OK] to take the default setting.

Step 4: Set the resolution

1 Click the Output Size drop-down   *The Output Size dialog box pops up*
list and select Specify Output Size.   *(Figure 14.43).*

2 Click the lock icon 🔒 to lock the Image Aspect to 1.333.

3 Change the Width to 2048.

4 Click [OK].

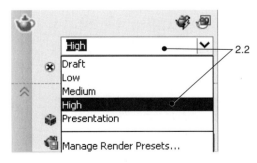

Figure 14.42
Set the quality setting.

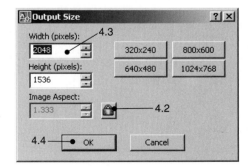

Figure 14.43
Output Size dialog box.

5 Click the QSAVE tool to save the drawing file.

- A high-quality rendering is a demanding job for your computer. Sometimes, it may cause the computer to crash or freeze. It is a good idea to save your work before starting a big rendering job.

6 Click the Render tool icon 🖼 to start the rendering process.   *AutoCAD starts to write the image file.*

7 Quit AutoCAD.

Construct the Space Model with ADT

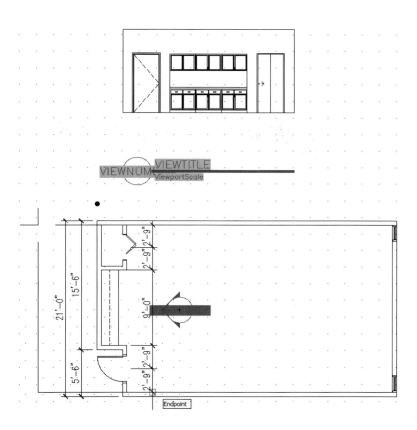

- Get to Know the ADT User Interface
- Start a New Drawing
- Create Walls
- Make Changes to the Plan
- Create Cabinets
- Dimension in ADT
- Create an Elevation

Get to Know the ADT User Interface

Step 1: Start ADT

1 Start the ADT program.

You are prompted to select a workspace (Figure 15.1).

2 Choose the Design **workspace and click [OK].**

You are asked if you want to view a new feature workshop.

3 Check Maybe Later **and click [OK].**

The ADT program window opens (Figure 15.2).

The ADT user interface is similar to that of AutoCAD. However, it has fewer menu items and the tool palette is prominent. In ADT, the tool palette starts the object creation process. It is, therefore, used more than the toolbars. The tool palette is very dynamic and may take many different forms. It may float on the drawing window, it may be docked into the drawing window frame, or it may be anchored to the side of the drawing window. It can also be set to hide automatically when the cursor is not on it in order to reduce visual interference with the drawing elements in the drawing window.

Step 2: Experiment with tool palette control

Because the tool palette is important in the use of ADT, we will play with the tool palette to learn all its tricks in the following experiments.

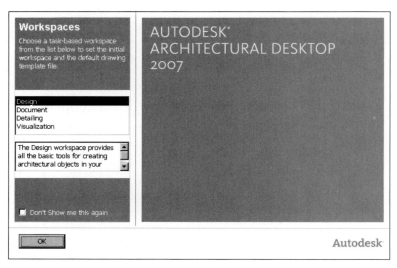

Figure 15.1
Select ADT workspace.

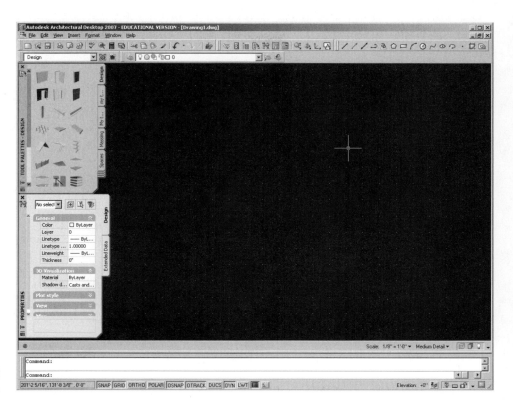

Figure 15.2
ADT user interface.

Experiment 1: Turn the tool palette on and off

1 Click the tool palette toolbar icon .   *The tool palette disappears.*

2 Click the tool palette toolbar icon   *The tool palette reappears.*
again.

- You may also close the tool palette by clicking the close button on the tool palette title bar.

Experiment 2: Set the tool palette Auto-hide mode

Because the opened palettes occupy a substantial area in the drawing window, we want to close them when they are not in use. Setting them to auto-hide mode will make them close when the cursor is away from them.

1 Click the Auto-hide button near   *The tool palette closes, with only its title bar*
the bottom of the tool palette title   *remaining on the screen (Figure 15.4). The*
bar (Figure 15.3).   *Auto-hide mode is on, and the button*
     changes to one larger arrow.

2 Move the cursor over the tool   *The tool palette opens.*
palette title bar.

3 Move the cursor away from the   *The tool palette closes.*
tool palette.

4 Click the Auto-hide button   *The Auto-hide mode is turned off.*
on the tool palette title bar.

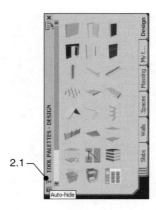

Figure 15.3
Set tool palette Auto-hide.

Figure 15.4
Tool palette in Auto-hide mode.

Experiment 3: Dock the tool palette

1 Click the Properties button at the lower end of the tool palette title bar.

The tool palette properties menu opens.

2 Choose Allow Docking from the tool palette properties menu.

3 Drag the tool palette by its title bar to the right side over the window frame and release it until a rectangle appears.

The tool palette is docked into the frame (Figure 15.5). The title bar is now two horizontal lines flanked by the Minimize and Close buttons.

4 Drag the tool palette by its title bar away from the window frame and release until a smaller rectangle appears.

The tool palette is floating in the drawing window.

Experiment 4: Anchor the tool palette

1 Click the tool palette properties button and choose Anchor Right from the pop-up menu.

The tool palette is anchored to the right window frame (Figure 15.6).

2 Move the cursor over the anchored tool palette.

The tool palette opens.

3 Move the cursor away from the tool palette.

The tool palette closes.

4 Move the cursor over the anchored tool palette and click the Auto-hide button near the bottom of the title bar.

The Auto-hide mode is turned off.

5 Click the Minimize button .

The Auto-hide mode is on and the palette closes.

Figure 15.5
Tool palette is docked.

Figure 15.6
Tool palette is anchored.

Start a New Drawing

An ADT drawing has many settings to control the behavior of the building components (called AEC objects). Using a template can simplify the task of setting up a drawing and avoid starting a new drawing with the wrong settings, which will cause you more trouble in the future. For this reason, you should always start a new drawing with a known template.

Step 1: Start a new drawing

1 Enter the command NEW.

The Select template dialog box pops up (Figure 15.7).

2 Double-click Aec Model (Imperial Stb).dwt.

A new drawing opens.

Step 2: Check and adjust the new drawing settings

Before you start creating building components, you should make sure the drawing settings can support your work.

1 Enter the LIMITS command to check the drawing limits.

- The drawing limit setting defines a work area of 288′ by 192′. That is more than adequate for your space.

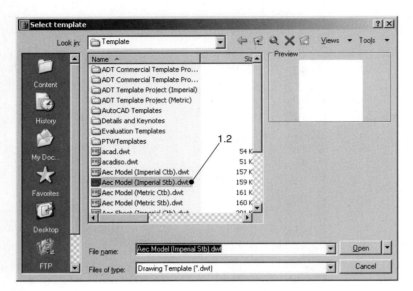

Figure 15.7
Select a template to start a new drawing.

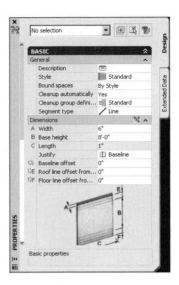

Figure 15.8
Wall properties are shown on the
Properties palette.

2 Enter the GRID command to change the drawing grid from 10′ to 2′.

3 Enter the SNAP command to change the snap setting to 1″.

4 Save the current drawing as ch15.dwg.

Create Walls

Step 1: Create boundary walls

1 Move the cursor over the anchored tool palette to open it.

2 Click the Design tab if it is not already open.

3 Click the wall tool (at the upper left corner).

The parameters of the wall are shown in the Properties palette (Figure 15.8).

- If the Properties palette is not shown, click the Properties toolbar icon 🖼 to bring it up.

4 Change the Dimensions parameters as follows:

See Figure 15.9.

B (Base height) = 10′
Justify = right

5 Click in the drawing area near the lower left corner to define the starting point.

6 Pull the rubber band wall up and enter 20′.

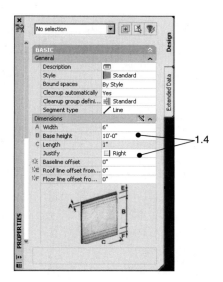

Figure 15.9
Change wall parameters.

Figure 15.10
Finished boundary walls.

7 Pull the rubber band to the right and enter 34′.

8 Enter option OR to enclose the space. Pull the rubber band down and click to indicate the direction of the enclosure.

The wall forms a rectangular enclosure.

9 ZOOM in to look at the walls.

See Figure 15.10.

Step 2: Examine the walls in an axonometric view

1 Right-click an existing toolbar and choose Views.

2 Place the Views toolbar next to the Layer toolbar.

3 Right-click an existing toolbar and choose Visual Styles.

4 Place the Visual Styles toolbar next to the Views toolbar.

5 Use the Views toolbar to switch to the SW axonometric view.

You can see that the walls are 3D objects (Figure 15.11).

Step 3: Add a door

1 Open the design tool palette and click the door tool.

2 Look at the door parameters as shown in the properties tool palette (Figure 15.12).

The dimensions of the door happen to be what you want (3′ w × 7′ h).

3 Change the Position along wall from "Unconstrained" to "Offset/Center."

4 Set the Automatic offset to 3″.

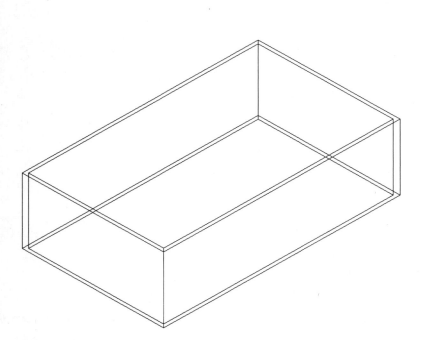

Figure 15.11
Axonometric view of the walls.

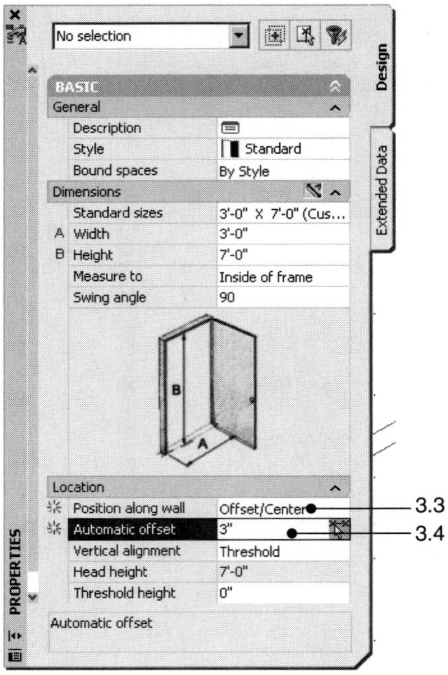

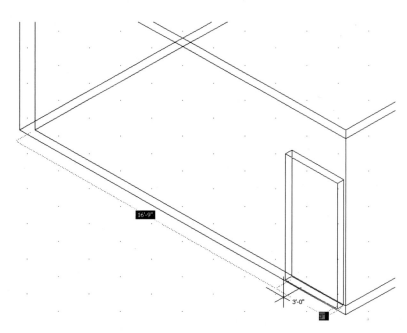

Figure 15.12
Set the parameters of the door.

5 Click the wall to the left near the corner where the door is supposed to be.

The location of the door is indicated by dimensions (Figure 15.13).

6 Make sure the distance to the corner of the space is 3″, and click to set.

7 Hit [Enter] to terminate the command.

Figure 15.13
Locate the door.

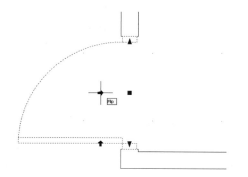

Figure 15.14
Flip the door using grips.

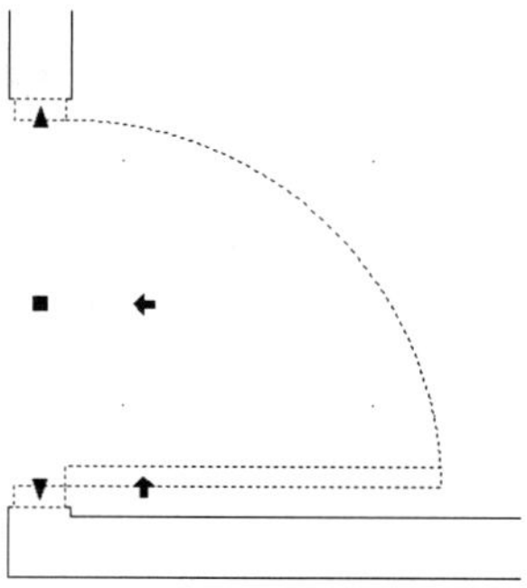

Figure 15.15
The door is flipped.

8 Switch to the plan view.

- You can see that the door is swung out. Because the designer's sketch shows that the door is swung in, you need to change it.

9 Click the door.   *The grips show.*

10 Click the arrow pointing to the   *The door flips into the space*
right (Figure 15.14).   *(Figure 15.15).*

- If your door is not swung to the wall, click the arrow pointing down to flip the door one more time.

11 Hit the [Esc] key to finish.

Step 4: Add windows

1 Open the tool palette and click the Windows tab.

- If you don't see the Windows tab, it is buried in the stacked tabs due to the limited height of the tool palette. Click the stacked tables to bring up a pop-up menu and choose Windows.

2 Click the picture window tool icon ▣.

3 In the Properties palette, change the parameters as follows:

Dimension
A (Width) = 2′
B (Height) = 10′
Location
Position along wall = Offset/Center
Automatic offset = 0
Head height = 10′

4 Click the wall to the right near the   *The location of the window is shown with*
lower corner.   *dimensions (Figure 15.16).*

5 Click to set.

6 Move the cursor to the upper   *The window is shown at the top of the*
portion of the same wall.   *wall (Figure 15.17).*

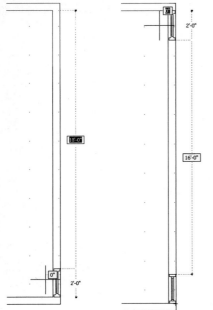

Figure 15.16
Create the
first window.

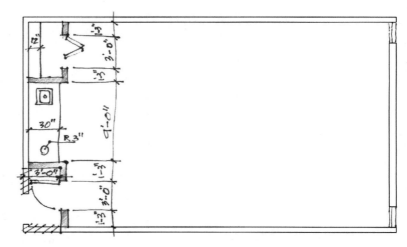

Figure 15.17
Create the second
window.

Figure 15.18
Designer's sketch of wall modification.

7 Click to set.

8 Hit [Enter] to terminate the command.

Step 5: Layer management

In ADT, layer management is automatic. When you add a building component, it is automatically created in a layer according to the AIA layer standard by default.

1 Click a wall and look at the layer toolbar.

2 The layer toolbar shows that the wall is in the layer A-wall.

3 Hit [Esc] to cancel.

Make Changes to the Plan

Now, let us modify the plan based on the designer's sketch. See Figure 15.18.

Step 1: Duplicate walls with the COPY command

Similar to lines, a wall can be copied. You can use the COPY command to create the new vertical wall with a door.

1 Start the COPY command.

2 Select both the wall and the door.

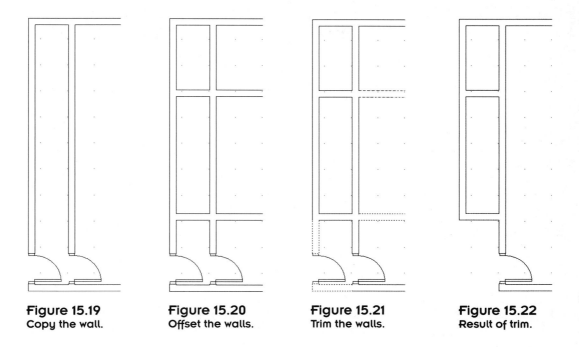

Figure 15.19
Copy the wall.

Figure 15.20
Offset the walls.

Figure 15.21
Trim the walls.

Figure 15.22
Result of trim.

3 Place the copy 3 feet to the right.   *See Figure 15.19.*

4 Terminate the COPY command.

Step 2: Duplicate walls with the OFFSET command

Walls can be duplicated using the OFFSET command, just as you do with lines.

1 Use the OFFSET command to create walls.   *See Figure 15.20.*
Offset distance for horizontal walls = 5′6″
from top and bottom.

Step 3: TRIM the walls

Walls can be trimmed in the same way as a line can be trimmed.

1 TRIM the walls as shown in Figures 15.21 and 15.22.

- When you trim the wall with the door, the door disappears with the trimmed wall. This is because the door is anchored in the wall. When the wall is gone, the door goes with it.

Step 4: Relocate the door

1 MOVE the door up 12″.

- Because the door is anchored in the wall, the door opening moves with the door.

2 Use the grips to flip the door to   *See Figure 15.23.*
match the sketch.

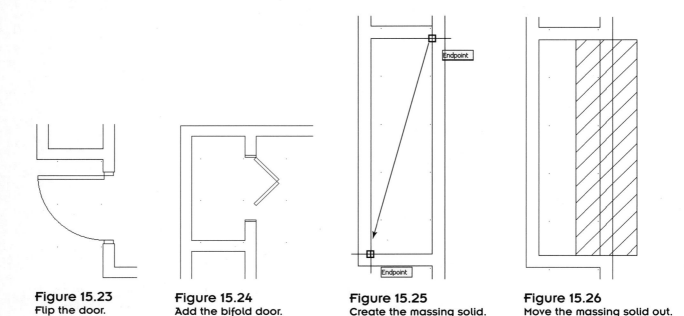

Figure 15.23
Flip the door.

Figure 15.24
Add the bifold door.

Figure 15.25
Create the massing solid.

Figure 15.26
Move the massing solid out.

Step 5: Add the bifold door

1 ZOOM to look at the closet.

2 Open the tool palette and click the Doors tab.

3 Click the bifold door tool icon ▮.   *The dimension and location settings happen to be what we want (3' w × 7' h).*

4 Click the wall and center the door relative to the closet.   *See Figure 15.24.*

Step 6: Add a wall opening

You need to carve out an opening on the wall for the counter area.

1 Open the tool palette and click the Massing tab.

2 Click the box tool icon ▣.

3 Click (with the object snap on) the   *See Figure 15.25.* inside corners of the counter space.

4 Enter 7' for height.

5 Hit [Enter] to accept the default value 0 for rotation.

6 Hit [Enter] to terminate the command.

7 MOVE the massing box 12 inches   *See Figure 15.26.* to the right to make it cross the wall.

8 Switch to the SE axonometric view.

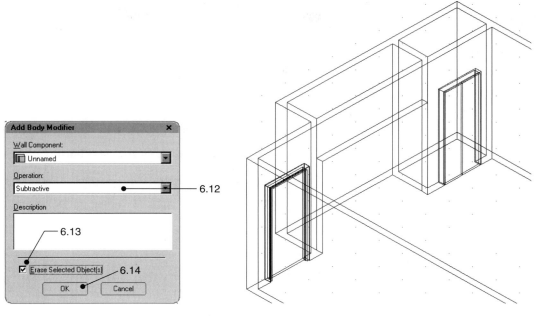

Figure 15.27
Add the wall body modifier.

Figure 15.28
Create the wall opening.

9 Click the wall crossing the massing box and right-click to choose Body modifier> Add.

10 Click the massing box.

11 Hit [Enter].   *The Add Body Modifier dialog box pops up (Figure 15.27).*

12 Change the Operation to "Subtractive."

13 Check the box "Erase Selected Object(s)."

14 Click [OK].   *The opening on the wall is created (Figure 15.28).*

Create Cabinets

In ADT, you can find tools to create the cabinets from the tool catalog library by using the Content Browser. The tools are different from the blocks you get from the Design Center. A major difference of the objects created with these tools is that they are view-dependent, which means they look different in different views.

Step 1: Load the tools

1 Open the tool palette and click the Design tab.

2 Click the Content Browser tool icon   *The Catalog Library page pops up.*
   [icon] (on top of the screen).

3 Find the cabinet tools in Design Tool Catalog – Imperial > Furnishing > Casework > Base Cabinet.

4 Use the i-drop tool to place the 36″ wide base cabinet tool onto your Design tool palette.

5 Find the wall cabinet tool in Design Tool Catalog – Imperial > Furnishing > Casework > 24in. High Wall.

6 Use the i-drop tool to place the 36″ wide wall cabinet tool onto your tool palette.

7 Close the Content Browser by clicking the close button at the upper right corner.

Step 2: Insert the base cabinet

1 Switch to the SW axonometric view.

2 ZOOM in to look at the counter area.

3 Click the base cabinet tool 🗔.

4 Place the cabinet unit in the space (by snapping the corner of the wall).   *See Figure 15.29.*

5 Insert the next unit.

6 Insert the next unit. Hit [Enter] to terminate the command.   *See Figure 15.30.*

Step 3: Insert the wall cabinet

1 Click the wall cabinet tool 🗔.

2 Insert the wall cabinet unit using the corner of the base cabinets as insertion points.   *See Figure 15.30.*

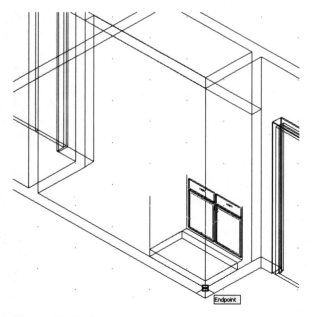

Figure 15.29
Place the first base cabinet.

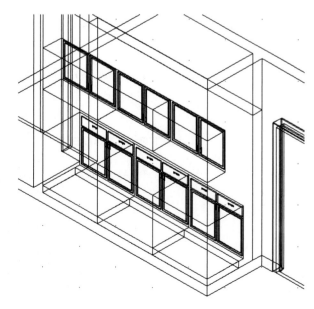

Figure 15.30
Cabinets are created.

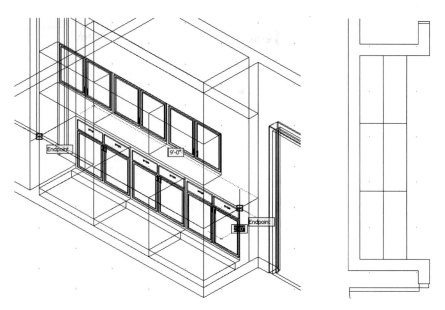

Figure 15.31
Create the countertop.

Figure 15.32
Top view of the cabinets.

Step 4: Create the countertop

The base cabinet needs a countertop. You will create a 3D solid box using the BOX command to represent the countertop.

1 Disable the Dynamic UCS by clicking [DUCS] on the status line.

2 Use the BOX command to create a box on top   *See Figure 15.31.*
of the base cabinet (height = 2″).

3 Create a new layer and name it COUNTERTOP.

4 Place the countertop on that layer.

Step 5: Control the object display

Switch to a plan view (Figure 15.32). You can see that the lines between the units are excessive. An easy solution to this problem is to turn off the display of the top views of the cabinet units and draw a line to represent the wall cabinet units.

1 Draw a line tracing the front edge of the wall cabinet units.

2 Switch to the SE axonometric view.

3 Click a wall cabinet unit.

4 Right-click and choose Edit Multi-   *The Multi-View Block Definition Properties*
View Block Definition.   *dialog box pops up (Figure 15.33).*

5 Click the View Block tab.   *See Figure 15.34. The General display*
representation and the view block
I_Case_Wall_24H_36in Wide_P are
highlighted by default.

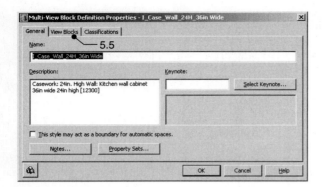

Figure 15.33
Set the cabinet display settings.

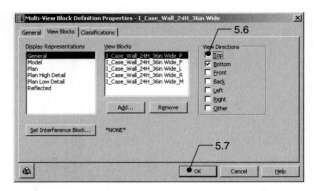

Figure 15.34
Set the cabinet display settings.

6 Uncheck the box Top.

This means that the cabinet will not be shown in the top view.

7 Click [OK].

8 Click a base cabinet unit.

9 Right-click and choose Edit Multi-View Block Definition.

The Multi-View Block Definition Properties dialog box pops up. The General display representation and the view block I_Case_Wall_ 24H_36in Wide_P are highlighted by default.

10 Uncheck the box Top.

11 Click [OK].

12 Switch to the plan view.

The lines between the cabinet are no longer there (Figure 15.35).

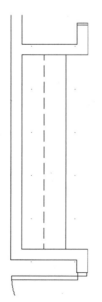

Figure 15.35
Top view of cabinets.

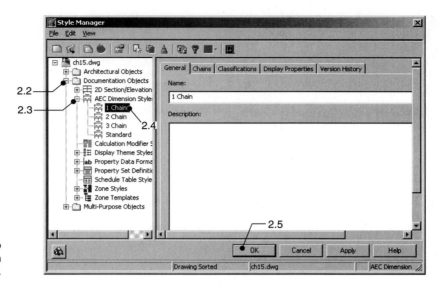

Figure 15.36
Find the AEC dimension
style in Style Manager.

13 Create a layer for the wall cabinet and change the linetype to Hidden2.

14 Place the wall cabinet line onto the new layer.

Dimension in ADT

In ADT, we will use a new type of dimension tool that is called AEC dimension. You will learn more about the AEC dimension as you work with it.

Step 1: Create a new tool palette

1 Right-click the title bar of the tool palette and select new palette. A new palette is created with the name "New Palette."

2 Right-click the new palette tab and choose Rename Palette.

3 Name it as "my tools."   *You will add the dimension tool here later.*

Step 2: Create a dimension tool with Style Manager

1 Click Format on the menu bar and choose Style Manager.   *The Style Manager window opens (Figure 15.36).*

2 Under drawing ch15.dwg, click the plus sign by the folder named Documentation Objects to see the contents.   *A subtree appears under the folder.*

3 Click the plus sign by AEC Dimension Styles to see all the dimension styles.   *A list of five dimension styles appears.*

4 Drag the style 1 Chain and drop it onto the My tools tab of the tool palette.   *The 1 Chain dimension tool appears on the tool palette.*

5 Click [OK] to close the Style Manager window.

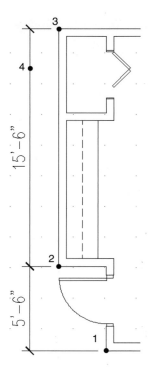

Figure 15.37
Create AEC dimension.

Step 3: Create a string of dimensions

1 **Click the dimension tool on your tool palette and look at the command line to interact with ADT.**

Command: DimAdd

Select Objects or [Pick points]: **P** ↵

pick points: **pick point 1**   *(Figure 15.37)*

pick points: **pick point 2**

pick points: **pick point 3**

pick points: ↵

Specify insert point or [Style/Rotation/Align] **pick point 4**

3 associative points added.

- When the dimensions created in ADT are compared with the dimensions created in AutoCAD tools, there are a few major differences.

  1. The AEC dimension acts as a whole string instead of individual segments.

  2. The AEC dimension is dependent on the display configurations. When you switch to the High Detail display configuration, the dimension texts and features become smaller.

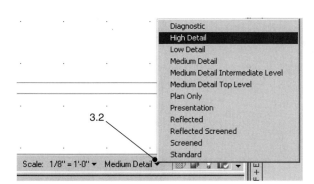

Figure 15.38
Change the display configuration.

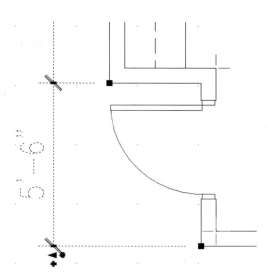

Figure 15.39
The grips of the AEC dimension.

2 Switch to the High Detail display configuration by clicking the arrow next to Medium Detail at the lower right corner of the drawing window (Figure 15.38).

The dimension text and features become smaller.

3 Switch back to Medium Detail.

Step 4: Adjust the dimensions using grips

The AEC dimensions can be adjusted using the grips. In this step, you may experiment with them and check out their functions.

1 Click the dimension.   *The grips pop up (Figure 15.39).*

- The triangle allows you to move the dimension line location (of all chains).
- The square is the anchor point of the dimension measure point. You can click and move it.
- The plus sign allows you to add dimension points.
- The minus sign allows you to delete an extension line.
- The dot is a switch to the second set of grips to allow you to adjust individual dimension features.

2 Click the dot to switch to the second set of grips.   *See Figure 15.40.*

- The squares near the dimension text allow you to relocate the dimension text.
- The cyan triangles allow you to move the starting points of the extension line.
- The magenta triangles allow you to move the dimension chain.
- The dot allows you to switch back to the previous grip set.

3 Hit [Esc] to exit.

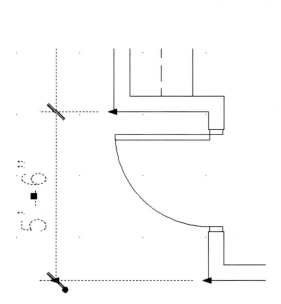

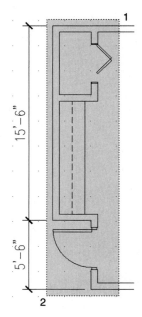

Figure 15.40
The second set of grips in the AEC dimension.

Figure 15.41
Select the AEC objects.

Step 5: Create dimension by selecting objects

1 Click the AEC dimension tool on the tool palette to start a dimension command and look at the command line to interact with ADT.

Command: DimAdd

Select Objects or [Pick points]: **pick point 1**   *(Figure 15.41)*

Specify opposite corner: **pick point 2** 11 found

2 were filtered out

Select Objects or [Pick points]: ⏎

Specify insert point or [Style/Rotation/Align] **pick point 3**   *(Figure 15.42)*

● You may need to move the cursor around before the dimension line becomes vertical.

9 added   *(Figure 15.43)*

● In comparison with the previous tool, this tool is object based. It will automatically create the dimensions about the selected objects, including the object anchored in the objects. Adjustment can be made using the grips in the same way as you did in the previous experiment.

2 Use grips to delete the extension lines   *See Figure 15.44.*
that mark the wall thickness.

Step 6: Change dimension style

Let us assume that we want to add an overall dimension over the first dimension string you created. A simple way of doing so is to change the dimension style from 1 chain to 2 chain.

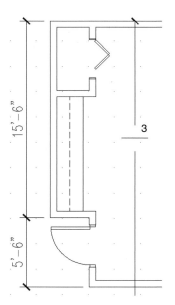

Figure 15.42
Pick the insert point.

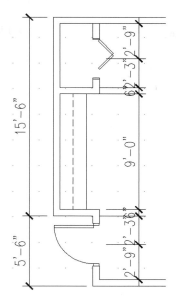

Figure 15.43
The created dimensions.

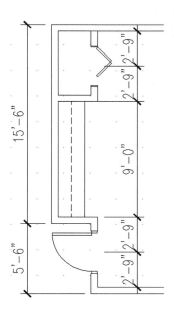

Figure 15.44
Finished dimension.

1 Click the dimension outside the room.

2 In the Properties palette, change the style to 2 Chain.

3 Use grips to delete the extension line in the middle and adjust the location of the dimension line as required.

See Figure 15.45. The second chain dimension appears.

See Figure 15.46.

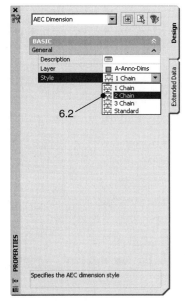

Figure 15.45
Change the dimension style.

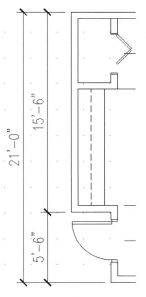

Figure 15.46
The finished overall dimension.

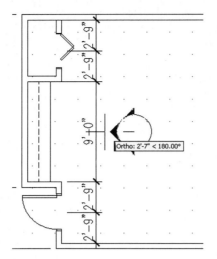

Figure 15.47
Insert the elevation mark.

Figure 15.48
The Place Callout dialog box.

Create an Elevation

In ADT, elevations can be generated automatically using the elevation mark tool.

Step 1: Load the elevation mark tool

1 Click the Content Browser toolbar icon .

The Catalog Library opens.

2 Find the elevation mark tools in Sample Palette Catalog – Imperial > Document > Callouts.

3 Drag and drop Elevation Mark A1 onto your tool palette.

4 Close the Catalog Library.

Step 2: Place the elevation mark

1 Click the Elevation Mark A1 tool on your tool palette.

2 Click in the space in front of the counter to insert the elevation mark.

See Figure 15.47.

3 Pull and click to indicate the viewing direction toward the counter.

The Place Callout dialog box pops up (Figure 15.48).

4 Click the Current Drawing button and look at the command line to interact with ADT.

Specify first corner of elevation region: **pick point 1**   *(Figure 15.49)*

Specify opposite corner of elevation region: **pick point 2**

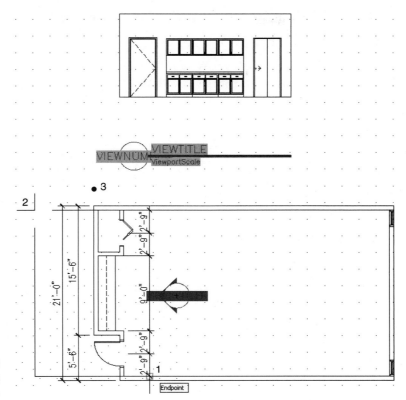

Figure 15.49
The elevation is
generated.

NOTE: The objects in the defined rectangular area will be processed to generate the elevation

Specify insertion point for the 2D elevation result: **pick point 3**

The elevation is generated (Figure 15.49).

Step 3: Fill in the elevation reference numbers

1 Double-click VIEWNUMBER in the elevation symbol in the floor plan.

The Enhanced Attribute Editor pops up (Figure 15.50).

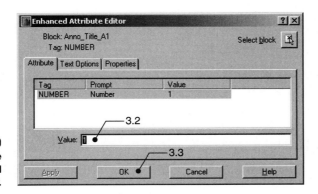

Figure 15.50
Change the attribute
value in the Enhanced
Attribute Editor.

2 Change the value from VIEWNUMBER to 1.

3 Click [OK].

4 Double-click VIEWTITLE in the   *The Enhanced Attribute Editor pops up.*
drawing title of the elevation.

5 Change the value of TITLE to ELEVATION.

6 Change the value of SCALE to $^1/_4'' = 1'-0''$.

7 Click [OK].

8 Double-click VIEWNUMBER in   *The Enhanced Attribute Editor pops up.*
the elevation bubble under the
elevation.

9 Change the value from VIEWNUMBER to 1.

10 Click [OK].

- If you make changes to the model, you can regenerate the elevation to update the drawing. To regenerate, click the elevation and right-click to choose regenerate. When the Generate Section/Elevation dialog box pops up, click [OK].

11 Save file and exit ADT.

Create the Reflected Ceiling Plan

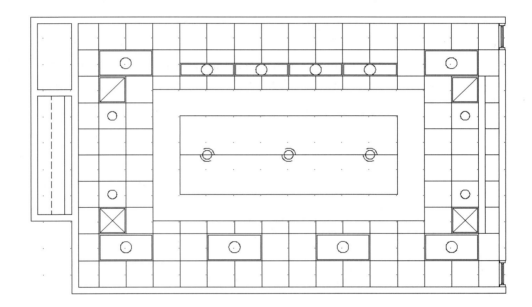

- ● Create the Ceiling Grid
- ● Create the Ceiling Cove
- ● Add Light Fixtures
- ● Finish the Ceiling Plan

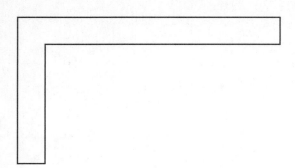

Create the Ceiling Grid

A ceiling grid in ADT is a special object for creating a reflected ceiling plan. It serves as a 2D visual representation of the ceiling tiles and provides anchor points for light fixture symbols. Its display has been set to show only in the reflected display configuration.

Step 1: Create a boundary of the ceiling

1 Start ADT.

2 Open the ch15.dwg drawing and save it as ch16.dwg.

3 Freeze layers A-Anon-Dims, A-Elev-Line, A-Elev, A-Elev-Iden, and G-Anno-Ttlb.

4 Use the RECTANGLE command (REC) 🔲   *See Figure 16.1.*
to create an enclosed polyline boundary
of the ceiling plane.

Step 2: Switch to the reflected display configuration

Because the ceiling grid is visible only in the reflected display configuration, we need to switch to the Reflected display configuration.

1 **Click the arrow next to Medium Detail**   *See Figure 16.2. The drawing*
at the lower right corner of the drawing   *changes to show the reflected plan*
window and choose Reflected.   *while the doors disappear.*

Figure 16.1
Create a boundary of the ceiling plane.

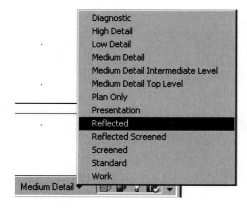

Figure 16.2
Change the display configuration.

Step 3: Create a ceiling grid

1 Open the design tool palette and click the ceiling grid tool 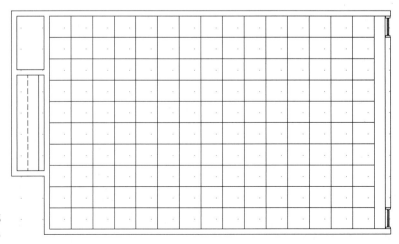.

2 Look at the command line and respond as shown below.

Command: CeilingGridAdd

Insertion point or [WIdth/Depth/XSpacing/YSpacing/XDivide by toggle/YDivide by

toggle/Set boundary/SNap to center/Match]: **S↵**   *S is for Set boundary.*

Select a space or closed polyline for boundary:: **select the rectangle**

Insertion point or [WIdth/Depth/XSpacing/YSpacing/XDivide by toggle/YDivide by

toggle/Set boundary/SNap to center/Match]: **pick the lower left corner of the room**

Rotation or [WIdth/Depth/XSpacing/YSpacing/XDivide by toggle/YDivide by

toggle/Set boundary/SNap to center/Match] <0.00>: **hit [Enter] to accept the
default value**

Insertion point or [WIdth/Depth/XSpacing/YSpacing/XDivide by toggle/YDivide by

toggle/Set boundary/SNap to center/Match/Undo]:   *The ceiling grid is inserted*
hit [Enter] to terminate the command   *(Figure 16.3).*

Step 4: Adjust the ceiling grid size

The ceiling grid is a little short on the right to cover the whole area because the default size is set at 20′ by 30′. You could have set a larger size before adding it to the drawing, but you will follow this procedure to learn how to adjust the size after it is created.

1 Click the ceiling grid.   *The grips show.*

2 Click the grip at the upper right corner and pull   *See Figure 16.4.*
it to the right beyond the room boundary wall.

3 Click to set and hit [Esc].

Figure 16.3
Ceiling grid is inserted.

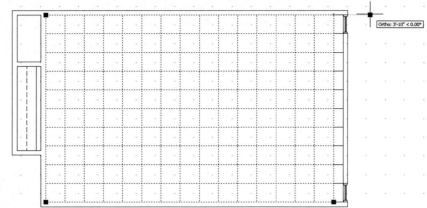

Figure 16.4
Adjust the ceiling grid size
using grips.

Step 5: Align the ceiling grid

The ceiling grid is not centered in the space. You need to adjust the alignment.

1 Draw a diagonal line across the ceiling area.

2 Start the MOVE command (M).

3 Select the ceiling grid and hit [Enter] to finish selection.

4 Move the cursor to the middle of the ceiling grid. *See Figure 16.5. A circle appears with the tag Center when the cursor is on the center point of the grid.*

5 Click to pick the center point of the ceiling grid.

6 Use the midpoint object snap to catch the midpoint of the diagonal line. *See Figure 16.6. The grid is centered.*

7 Erase the diagonal line.

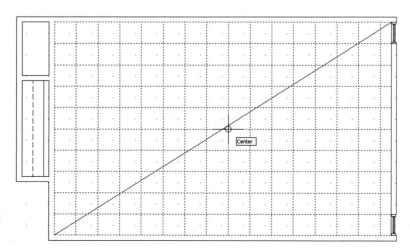

Figure 16.5
Pick the center point of
the ceiling grid.

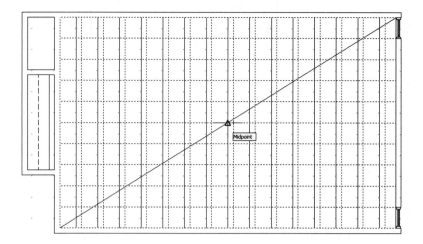

Figure 16.6
Ceiling grid alignment.

Create the Ceiling Cove

In the following steps, you will create the ceiling cove. See the designer's sketch (Figure 16.7) for reference.

Step 1: Create the boundary

Similar to the ceiling boundary you created at the beginning of this chapter, you will create the boundary of the drywall ceiling by cutting a hole. The boundary needs to be an enclosed polyline.

1 Use the RECTANGLE command (REC) ▢   *See Figure 16.8.*
   to create the outer boundary of the cove.

2 Move the rectangle up 12 inches.

Step 2: Clip the ceiling grid

1 Click the ceiling grid.

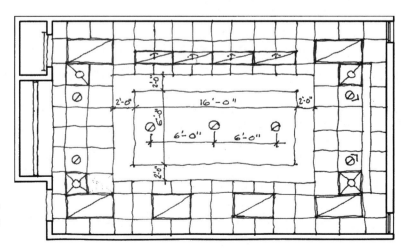

Figure 16.7
The designer's sketch of
the reflected ceiling plan.

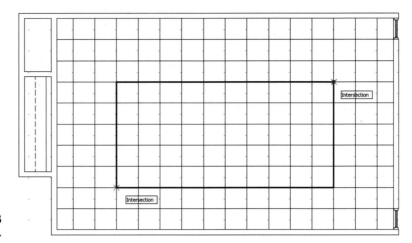

Figure 16.8
Create a rectangle.

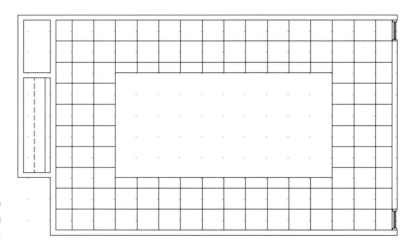

Figure 16.9
Clip the grid to add a
hole.

2 Right-click and choose Clip. Look at the command line and respond as shown below.   *See Figure 16.9.*

Ceiling grid clip [Set boundary/Add hole/Remove hole]: **A↵**   *A is for "Add hole".*

Select a closed polyline or AEC object for hole: **select the rectangle**

Ceiling grid clip [Set boundary/Add hole/Remove hole]: **hit [Enter]**

3 Use the OFFSET command (O) to create the opening of the cove (offset = 24″).   *See Figure 16.10.*

Add Light Fixtures

Lighting symbols can be found in the Design Center. These symbols are used with the ceiling grid.

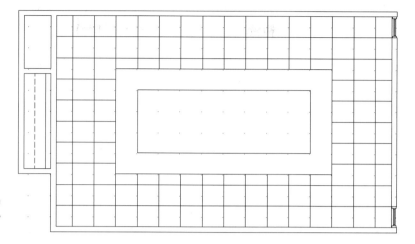

Figure 16.10
Use **OFFSET** to create the opening of the cove.

Step 1: Import the lighting fixture symbol

1 Click the Design Center icon 🖼️ on the Standard toolbar.

The Design Center window pops up (Figure 16.11).

2 Click the AEC Content tab.

3 Find the 2 × 4 light symbol in the folder **Architectural Desktop** > **Imperial** > **Design** > **Electrical** > **Lighting** > **Fluorescent**.

4 Click on the 2 × 4 symbol.

● An image is shown in the preview window. The description below the preview window indicates that it is a 2 × 4 fluorescent fixture and it is also "in Masking Block," which means it can cover the ceiling grid.

5 Drag the symbol (not the preview image) and drop it into the drawing.

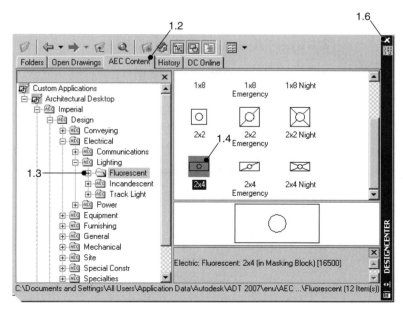

Figure 16.11
Find the lighting symbol in the Design Center.

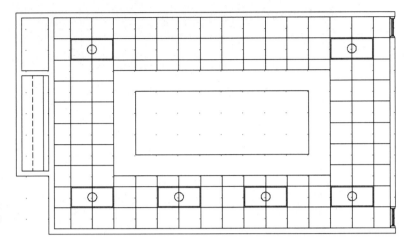

Figure 16.12
Attach 2 × 4 light symbols
to the ceiling grid.

6 Close the Design Center.

7 At the "Select Layout Node" prompt, click at an intersection of the ceiling grid.

This will anchor the light symbol on the ceiling grid.

8 Turn off object snap.

9 Move the lighting fixture to a location according to the designer's sketch.

The light symbol will snap automatically to the intersection of the ceiling grid.

10 Use the COPY command to duplicate the lights.

See Figure 16.12.

Step 2: Mask the ceiling grid in the middle of the light fixture

1 Select all the light symbols.

2 Right-click and choose Attach Objects.

3 At the "Select AEC object to be masked" prompt, select the ceiling grid.

The Selected Display Representations dialog box pops up and Reflected is highlighted. See Figure 16.13.

4 Click [OK].

The ceiling grid lines in the middle of the light are masked (Figure 16.14).

5 Repeat the procedure and add fluorescent 1 × 4 fixtures according to the designer's sketch.

6 Mask the ceiling grid line.

See Figure 16.15.

Step 3: Add the recessed cans

1 Open the Design Center.

2 Open the Incandescent folder.

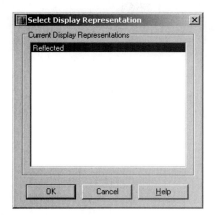

Figure 16.13
Mask the ceiling grid.

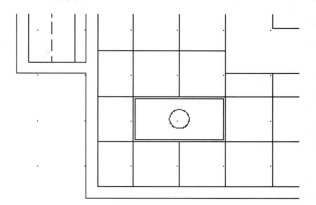

Figure 16.14
Mask the ceiling grid.

3 Drag the symbol named "Round" and drop it into the drawing.

4 Hit [Enter] to accept the default 0 for rotation.

5 Close the Design Center.

6 Move the symbol near the wanted location.

7 ZOOM in to look at the symbol closely.

8 Use the MOVE command with object snap to place the center of the light at an intersection of the ceiling grid.   *See Figure 16.16.*

9 MOVE the light to the center of the ceiling tile, using 12,12 as displacement.   *See Figure 16.17.*

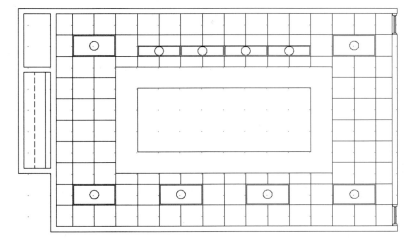

Figure 16.15
Insert and mask the 1 × 4 light symbols.

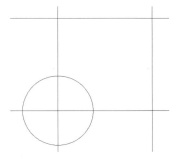

Figure 16.16
Move the light symbol to an intersection.

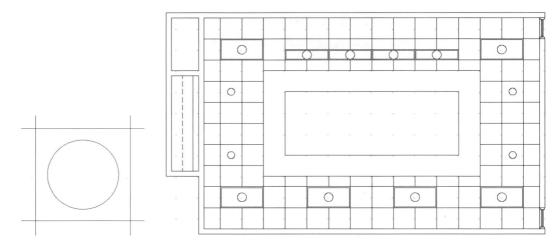

Figure 16.17
The symbol is centered.

Figure 16.18
Duplicate the recessed cans.

Step 4: Reduce the size of the symbol

1 Click on the light symbol and right-click   *The Properties palette opens.*
to choose Properties.

- The scale values for X, Y, and Z are all 9. The actual diameter of the symbol is
18″, which means that the original size of the block geometry is 1″ in radius.

2 Change the scale factors to 4.

3 Turn on OSNAP.

4 Use the COPY command (CP) to duplicate.   *See Figure 16.18.*

Step 5: Add recessed lights in the middle of the cove

Tools in ADT can help locate AEC objects. Because there is no ceiling grid in the cove,
you need such help to locate the recessed cans in that area.

1 Draw a horizontal middle line in the   *See Figure 16.19.*
cove opening.

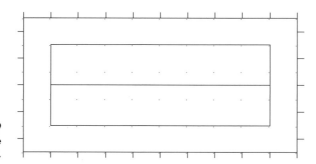

Figure 16.19
Draw a middle line in the
cove opening.

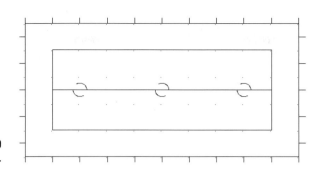

Figure 16.20
Set the Layout Curve.

2 Click the Content Browser toolbar icon to open the Catalog Library, and proceed to Stock Tool Catalog > Parametric Layout & Anchoring Tools.

3 Use the i-drop tool to drop the Layout Curve into the drawing, and look at the command line to interact with ADT.

Select a curve: **select the middle line**

Select node layout mode [Manual/Repeat/Space evenly] <Manual>: **S⏎**

Start offset <0″>: **24⏎**

End offset <0″>: **24⏎**

Number of nodes <3>: ⏎   *Circles are placed on the line to represent nodes (Figure 16.20).*

4 Click the Content Browser toolbar icon to reopen the Catalog Library.

5 Use the i-drop tool to drop Node Anchor into the drawing and look at the command line to interact with ADT.

Node anchor [Attach object/Set node/Copy to each node]: **C⏎**

Select object to be copied and anchored: **select one of the recessed can symbols**

Select layout tool: **select the purple circle on the line**

3 object(s) copied.   *See Figure 16.21.*

Node anchor [Attach object/Set node/Copy to each node]: ⏎

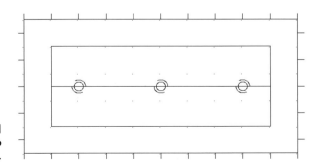

Figure 16.21
Attach light symbol to nodes.

Step 6: Layer management

Because the lights are anchored on the line, erasing the line will erase the lights. We need to use a layer to control its visibility.

1 Place the middle line on the layer G-Grid-Nplt.

Finish the Ceiling Plan

Step 1: Add air diffusers

1 Click the Design Center toolbar icon ▣ to open the Design Center.

2 Open Mechanical > Air Distribution folder.

3 Drag and drop Diffuser Return into the drawing.

4 Place it on the ceiling grid by clicking an intersection.

5 MOVE it to the correct location according to the sketch.

6 Drag and drop Diffuser Supply into the drawing window.

7 Place it on the ceiling grid by clicking an intersection.

8 MOVE it to the correct location according to the sketch.

9 Close the Design Center.

10 Duplicate the diffusers.   *See Figure 16.22.*

Step 2: Create the drop-down screen slot

1 Use the PLINE command to draw a   *See Figure 16.23.*
rectangle 6″ × 12′. Be sure to use the
Close option at the end of the command
to make it an enclosed boundary.

2 Click the ceiling grid.

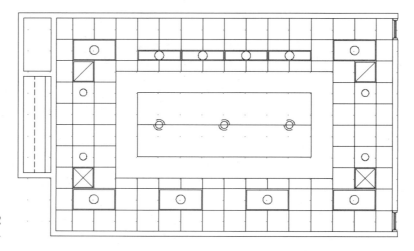

Figure 16.22
Insert the air diffusers.

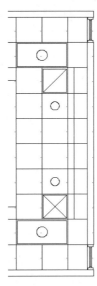

Figure 16.23
Draw the screen slot boundary.

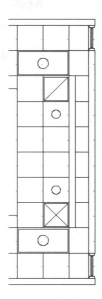

Figure 16.24
Clip the ceiling grid in the slot.

3 **Right-click, choose Clip, look at the command line, and respond as shown below.**

Ceiling grid clip [Set boundary/Add hole/Remove hole]: **A↵**

Select a closed polyline or AEC object for hole: **select the rectangle**

Ceiling grid clip [Set boundary/Add hole/Remove hole]: ↵   *See Figure 16.24.*

Step 3: Layer management

1 **Switch to the Medium Detail display configuration.**   *See Figure 16.25.*

● You can see that while the ceiling grid and light symbols disappear, the cove lines, the ceiling boundary, and the slot remain visible. You can simply place them in a layer and turn it off.

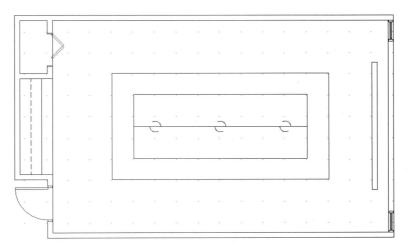

Figure 16.25
Switch to the Medium
Detail display
configuration.

2 Create a new layer and name it A-clng-line.

3 Set the Plot Style to Medium.

4 Place the lines on the new layer so that you can turn it off when you need to.

5 Switch back to the Reflected display configuration.   *See Figure 16.26.*

6 Save the file and exit ADT.

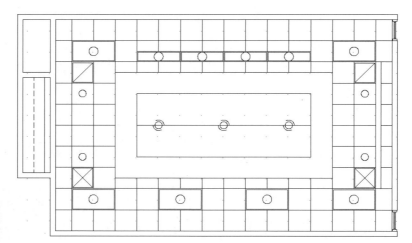

Figure 16.26
Finished reflected
ceiling plan.

Rendering with VIZ Render

- Create the Ceiling and Floor
- Add Furniture
- Prepare the Model and Link to VIZ Render
- Get to Know VIZ Render
- Set up Lighting
- Materials
- Radiosity

In this chapter, you will continue to work on the model to finish it and render it in VIZ Render. VIZ Render is a rendering program accompanying ADT. It is a simplified version of Autodesk VIZ.

Create the Ceiling and Floor

The ceiling grid you created in the previous chapter is only a 2D representation of the ceiling. To complete the 3D model of the space, you will borrow the 3D component from the AutoCAD model you created in Chapter 13. In the process, you will learn how to copy drawing elements from one drawing to another.

Step 1: Copy the drawing elements from Chapter 13

1 Start ADT.

2 Open drawing ch15.dwg and save it as ch17.dwg.

3 Open drawing ch13.dwg.

4 Switch to the SE axonometric view.

5 Freeze all layers except the following:
   Board, cove, drywall, floor, I-CLNG, I-CLNG-LITE, picture, and tray

6 Select all the objects on the screen.

7 Click Edit on the menu bar and choose Copy with basepoint.   *You are prompted to specify the base point.*

8 Select the southeast corner of the floor at the floor level.   *See Figure 17.1.*

Step 2: Paste the drawing elements

1 Switch to the ch17.dwg by the key combination [Ctrl] and [Tab].

2 Click Edit on the menu bar and choose Paste as Block.

3 Snap to the southeast corner of the wall as the basepoint.   *See Figure 17.2.*

Add Furniture

Step 1: Clean up 2D elements and purge unused elements

1 Turn on all the layers.

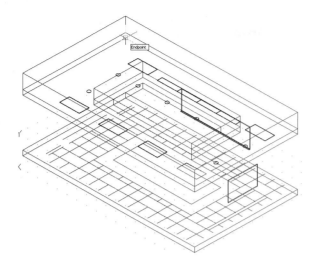

Figure 17.1
Copy with basepoint.

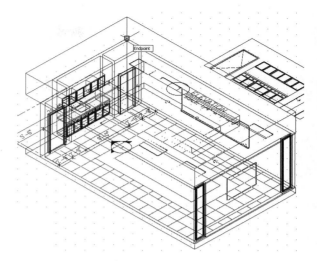

Figure 17.2
Paste as block.

2 Erase all the 2D lines on the floor.

3 Use the PURGE command to purge all the unused elements.

Step 2: Insert the conference table furniture group

1 Switch to the plan view.

2 Switch to the Medium Detail display configuration.

3 Click the Design Center toolbar icon ▦ to open it.　　　　*See Figure 17.3.*

4 Open the AEC Content tab.

5 Open the folder Table through the following path: Architectural Desktop > Imperial > Design > Furnishing > Furniture > Table.

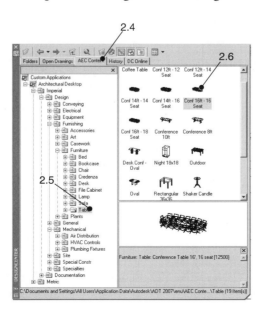

Figure 17.3
Find the conference table
in Design Center.

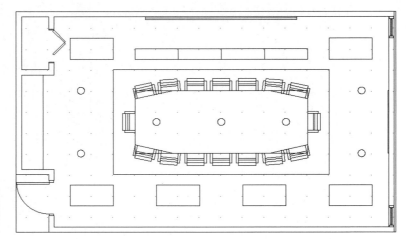

Figure 17.4
Locate the conference table at the center of the room.

6 Drag and drop the item "Conf 16ft – 16 Seat" into the drawing window.

7 MOVE it to the center of the space. *See Figure 17.4.*

- You may use the cove lines as a reference to align the table furniture group.

Prepare the Model and Link to VIZ Render

Step 1: Sort objects according to material assignment

The conference table and chairs are currently grouped together as a block, and they are on the same layer. This makes it difficult for you to assign different materials to them. You need to explode the block and put individual objects on different layers.

1 Switch to an axonometric view.

2 EXPLODE the conference table group three times until the color changes to white.

- The reason to switch to an axonometric view before using the EXPLODE command is to ensure that the 3D model is displayed. Because the conference table group is an AEC object, it has multiple views that are displayed in different views. Therefore, exploding the group in a plan view may have a different result.

3 Create two new layers: table and chair.

4 Put the table on the table layer and the chair on the chair layer.

Step 2: Delete named views

In the process of creating the elevation in Chapter 15, a view named Elevation was automatically created. Each named view in ADT will be transformed into a camera when you link the ADT model to VIZ Render. You need to clean up any unnecessary camera to simplify the model and ensure its proper display.

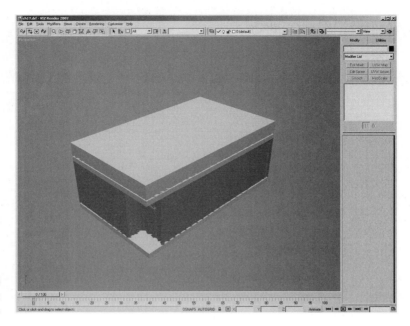

Figure 17.5
VIZ Render program
window.

1 Enter command VIEW (V).   *The View Manager dialog box*
                                       pops up.

2 Under Model Views, select the view Elevation and click [Delete].

3 If you have any other views or cameras, delete them as in 2.

4 Click [OK] to exit the View Manager dialog box.

5 Save the drawing.

Step 3: Link the model to VIZ Render

1 Click the small arrow ⬛ below the drawing window on the left to bring up the
shortcut menu.

2 Choose Link to VIZ Render.   *VIZ Render will start and the*
                                        ADT model will appear in the
                                        viewport as an exterior perspective
                                        view. See Figure 17.5.

● If the Missing External Files dialog box pops up, you may click [Continue] to
proceed. You will fix the problem later.

● When the File Link Settings dialog box pops up, click [OK].

Get to Know VIZ Render

Step 1: Switch to the four-viewport configuration

1 If you have any toolbar floating on the screen, close it.

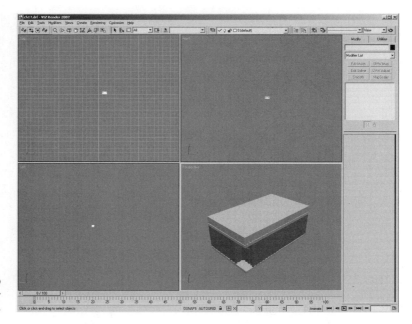

Figure 17.6
Four-viewport configuration.

2 Click the Minimize view tool icon on top of the viewport.

The viewport changes into a four-view configuration (Figure 17.6). The Minimize view tool icon changes into the Maximize view tool icon. Clicking it will bring back the one-view configuration.

● The perspective view is at the lower right corner. Only one of the four views can be active. The yellow frame indicates that the perspective view is active.

Step 2: View control: Zoom extent

1 Right-click inside the Top view viewport (upper left) to activate it.

2 Click the zoom extent icon.

The active viewport zooms to show the extent of the top view of the model.

3 Click the Zoom extent in all viewports icon.

The model shows in all viewports (Figure 17.7).

● You may click the Zoom extent tools a second time to center the model in the viewports.

Step 3: Load toolbars

VIZ Render loads toolbars in the same way as AutoCAD or ADT. Right-click on the title bar of any existing toolbar to bring up the toolbar list and choose the toolbar you want. The checked ones are already shown.

1 Right-click the title bar of a toolbar to bring out the toolbar list.

2 Select Transform.

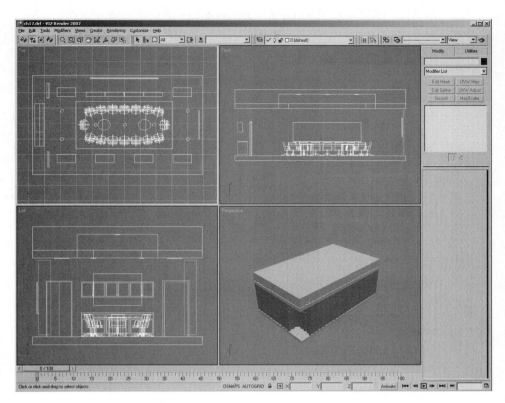

Figure 17.7
Zoom extent in all four viewports.

3 Repeat 1 and select Create.

4 Repeat 1 and select View Shading.

5 Dock the toolbars.

Step 4: Create a camera

1 Click the Target Camera tool icon ⬚.

2 Click near the room entrance door to locate the camera and pull the cursor to locate the target.   *See Figure 17.8.*

3 Move the cursor upward to raise both the camera and the target up to eye level and click to set.

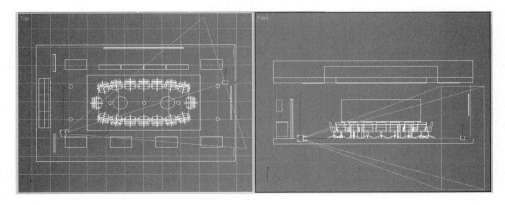

Figure 17.8
Set the camera.

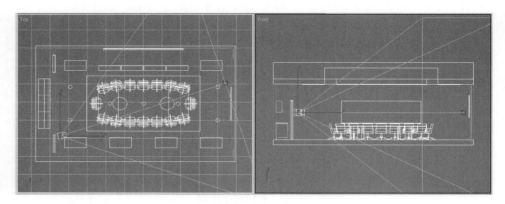

Figure 17.9
Set the camera height
and zoom.

4 Click [24mm] in the Stock Lenses group on the Modify panel on the right of the screen.

The cone of the camera is widened (Figure 17.9).

Step 5: Switch to the camera view

1 Right-click inside the perspective viewport to activate the viewport.

2 Type C.

The perspective viewport changes into the camera view (Figure 17.10).

Step 6: Render the model

1 Click the quick render tool [image] in the render toolbar.

The render window pops up (Figure 17.11).

● Before any light is created in the scene, default light is provided. It is uniform and has no shadow. You need to work on it.

2 Close the render window.

Figure 17.10
Camera view.

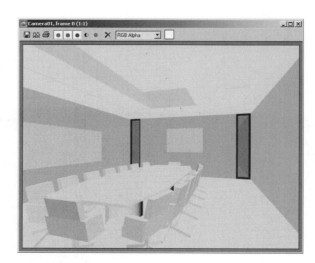

Figure 17.11
Result of a quick render.

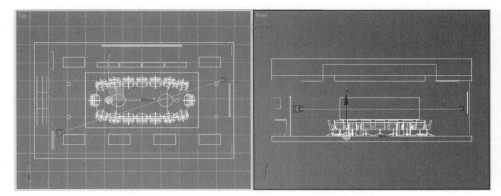

Figure 17.12
Place the light in the space.

Set up Lighting

In VIZ Render, lights are more realistic. They are all called photometric lights, and they behave according to the laws of physics. You have control of the intensity of the lights in terms of real physical measurements.

Step 1: Create a free point light

1 Click the free point light icon ⬚ on the Create toolbar.

2 Click in the top view at the location of the downlight in the cove.

The light is created, but it is placed on the floor level (Figure 17.12).

3 Click the move tool ⬚.

4 Right-click the Move tool icon.

The Move Transform Type-In dialog box pops up (Figure 17.13).

5 Type 12'11" in the box for Absolute World Z coordinate and hit [Enter].

The light is moved up into the cove (Figure 17.14).

6 Close the Move Transform Type-In dialog box.

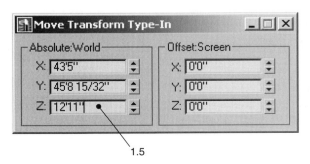

1.5

Figure 17.13
Enter the Z value to move the light up.

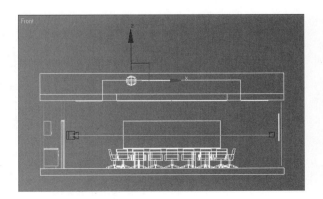

Figure 17.14
The light is moved into the ceiling cove.

Figure 17.15
Result of quick render.

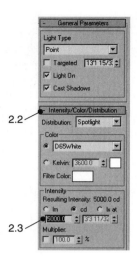

Figure 17.16
Change the light parameter.

7 Right-click the camera view and click the render tool to have a quick render of the scene.

See Figure 17.15.

8 Close the render window.

Step 2: Change the light distribution and intensity

When the light is created, the parameters of the light are shown in the modify panel on the right of the screen. You can change them there. The major parameters are intensity and distribution. The default distribution is isotropic, which means the light radiates in all directions equally, similar to a bare light bulb. Because a recessed downlight can be seen as a spotlight, you need to change the distribution to spotlight.

1 Click the drop-down list of distribution and choose Spotlight.

See Figure 17.16.

2 Look down on the lighting parameter panel to find [+ spotlight parameters] and click on it.

The default intensity value is 1500 cd (candela or candle power).

3 Change the intensity value to 5000.

4 Click the quick render tool to have a quick render.

See Figure 17.17.

5 Close the render window after checking the result.

Step 3: Duplicate the light

In VIZ Render, copy is accomplished by holding the [Shift] key while using a move command. You will use this method to duplicate the first light you just created.

1 Right-click the top view to activate it.

2 Click the move tool.

• The light should still be selected. If not, select the light.

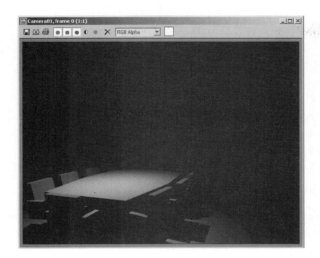

Figure 17.17
Result of quick render.

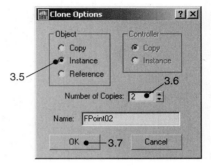

Figure 17.18
The Clone Options settings.

3 Move the cursor over the *x* axis arrow.   *The four-way move arrow appears.*

4 Hold down the Shift key, drag the light to the next downlight position, and release the mouse button.   *The Clone Options dialog box pops up (Figure 17.18).*

- Dragging the object by an axis restricts the movement along that axis.

5 Make sure Instance is checked.

- An instance is a clone of the original, but it is not independent of the original. When the parameters of either the original or the clone are changed, they both change as if they were connected. In comparison, a copy is independent of the original.

6 Change the Number of Copies to 2.

7 Click [OK].   *Two instances are created.*

8 Right-click the camera view and click the quick render tool ⟲ to have a quick render.   *See Figure 17.19.*

9 Close the render window after checking the result.

Figure 17.19
Result of the quick render.

Step 4: Create a target point light

There are two directional lights to light the picture on the wall. You need target point lights so that you can easily control the aiming. Instead of creating a target point light to begin with, you will create a free point light and change it into a target point light.

1 Create a free point light in the top view at the center of the recessed can in front of the picture.

The light is created on the floor level.

2 Click the Move tool and move it up (in the front view) near the ceiling.

See Figure 17.20.

3 Look at the lighting parameter panel to find the light type (under General Parameters).

4 Check the box before "targeted."

A target, shown as a small white box, is added right below the light (Figure 17.21).

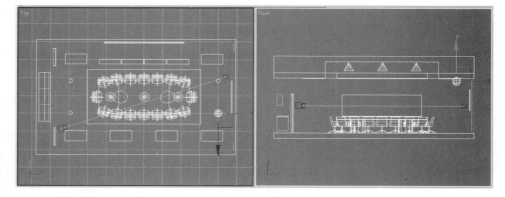

Figure 17.20
Create and move the first picture light.

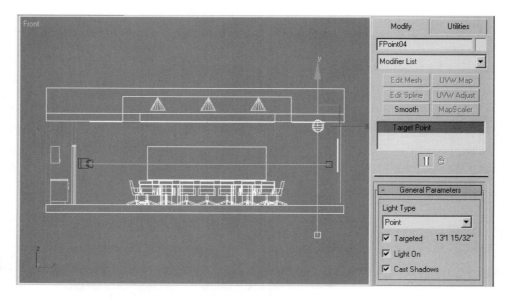

Figure 17.21
Turn on the light target.

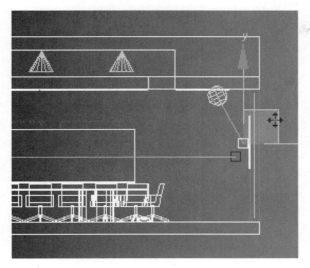

Figure 17.22
Move the target up.

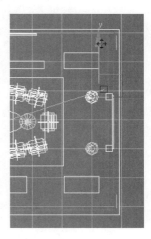

Figure 17.23
Duplicate the light.

5 Click to select the target.

6 Move the cursor a little above the *x* axis
to see the yellow square showing between
the two axes. Drag to move the target toward
the center of the picture in the front view.

See Figure 17.22.

- The yellow square indicates that you can execute free 2D moves on the plane
defined by those two axes.

Step 5: Duplicate the light

1 Click the line between the light and the target. This will select both the light
and the target.

2 Right-click in the top view to activate it.

3 Hold down the Shift key, drag the light along
the *y* axis (green), and place it on the other
side of the picture.

See Figure 17.23.

4 Click [OK] when the Clone Options dialog box pops up.

5 Move the targets to form a cross wash of the picture.   *See Figure 17.24.*

Step 6: Set the light parameters

1 Click one of the picture lights.

2 On the Modify panel, change the light distribution to spotlight.

3 Change the intensity to 5000 (cd).

4 Test-render the camera view.   *See Figure 17.25.*

5 Close the render window after checking the result.

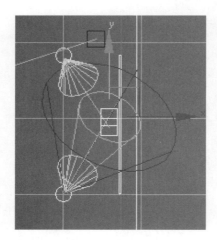

Figure 17.24
Aim the lights.

Figure 17.25
Result of quick render.

Step 7: Create area light for the 2 × 4 fluorescent lights

1 Click the free area photometric light tool icon ⬚.

2 Click in the top view over the 2 × 4 light at the lower left corner.

3 Look at the intensity settings.

4 Click to check the units from cd to lm.

5 Change the intensity value to 4000.

6 Move the light up to 9′11″.

7 Duplicate the light.

Step 8: Create linear light to light the cove

1 Turn off the chair layer (similar to what you do in AutoCAD) to simplify the top view and to reduce the text render time.

See Figure 17.26.

2 Click the free linear light tool icon ▱.

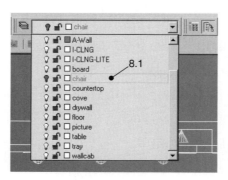

Figure 17.26
Turn off the chair layer.

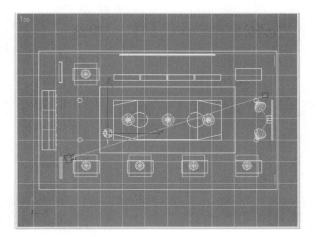

Figure 17.27
Place the first cove light.

3 Click in the top view near the edge of the cove.   *See Figure 17.27.*

4 Look at the Modify tab to find the [+ Linear Light Parameters] rollout.

5 Click the + sign to expand it.

6 Change the length value to 4′.

7 Change the intensity value to 3000 lm.

8 Click the rotation tool.

9 Right-click the rotation tool icon.   *The Rotate Transform Type-In dialog box pops up.*

10 Change the absolute world value for X to 180.   *This will turn the light upward to light the upper ceiling in the cove.*

11 Close the Rotation Transform Type-In dialog box.

12 Click the move tool.

13 Move the light up into the cove. Height = 11′1″.

14 Duplicate the light for both the left and right sides of the cove.   *See Figure 17.28.*

● To select multiple lights for duplication, hold down the [Ctrl] key and pick additional lights.

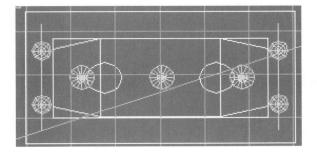

Figure 17.28
Duplicate the cove light.

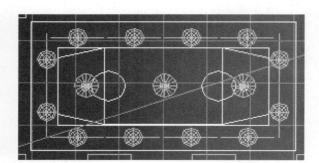

Figure 17.29
Duplicate the cove light.

Figure 17.30
Result of quick render.

15 Create one instance of the linear cove light in the cove.

16 Rotate it by setting the Absolute World value for Z to 90.

17 Move it into place and duplicate.   *See Figure 17.29.*

18 Test-render the camera view.   *See Figure 17.30.*

19 Close the render window after checking the result.

Step 9: Create a linear target light for the 1 × 4 wall washers

1 Click the free linear light tool icon ▨.

2 Click at the location of a 1 × 4 wall washer.

3 Move the light up near the ceiling. Height = 9′.

4 In the General Parameters rollout, check the box "Targeted."

5 Rotate the light 90° about the Z axis.   *A target is added. It is visible in both the front and left views.*

6 Click the move tool.

7 Select the target in the Left view.

8 Move it to the middle point of the whiteboard.   *See Figure 17.31.*

9 Look at the Modify panel to find the [+ Linear Light Parameters] rollout.

10 Click the + sign to expand it.

11 Change the length value to 4′.

12 Change the intensity value to 2000 lm.

Step 10: Duplicate the light

1 Right-click the top view to activate it.

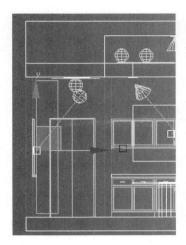

Figure 17.31
Aim the light at the whiteboard.

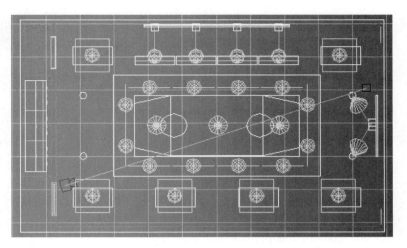

Figure 17.32
Duplicate the lights for the whiteboard.

2 Click the aiming line between the first whiteboard light and the target.

3 Hold down the Shift key and move the light to the next light position.

4 In the Clone Options dialog box, set the   *See Figure 17.32.*
Number of Copies to 3 and click [OK].

5 Test-render the camera view.   *See Figure 17.33.*

6 Close the render window after checking the result.

Materials

Step 1: Create a light material for the light objects

1 Open the materials palette.

2 Click the Scene—Unused tab.

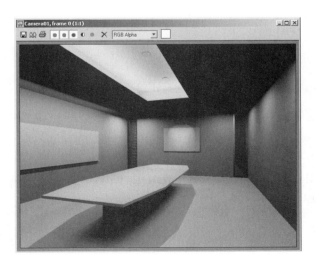

Figure 17.33
Result of quick render.

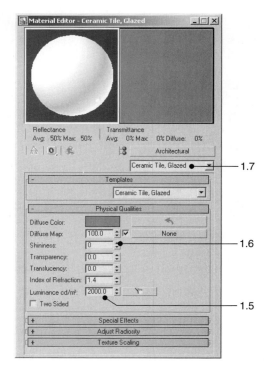

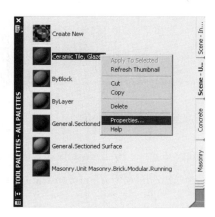

Figure 17.34
Create a new material.

Figure 17.35
Set the material parameters.

3 Click the Create New material at the top of the palette.

A new material is created with the name "Ceramic Tile, Glazed" (Figure 17.34).

4 Right-click the new material and choose Properties.

The Material Editor dialog box pops up (Figure 17.35).

5 Change the value for Luminance to 2000.

6 Change the value for Shininess to 0.

7 Name the material as light.

8 Close the Material Editor dialog box.

Step 2: Assign the material to the light object

1 Click one of the fluorescent light objects in the camera view to select it.

2 Look at the Modify palette to make sure the name shown at the top of the palette is the object you want. (The name of the light object should be "3dsolid.")

3 Right-click the created material on the material palette and choose Apply To Selected.

The bright white material appears in the camera view. It disappears from the Scratch tab (because it is moved to the **Scene—In Use** *tab).*

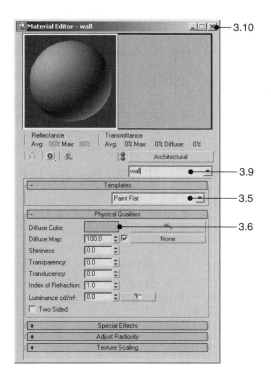

Figure 17.37
Create a solid color material for the wall.

Figure 17.36
Apply the light material on light objects.

4 Click the Scene—In Use tab.

5 Click one of the recessed can light objects.

6 Right-click the light material and choose   *See Figure 17.36.*
Apply To Selected.

Step 3: Create a new material for the wall

1 Open the materials palette.

2 Click the Scene—Unused tab.

3 Click the Create New material at the top of   *A new material is created*
the palette.   *with the name "Ceramic*
    Tile, Glazed."

4 Right-click the new material and choose   *The Material Editor dialog*
Properties.   *box pops up (Figure 17.37).*

5 Change the template to Paint—Flat.

6 Click the diffuse color swatch.   *The color selection dialog box*
    pops up.

7 Select a beige color (RGB = 205, 169, 121).

8 Close the Color Selection dialog box.

9 Rename the material as "wall."

10 Close the Material Editor dialog box.

11 Drag and drop the material onto the wall in the camera view.   *The color appears.*

Step 4: Create a new material for the picture

1 Click the Scene—Unused tab.

2 Click the Create New at the top of the palette.   *A new material is created with the name "Ceramic Tile, Glazed."*

3 Right-click the new material and choose Properties.   *The Material Editor dialog box pops up.*

4 Change the name of the material to "picture."

5 Click the Diffuse Map button (currently showing "None").   *The Material/Map Browser dialog box pops up (Figure 17.38).*

6 Double-click Bitmap.   *The Select Bitmap Image File dialog box pops up (Figure 17.39).*

7 Find the image file water lilies.jpg in the Sample Pictures folder and double-click it.   *The image appears on the Material Editor dialog box (Figure 17.40).*

8 Clear the checks under Tile.   *The image disappears.*

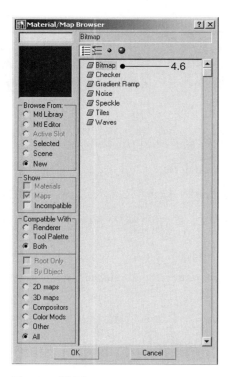

Figure 17.38
Material/Map Browser.

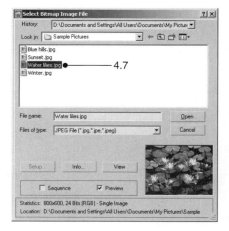

Figure 17.39
The Select Bitmap Image File dialog box.

Figure 17.40
The Material Editor at the Bitmap level.

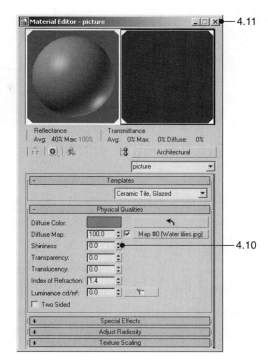

Figure 17.41
The Material Editor at the material level.

9 Click the Go to Parent button [icon].

The Material Editor dialog box returns to the previous level (Figure 17.41).

10 Change the Shininess value to 0.

11 Close the Material Editor dialog box.

12 Drag and drop the material onto the picture.

- The image does not show and the picture looks darker. The picture is not shown because the picture object created in AutoCAD does not have a mapping coordinate to let VIZ Render know how to handle the image. You need to set a mapping coordinate.

Step 5: Set mapping coordinates

1 Click the picture to select it.

2 Click the [UVW Map] button on the Modify panel.

See Figure 17.42. Some colored strips show on the picture. This is the result of the image being mapped on top of the picture.

3 Change the Mapping setting from Planar to Box.

The image appears on the picture, but it is a little small and not aligned on center.

Figure 17.42
Set UVW Mapping.

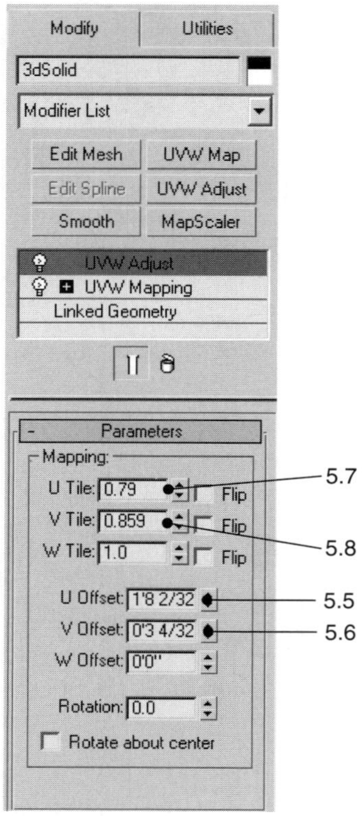

Figure 17.43
Adjust UVW map settings.

4 Click the button [UVW Adjust]   *See Figure 17.43.*
on the Modify panel.

5 Adjust the U Offset to make the image move to the left of the picture object.

6 Adjust the V Offset to make the image move to the bottom of the picture object.

7 Reduce the U Tile value to make the image wider.

8 Reduce the V Tile value to make the image taller.

9 Stop adjusting until the image fits the picture object.

Step 6: Import a wood material from the catalog library

1 Click the Content Browser icon [icon].   *The Content Browser pops up with the*
catalog library home page.

2 Click Render Material Catalog> Woods and Plastic>Finish Carpentry.

3 Click Next to turn to the second page.

4 Use the i-drop tool to drop the material "Woods & Plastic.Finish
Carpentry.Wood.Mahogany" onto the conference table.

5 Close the Content Browser.

6 Click the Scene—In Use tab in the Materials palette.

7 Right-click the mahogany material and choose Properties.

The Material Editor dialog box pops up (Figure 17.44).

8 Check the box Two Sided. This will make the table supports look complete.

● Because you exploded the table many times when trying to separate it from the chairs, it now has many parts. Dropping the material on the table applies only one part of the table. You need to select all the pieces before applying the material.

Step 7: Apply the wood material to the entire table

1 Click the Selection Floater tool icon ▐▙.

The Selection Floater dialog box pops up (Figure 17.45).

2 Click the table to select a part of it.

The selected item is highlighted on the list.

3 Check the box "Select Subtree."

4 Look up the list to find the header (the item without indentation) above the selected item.

5 Click the header item.

The subtree items are all highlighted.

6 Click [Select].

All the table components are selected.

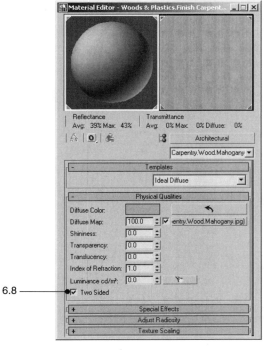

Figure 17.44
Make the material two-sided.

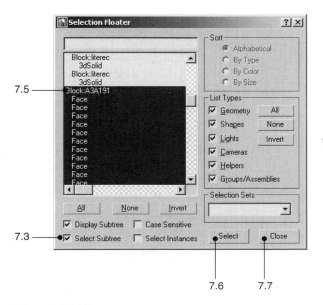

Figure 17.45
Select the table parts.

7 Close the Selection Floater.

8 Open the Scene—In Use tab of the Materials palette.

9 Right-click the mahogany material and choose Apply to Selected.

The mahogany material is applied to the entire table.

Step 8: Import a black leather material for the chairs

1 Turn on the chair layer.

2 Click the Content Browser icon .

3 Click Render Material Catalog>Furnishings>Fabrics.

4 Use the i-drop tool to drop the material "Furnishings.Fabrics.Leather.black" onto the chairs.

5 Close the Content Browser.

● Like the table, the material is applied only to some parts of the chair. You need to select all the chair components and apply the material.

6 Follow the procedure described in Step 4 to apply the black leather material to all the chairs.

7 Test-render the perspective view.

See Figure 17.46.

● The test render shows that the texture of the material is too large for the chair. You need to reduce the texture scale.

Step 9: Adjust the texture scale

1 Open the Scene—In Use tab.

2 Right-click the black leather material and choose Properties.

The Material Editor dialog box pops up (Figure 17.47).

3 Click the [+ Texture Scaling].

The rollout expands.

4 Change the values of the width and height to 6".

5 Test-render the perspective view.

See Figure 17.48.

Figure 17.46
Result of quick render.

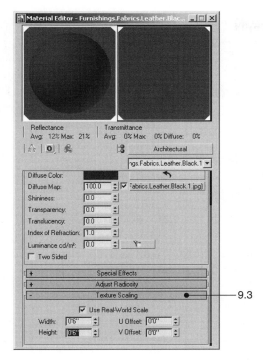

Figure 17.47
Adjust the texture scale.

Figure 17.48
Result of quick render.

Step 10: Import the ceiling tile material

1 Click the Content Browser icon [ ].

The Content Browser pops up with the Catalog Library home page.

2 Click Render Material Catalog>Finishes>Ceiling.

3 Use the i-drop tool to drop the material "Finishes.Ceiling.Acoustical Tile.Exposed Grid.2 × 2.Fissured.White" onto the ceiling.

4 Close the Content Browser.

- The texture appears on the ceiling in the perspective viewport. The pattern is distorted, and you need to turn on the texture correction function.

5 Right-click the text "camera" at the upper left corner of the perspective viewport and choose Texture Correction.

- The ceiling tile pattern appears normal, and the size appears to be correct. But the tiles are not aligned correctly with the lights.

Step 11: Adjust the mapping coordinates

1 Click the ceiling to select it.

2 Click [UVW Adjust].

3 Adjust the U Offset and V Offset to align the tile to the lights.

Step 12: Import more materials

1 Import the material "Finishes.Flooring.Cork" and map it onto the floor.

2 Adjust the Texture Scaling to 2′.

3 Import the material "Finishes.Gypsum Board.Painted.White" and apply it to the cove and the cove opening.

4 Test-render the camera view.   *See Figure 17.49.*

5 Close the render window after checking the result.

Step 13: Partial change of the wall texture

From the result of the quick render (Figure 17.49), you can see that some variation of wall texture may enhance the aesthetic quality of the space. Let us change the end wall into a brick wall. Because the walls are now all connected as a single entity when material is assigned to them, you need to separate the end wall from the rest of the walls.

1 Click the end wall.

2 Click [Edit Mesh] on the Modify panel.   *A File Link Message pops up.*

3 Click [OK].   *The selection rollout appears on the Modify panel (Figure 17.50).*

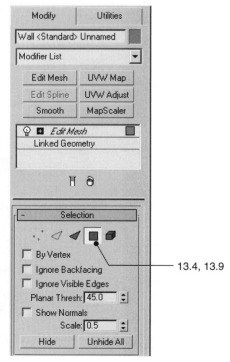

13.4, 13.9

Figure 17.49
Result of quick render.

Figure 17.50
Select the polygon.

4 Click the Polygon icon.

5 Click the end wall to select the surface polygon.

The selected surface turns red.

6 Click to open the Masonry tab on the Materials palette.

7 Right-click Masonry.Unit Masonry. Brick.Modular.Stack and choose Apply to Selected.

A Material Propagation Warming dialog box pops up.

8 Click [Yes].

9 Click the Polygon icon to deselect it.

The brick texture shows on the end wall.

Step 14: Correct the missing bitmap problem

The problem of the missing bitmap may have been bothering you from the beginning. It is caused by the material that came with the bifold door you created in ADT. You need to reassign a material to it.

1 Click the bifold door in the Left view and select the entire group using the Selection Floater.

2 Click to open the Door-Windows tab on the Material palette.

3 Right-click Doors-Windows.Wood Door.Ash and choose Apply to Selected.

Radiosity

Radiosity is a method for simulating light reflection in space. In the rendered views lighted only with the spotlight, you have seen that there is no reflected light. The lack of reflected light is because you did not start the radiosity process.

Step 1: Start the radiosity process

1 Click the render scene tool icon 🖻 in the render toolbar.

The Render Scene: Photorealistic Renderer dialog box pops up (Figure 17.51).

2 Click the Radiosity tab.

3 Click the [+ Radiosity Meshing Parameters] rollout.

See Figure 17.52.

4 Check the box before Enabled.

5 Click the [− Radiosity Meshing Parameters] to close the rollout.

6 Click [Start] and wait for it to stop automatically.

- When the process stops, the lighting effect is shown in the camera view, and the models in the other three views are divided into meshes (Figure 17.53).

1.2

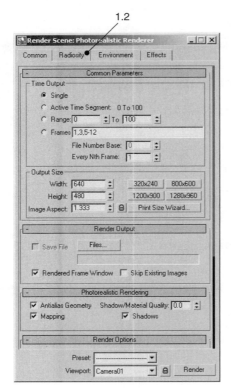

Figure 17.51
The Render Scene dialog box.

1.3, 1.5

1.4

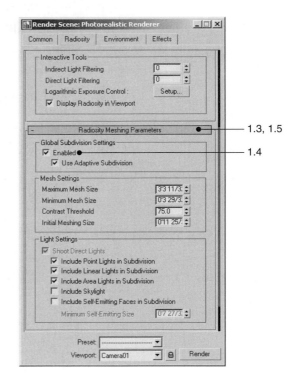

Figure 17.52
Set the radiosity meshing parameter.

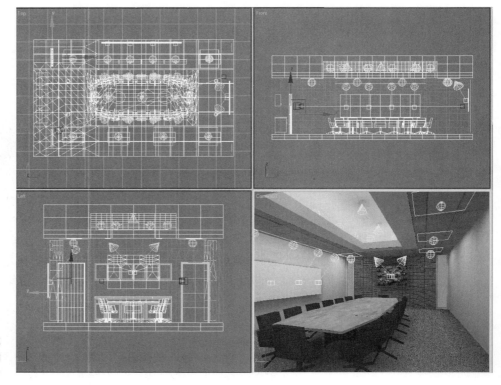

Figure 17.53
The result of radiosity
processing.

Step 2: Adjust the exposure

The exposure control simulates the adaptation of the human eye to different lighting conditions.

1 Click the Environment tab.   *See Figure 17.54.*

2 Click [Render Preview].

3 Change the value of Brightness if the image is either too dark or too bright.

Step 3: Set the background image

1 Check the box "Use map" under Background.

2 Click [None] and select the file Blue hills.jpg from the Sample Pictures folder provided with Windows.

3 Click [Render] to see the effect.   *See Figure 17.55.*

Step 4: Adjust the brightness of the table

From the text render, you can see that the table appears too bright. Mahogany is usually a dark wood. You need to adjust the brightness.

1 Open the Scene—Used tab on the material palette.

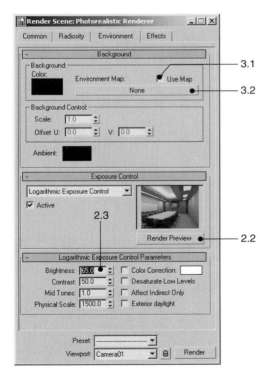

Figure 17.54
Exposure control.

Figure 17.55
Result of quick render.

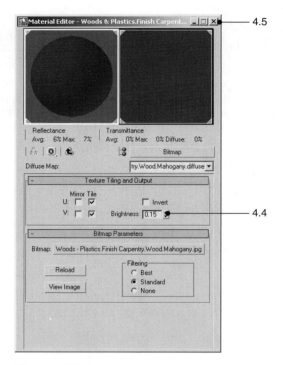

——— 4.5

——— 4.4

Figure 17.56
Adjust the texture output to darken the wood
texture.

2 Right-click the mahogany material and   *The Material Editor dialog box*
choose Properties.   *pops up.*

3 Click the diffuse map button that shows the image file name.

4 Under Texture Tiling and Output, change   *See Figure 17.56.*
the brightness value to 0.15.

5 Close the Material Editor dialog box.

6 Render the perspective view.

Step 5: Rendering output

When the lighting and material are set, you are ready for the final rendering output.
To create a good printout, you need a high-resolution image.

1 Click the Common tab in the Render dialog box.

2 Click [Print Size Wizard].   *The Print Size Wizard dialog box*
                                                pops up (Figure 17.57).

3 Set the paper size first.

4 Click the DPI value that you want (72 is for screen display, 150 is for a mid-
quality printout, and 300 is for a good quality printout).

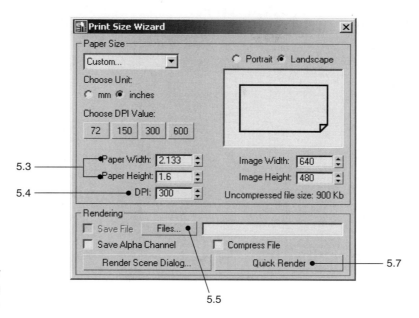

Figure 17.57
Print Size Wizard dialog box.

5 Click [Files. . .].

6 Find location and give a name. Click [Save].

7 Click [Quick Render]

8 Save the file and exit ADT.

Switch from the Autodesk Architectural Desktop User Interface to the AutoCAD User Interface

The following procedure can be used to switch from the Autodesk Architectural Desktop user interface to the AutoCAD user interface.

1 **Start the Autodesk Architectural Desktop 2007 program.**

The Autodesk Architectural Desktop 2007 front page shows (Figure A.1). You are prompted to choose a workspace to start.

2 **Click to select Design and click [OK].**

You are prompted to decide if you want to view the New Features Workshop (Figure A.2).

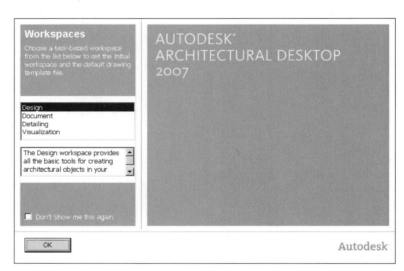

Figure A.1
Choose a workspace.

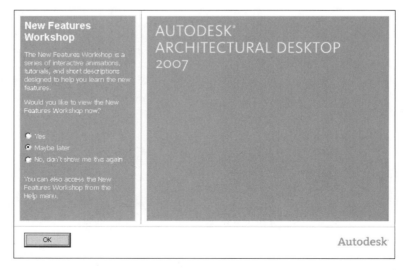

Figure A.2
ADT New Features Workshop prompt.

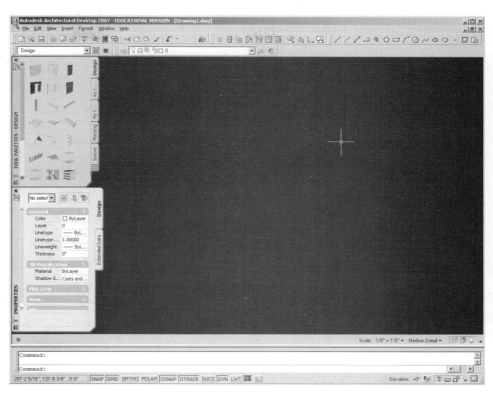

Figure A.3
The Architectural Desktop 2007 user interface.

3 Check Maybe later and click [OK].

The Autodesk Architectural Desktop 2007 opens (Figure A.3).

4 Type the command MENU and hit the [Enter] key.

The Select Customization File dialog box pops up (Figure A.4).

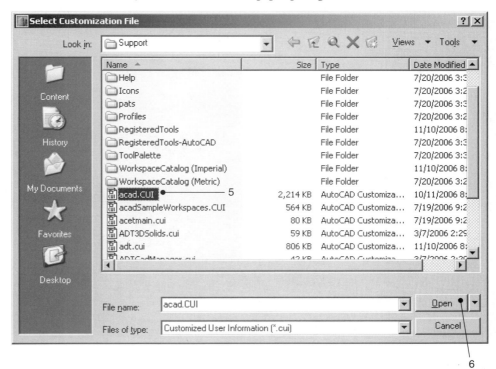

Figure A.4
Select the AutoCAD user interface file.

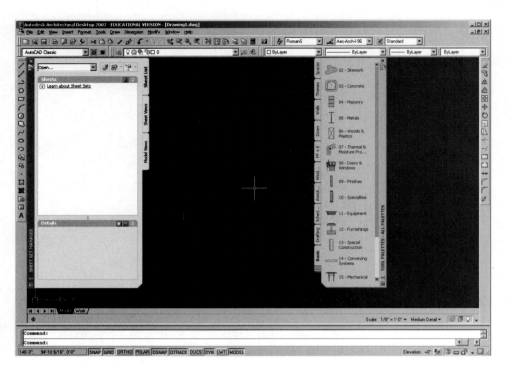

Figure A.5
The AutoCAD user interface.

5 Click the file named acad.CUI to select it.

6 Click [Open].   *The interface changes (Figure A.5).*

Switch from the AutoCAD User Interface to the Autodesk Architectural Desktop User Interface

The following procedure can be used to switch from the AutoCAD user interface to the Architectural Desktop user interface.

Step 1: Switch to the ADT user interface

1 Enter the command MENU.

The Select Customization File dialog box pops up (Figure B.1).

2 Click the file named adt.CUI to select it.

3 Click [Open].

The ADT user interface shows (Figure B.2).

Step 2: Load the dashboard

Because the 3D modeling and rendering tasks in Chapters 13 and 14 require the use of the dashboard, you need to load it.

1 Click Window on the menu bar and choose Dashboard.

The dashboard appears (Figure B.3).

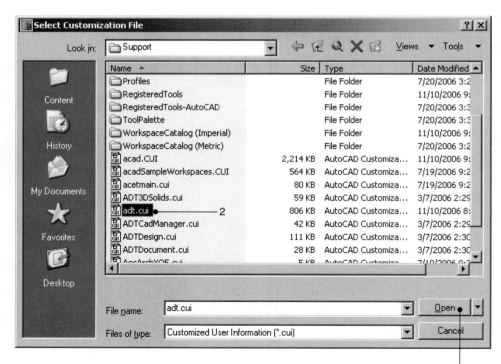

Figure B.1
Select the ADT user interface file.

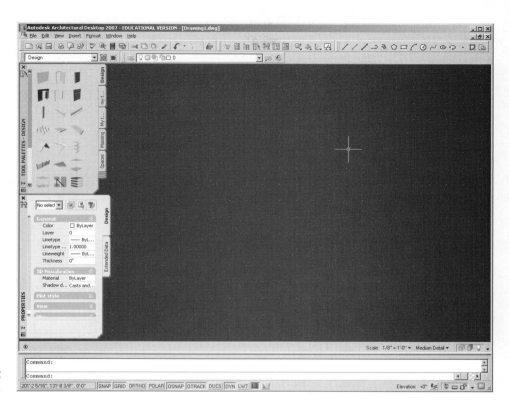

Figure B.2
The ADT user interface.

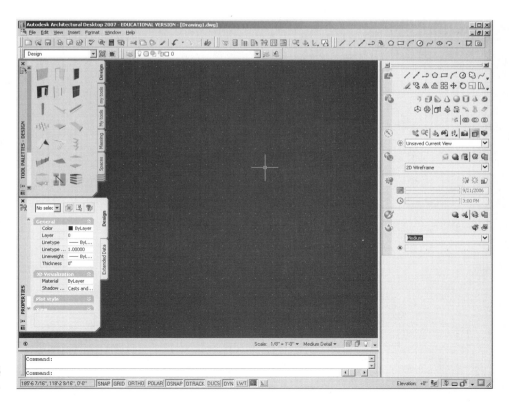

Figure B.3
Load the dashboard.

Index